DISABILITY RIGHTS AND RELIGIOUS LIBERTY IN EDUCATION

DISABILITY HISTORIES

Series editors: Kim E. Nielsen and Michael Rembis

Disability Histories explores the lived experiences of individuals and groups from a broad range of societies, cultures, time periods, and geographic locations who either identified as disabled or were considered by the dominant culture to be disabled. Conceiving of disability and disabled experiences broadly, and spanning a range of embodiments, the series highlights innovative approaches to disability history that deepen our understanding of the past.

A list of books in the series appears at the end of this book.

DISABILITY RIGHTS AND RELIGIOUS LIBERTY IN EDUCATION

THE STORY BEHIND
Zobrest v. Catalina Foothills School District

Bruce J. Dierenfield and David A. Gerber

UNIVERSITY OF ILLINOIS PRESS
Urbana, Chicago, and Springfield

1 2 3 4 5 C P 5 4 3 2 1
♾ This book is printed on acid-free paper.

Library of Congress Control Number: 2020937180

For Kate and Elizabeth, and for the deaf who must navigate a world that is stacked against them.

—Bruce J. Dierenfield

To all those who have campaigned for equality and justice for people with disabilities.

—David A. Gerber

CONTENTS

ACKNOWLEDGMENTS

In reconstructing the story of the Zobrest lawsuit, the authors were fortunate to have the assistance of a number of generous individuals who helped us in getting to know the principal actors, finding documentary resources, and analyzing the many interpretive problems that confronted us. Some of those with whom we did oral history interviews or extensive written questionnaires found us coming back to them repeatedly with reformulated questions, probing more deeply at their initial answers for facts or to fill in gaps and clarify inconsistencies as well as for greater understanding of their roles and perspectives. We owe these patient people, in particular, a deep debt of gratitude for allowing us to return to them with questions on multiple occasions: Judge Thomas Berning, the late Terry Downey, Denise Jensen Erickson, John Richardson, and James Santeford. Ginny Ball Duncan has been a constant, ever-patient resource, assisting us in understanding both the Zobrests and her late father, William Bentley Ball. We wish to acknowledge also those who helped us find documentary materials or to organize documentary materials for our analysis: Cathy Allen, Kathleen DeLaney, Wanda Martinson, Philip Murren, Rev. Rob Schenk, Tinsley Yarbrough, and Marsha Zubrow. Professor Susan Burch has been of help on many occasions in thinking about the singular issues presented by deafness and hearing impairment in a world dominated, too often unreflectively, by the hearing. We gratefully acknowledge, too, the editorial assistance of Jane Morris and Irene Sipos.

Finally, special thanks must go to the Zobrest family: Sandi, Larry, Jim, and Sam. We want to record an especially deep sense of gratitude to Sandi Zobrest, a woman of extraordinary fortitude, for her patience in the face of incessant questioning over the course of more than two years and for opening her files of correspondence with her attorneys, friends, the media, and sources she contacted while fund-raising on behalf of legal expenses and payment of Jim's sign language interpreter. Few people have been as continuously placed under a microscope by strangers, claiming a variety of sources of authority and a variety of interests, as Jim Zobrest. His experience of education was a protracted process of probing to discover his weaknesses and strengths—physical, intellectual, and psychological. His lawsuit brought him into the public eye for the national and local media to inspect. Now, historians are asserting their claims on him. Some might have responded by saying, in effect, "Enough!" But Jim Zobrest shared memories of his distant adolescence with us and allowed us permission to examine the records of his schooling that are housed at the offices of the Catalina Foothills School District. He aided us greatly in moving his position in history from that of the object of a U.S. Supreme Court decision to that of a three-dimensional historical actor in his own right. In addition to the family interview we did with the Zobrests in June 2015, in which Sandi interpreted for him and Jim answered some of our questions with oral speech, we communicated one-on-one with Jim by email. Also, a number of the emails exchanged with Sandi Zobrest that are cited in the endnotes of this volume, especially those dealing with questions of memory of events in the 1980s and 1990s, were answered after collaboration between Jim and Sandi. We have endeavored to take seriously his dawning aspirations and his dilemmas as a teenager, especially to the extent that deafness led him, relatively early in life, to be more acutely aware of them.

Much of this book, especially the early chapters prior to the more scholarly treatment of constitutional doctrine and formal legal processes, is an attempt at experiential history. That is, we strive to understand the world through the Zobrests' perspectives and to examine the choices they made, principally mainstreaming Jim's education as the logic of their situation and their aspirations for Jim asserted themselves in their decision making. But to the extent we often do so critically, the narrative tends simultaneously to take on three perspectives. First, there is mainstreaming, from the Zobrests' perspective, which is the story of their struggle to mobilize existing public resources, available under the law, to further Jim's education in schools, both public and Catholic, which in his experience were exclusively populated by hearing students. This is the goal that ultimately led the Zobrests to the U.S. Supreme Court in 1993, where they achieved a notable victory on behalf of the goals they advanced for Jim's education. Here, we are led ultimately to investigate the development not only of law addressing disability and education but also the constitutional jurisprudence addressing the relations between church and state. Second, there is the evaluation of mainstreaming, from within its goals of normalization as it was implemented, often tentatively and unevenly in the Zobrests' experience. Third, there is the critique of mainstreaming advanced from within the Deaf community, a critique that rejects the premise of normalization. In light of these dimensions of the book, it seems appropriate to tell the story through the lens of the Zobrests' aspirations and understandings, even while at times the authors bring their own critical reflections on the choices made by Sandi and Larry Zobrest. The authors are conscious of the tensions in such a complex interpretive stance and hope that the Zobrests are able to find the efforts made in this book to understand those choices both fair and truthful.

DISABILITY RIGHTS AND RELIGIOUS LIBERTY IN EDUCATION

INTRODUCTION

The historian of disability Douglas Baynton has observed that when we set off purposely to look for it, we find that disability is everywhere throughout history.[1] A corollary to Baynton's axiom is that if disability is everywhere, we may find many disparate phenomena, some of them apparently distant and some of them proximate, intersecting with disability, either predictable and easily imagined or requiring us to stretch our imaginations.[2]

That corollary may well prove true for readers of this book, which narrates the legal and social history of a lawsuit that brought together two disparate sources of late twentieth-century American public discourse and disagreement—disability law in primary and secondary education and church-state constitutional law. In doing so, it joined the two in a tenuous but ultimately consequential dialogue that eventually, after five years of slowly winding its way through local and state justice agencies, legal advocacy organizations and attorneys' offices, and the lower federal courts, was heard in the Supreme Court of the United States on a frigid day in February of 1993.

That lawsuit, which became known to the Supreme Court as *Zobrest v. Catalina Foothills School District*,[3] was about issues that emerged at an intimate level of American family life—the decision of middle-class parents living in a suburb above the desert plain of Tucson, Arizona, about the welfare of Jim, their hearing impaired son. The Zobrests, Larry and Sandi, were living in Erie, Pennsylvania, when Jim, their first child, was born in 1974 and, less than a year later, was pronounced "profoundly deaf" after routine examinations.[4] Thereafter, the course of where and how the Zobrests lived was to be greatly determined by their efforts to provide Jim with the opportunities they sought, within the choices they determined were available to them, to launch him successfully into adult life. Typically for hearing parents of a deaf child, Larry and Sandi envisioned the trajectory for Jim's life in terms of integration into the mainstream hearing society of which they were a part. For them, deafness was a defect to be corrected, not as for contemporary hearing impaired activists an alternative way to live, with its own identity, community, and culture, rooted in a language, American Sign Language (ASL). They did not know the deaf world when they confronted the options before them, but they knew for certain that access to the mainstream and opportunity to get on successfully in life lay with the hearing majority. Moreover, they wanted above all else to be able to communicate with their son and have him integrated into their family life. In consultation with educators, speech therapists, audiologists, and other professionals engaged in the education of the hearing impaired, they sought schooling and training for Jim that would, as much as possible, correct and compensate for his hearing loss. In the process, as Jim was molded in the image of the hearing world, his parents also would be changed. They continually armed themselves with information about deaf education and training and about the laws facilitating the education of children with disabilities. Sandi became a skilled practitioner of the methods of Total Communication, a way of communicating for and with the hearing impaired. Probably most unlikely of all, with Jim's welfare in mind, they ultimately set off on the quest for justice that led them to the nation's highest court and to a place in the history of American constitutional law.

The Zobrests moved to Tucson because after Jim left a private preschool in Erie, Pennsylvania, the Gertrude A. Barber Center (now the Barber National Institute), for children with disabilities, he would have eventually been sent to the public schools in Erie. The Erie schools were then being strongly criticized by local parents for inadequately meeting the needs of children with disabilities. An alternative was the schools for deaf children operated by the state of Pennsylvania, but these were widely dispersed around the state, and enrollment would have meant sending a small child to board far away from home. Barely beyond being a toddler, little Jim Zobrest would have become a commuter, visiting his family on weekends, a possibility that the Zobrests regarded as intolerable.

On the other hand, they had high hopes for what they had learned about the state-operated Arizona School for the Deaf and the Blind (ASDB), which is located on the westside of Tucson. They had relatives in Tucson and were expecting that their resettlement in the West would be eased by both a family support network and opportunities for making a living, and perhaps starting their own business, in the Sunbelt city's rapidly expanding economy. That resettlement in 1977 would not be permanent. They left after several months to return to Erie, but they returned to Tucson to stay in 1980.

Sandi and Larry Zobrest would have their struggles, at times very severe ones, making a living in Tucson, partly connected to business reversals in a dry-cleaning business they were attempting make a go of, and partly connected to legal and educational expenses they incurred in their continuing quest to get Jim the best schooling they believed possible. The legal and educational expenses resulted from the protracted disagreement with the Catalina Foothills School District that produced their lawsuit. They eventually had to declare personal bankruptcy.

The ASDB proved disappointing for the Zobrests because they came to feel that Jim was not getting an education that would prepare him for a regular public high school and, beyond that, a college education. They also believed the discipline there, inside and outside the classroom, was lax. Jim spent the last year of elementary school and then the two years of junior high school at a suburban public school within the Catalina Foothills district. He joined a generation of students with disabilities throughout the nation that pioneered in a radical, progressive, and, for deaf children in particular, controversial experiment in mainstreaming disabled children in the public schools.

DISABILITY EDUCATION LAW EVOLVES

Up to that point, the access of children with disabilities to a free public education was random, and their presence was seen largely as an inconvenience to many public school systems, which lacked ideas for confronting the challenges of educating special needs students and believed that educating them was too expensive in light of the low teacher-student ratio that was necessary to address their needs.[5]

But times were rapidly changing as far as the expectations for what was both right, from the standpoint of justice and fairness, and possible for people with disabilities. The moral scope of the civil rights movement was extending itself beyond race and gender to encompass those with disabilities, the nation's largest minority. Other periods of time had seen public self-advocacy and protest by people with disabilities.[6] But the 1970s and 1980s were filled with an unprecedented wave of lawsuits and of organized protests by people with disabilities, including the deaf and hearing impaired, demanding social inclusion, equal opportunity, accessible transportation and public buildings, and the most ordinary of rights—the right to have authority in speaking for themselves. The nation's most unanticipated civil rights movement was taking shape, manifesting itself here and there, from Berkeley, California, to

Washington, D.C., in dramatic protest demonstrations, such as those staged by the deaf students at Gallaudet University in 1988 demanding that the board of trustees name a new university president who was Deaf and shared their language (ASL), history, and group identity. The disability rights protests had a great many well-wishers in the general public and in the cases, for example, of Senators Hubert Humphrey, Edward M. Kennedy, and Tom Harkin, and President George H. W. Bush, among the nation's political leaders. Human life is constructed such that few of us can get through it without at some point in time having a disability or having a family member—as did all four of these political leaders—a friend, or a coworker who does. The result of the calls for change was a series of dramatic legislative breakthroughs, from the 1973 Rehabilitation Act, which established the principles of nondiscrimination for people with disabilities in all activities and programs that received federal financial support and of integrated educational opportunities for students with disabilities, to the 1990 Americans with Disabilities Act, the symbolic culmination of this legislative trend. A comprehensive civil rights act covering employment in the public and private sectors, public services, public accommodations, and telecommunications, the 1990 law was written by Senator Harkin and signed enthusiastically into law in an imposing ceremony on the White House lawn by President Bush.[7]

A hallmark in this legislative process of liberation for the nation's disabled citizens was the Education for All Handicapped Children Act (EAHCA), passed by Congress in 1975 and signed by President Gerald Ford. Public Law 94-142, the law's prosaic title, is often referred to grandly as the *Bill of Rights for the Education of Handicapped Children*, because it established a right to equal educational opportunities in the same way that the first ten amendments to the Constitution established such inalienable rights as, for example, free speech or trial by jury. (In 1990, the EAHCA was reauthorized by Congress and renamed the Individuals with Disabilities Education Act, or IDEA.) The new law, a mandate for what came to be widely known as *mainstreaming*, was a response both to the inadequacies of the 1973 law and to a variety of understandings touching directly upon the status of students with disabilities. Section 503 of the 1973 law had spoken to education, opposing the segregation of disabled students unless it was necessary for a program's effective functioning on a student's behalf. But Section 503 contained no funding mechanism to help implement its goals, and it failed at the basic task of defining a process of making those goals achievable. Meanwhile, recent government-funded research revealed that more than half of the nation's disabled children were woefully neglected when it came to education. About

37 percent (3 million) of the 8 million children with disabilities were not receiving an adequate education and were often set off in segregated programs in public schools or in segregated state or private institutions. Another 22 percent (1.75 million) were receiving no schooling at all, some of them languishing in segregated state or private institutions, while many others were shut in at home. Research had also revealed that most students with disabilities, especially physical disabilities, did not perform better academically in segregated classes than in regular classrooms. Segregated programs seemed to bring no educational benefits while posing all of the social, cultural, and political disadvantages that segregation always brings with it.[8]

The EAHCA offered a radically different approach to the mostly ineffective and neglectful past educational approaches to the education of children with disabilities, and its definition of *disability*, totaling thirteen categories of conditions, was expansive enough to encompass physical and mental disabilities as well as chronic illnesses ("emotional disturbances" and "health impairments"). It mandated that these children were entitled to a "free, appropriate public education" in "the least restrictive environment" that could be created for them within tax-supported public schools. The law mandated further that they must have access to nondiscriminatory testing, evaluation, and placement procedures in the service of informed and appropriate placement within public schools. These requirements were to be accomplished by school administrators in consultation with parents drawing up an Individualized Education Program (IEP) for each child. The EAHCA included a federal funding mechanism to support public school systems in paying the considerable costs of what would become increasingly popularly known as *special education*—all of the technological, pedagogical, and otherwise assistive materials and devices needed to ensure successful outcomes for students within the public schools.[9]

Controversies over the interpretation of the law soon appeared. This was clear in the early Supreme Court decision testing the limits of the EAHCA. Two of the most important of these decisions involved hearing impaired students. One of the two lawsuits had arisen over costs. The expenses involved, in fact, had become a matter of intense debate, because it was soon understood by public school administrators that the various costs of educating many students with disabilities involved resource inputs that were considerably more expensive than those of educating their nondisabled peers. It was certainly not sufficient, however, to adopt a neutral stance, putting these students in an integrated classroom and inviting them to fend for themselves. Deaf and hearing impaired students routinely needed combinations of speech therapy, training in speechreading, audiological monitoring, hearing aids, instruction in signed language, and signed language interpretation* to succeed in an integrated setting. The Supreme Court addressed the issue of costs and related goals in 1982 in the case of *Board of Education of the Hendrick Hudson Center School District v. Rowley*. The court majority held that a public school district did not have to provide signed language interpretation to ten-year-old Amy Rowley, a hearing impaired student from Cortlandt, New York, in light of the fact that it was already supplying her with speech therapy, a wireless hearing aid, and a TTY (a teletypewriter machine with a keyboard and screen linked for transmission to the standard telephone lines). The district was spending three times more on Amy's education than it was spending on a hearing child's education. Amy's attorney, Michael A. Chatoff, the first deaf lawyer to plead before the Supreme Court, argued that Amy would be getting a lot more from her schooling if she had the services of a signed language interpreter. The court's majority decision, written by Justice William Rehnquist, however, noted that Amy was doing well enough in school without one. She was not entitled by the EAHCA to an education geared to bringing out her individual potential, Rehnquist reasoned, but instead to a "free, appropriate one," as similar to that of her peers as was practically possible, even if it could not be exactly the same. While costs did not enter explicitly into the Zobrest lawsuit, the second of these two lawsuits involving hearing impairment, in the later twentieth-century era of pinched school budgets and conservative public fiscal policy, costs were implicitly a factor in the calculations of any school district about how it was going to spend its money.[10]

The other question soon arising under the EAHCA was one tested explicitly by the Zobrest lawsuit: what were the implications of the new law for students with disabilities who were *not* in public schools or public institutions? The law clearly established that the public had to fund a disabled child's education, whatever sort of institution or school parents chose for that education. About 13 percent of the nation's K–12 school children were in private schools. Although data are hard to come by, probably 10–12 percent of the nation's population of children with disabilities (as many as five hundred thousand[11]) were in private schools. As states lagged in

* "Signed language(s)" will be used to refer to the body of languages expressed in sign. "Sign language," in contrast, will be used for a particular language that is signed, such as and principally American Sign Language (ASL). "Sign language interpretation" and "sign language interpreter(s)" will be used to refer to the practice of interpretation and to practitioners, mostly professional, of interpretation. The words "interpretation" and "interpreter" may also be used, here and there, for stylistic variety, as will "signing" and "sign" as verbal form.

implementing the law to students in nonpublic settings, this commitment was underscored in a 1983 amendment to the law that required direct federal intervention, which was often necessary. But the law did not specify where those services were to be provided. As a consequence, the courts were left to sort out questions created by the location of the resources needed by a student, which might combine with the problem of the specific nature of the resources a child required at those locations, as it did in the Zobrest lawsuit. If, for example, a student were placed in a nonpublic setting by public school administrators in consultation with parents—because that nonpublic setting might somehow be better for the student's intellectual development—the law seemed to dictate that all the costs must be borne at that location by the public schools. Or, when a child was in an integrated private setting, such services might be made available at a neutral site or at a public school to which the student could commute. The law did not speak, however, to the issue dictated by the costs of the transportation the situation required.[12]

What if a student were in a nonpublic school as a result of a choice made by parents who rejected the option, even where it was available, of a free, accessible public education that was appropriate to a student's needs, because of a preference for an education founded upon religion? Most private schooling in the United States was provided, as it had been historically, by church-connected schools, which accounted for a quarter of the nation's K–12 institutions. Roman Catholic schools then had about 60 percent of the private school enrollment.[13] The courts exercised close scrutiny over church-state relations, especially in the realm of education, under the Establishment Clause of the First Amendment to the Constitution, and cases coming to the Supreme Court almost always involved the claims of Catholic education or of Catholic parents seeking access to Catholic education with public funds. Of course, the student could be invited to take advantage of public resources by commuting to a public school or to a neutral site. That might work for a deaf or hearing impaired student, for example, for speech therapy and audiological monitoring. But it was hardly practical for sign language interpretation, because by the very nature of the service rendered by the interpreter, he or she had to be at the student's side throughout the school day. In being paid with public money the interpreter became, in effect, a public employee. The Supreme Court had made it clear in two 1985 decisions (neither directly pronouncing on the circumstances in the Zobrest lawsuit) that public employees must not work in religious educational settings. It was one thing for a fire marshal, who was paid a salary by the local fire department, to inspect a parochial school once a year for fire hazards. It was quite another for a teacher or a teacher's aide, whose position is analogous to a sign language interpreter, to provide instruction at a parochial school throughout the school year and be paid by the state. The history of the resolution of that question, as it related to both the EAHCA and the Establishment Clause of the Constitution, is at the heart of the analytical narrative developed in this book. The vagueness with which the law addressed this complex set of contingencies would bedevil the Zobrests' lawsuit right up to the Supreme Court's 1993 decision, and it ultimately would serve at that time to sharply divide the nine members of the court. Throughout the five years in which the matter was before public officials in Arizona and in the federal courts, legal claims over rights and obligations made on the basis of disability and those made on the basis of religion, whether from a religious liberty perspective in the Zobrests' viewpoint, or a church-state separation perspective on the part of the Catalina Foothills School District, would compete with one another.[14]

JIM ZOBREST IN SCHOOL

Under the EAHCA, and through cooperative negotiations between the Zobrests and the Catalina Foothills School District, as long as he was in public school, Jim Zobrest profited from the services of a publicly funded speech therapist and a sign language interpreter, who accompanied him to class throughout the day. Tall, handsome, and athletic, Jim also starred on the school's basketball team and began to aspire to go on to play in high school and perhaps even beyond, in college or university. His interpreter also accompanied him to basketball practice and games. As was the case throughout the balance of Jim's education, he was the only deaf student in his school. As such, as this study hopes to make clear, his experience, that of a pioneer in the mainstreaming of a deaf student, provides a specific and dramatic instance of the identity and social and intellectual challenges a deaf student might face in an overwhelmingly hearing environment. These challenges mounted the concern and the opposition to mainstreaming among Deaf activists, who have preferred the capital *D* to mark their identity, and assisted, alongside fears among these same activists for the future of Deaf identity and culture, in producing a virtual civil war among the deaf and hearing impaired that continues into the present.[15]

Catalina Foothills did not have a high school of its own at the time Jim was about to graduate junior high school in 1988. Parents in the district were invited to choose a public high school for their children from a roster of existing high schools in the area. Larry and Sandi Zobrest shared with large numbers of American parents of adolescents at the time profound reservations about the social atmosphere and the quality of education that appeared to prevail at many urban American public high schools. They observed drugs, gangs, and casual violence between students that might interfere with learning and teachers who were growing demoralized trying to keep order. Many students did poorly on standardized tests; colleges and universities complained that first-year students seemed less and less ready for higher education. Public education was perceived to be losing its way. In contrast, tuition-based Roman Catholic private religious schools (customarily called "parochial schools"), once a backwater of American education that had long experienced difficulties keeping up with tax-funded public schools, now appeared attractive for their order and discipline, the dedication of their teachers—lay and clerical, in spite of relatively low pay—and the moral seriousness of the pedagogy and vision of community they advanced. Their relative isolation from a society that many felt was losing its way now had become a virtue.[16]

Salpointe Catholic High School, then Tucson's only Roman Catholic secondary school, was founded and maintained by Carmelite priests. Though heavily endowed, it had its own recent fiscal troubles, but under the leadership of its recent principals in the 1970s and 1980s, Father Frank McCarthy and his successor Father Leo McCarthy, it had begun to emerge from them. The Carmelites promised parents a curriculum pervaded by religion and dedicated to preparing their children for college, and they took pride in the ethos of responsibility and engagement it sought to pass on to its students. Salpointe's sports teams were called "Lancers." A prominently displayed lobby wall hanging at the school proudly announced its *Lancers Values*: **L**ove of Justice and Peace; **A**cademic Excellence; **N**urturing the Whole Person; **C**ommunity; **E**vangelization; **R**esponsibility and Respect; and **S**olidarity. Salpointe was becoming known as an elite destination for ambitious parents and students, Catholic and non-Catholic alike.[17]

The Zobrests were then practicing Catholics and felt that Jim needed additional religious training beyond that provided at home and attendance at Mass at their parish church. They liked the aspiration for excellence and seriousness of purpose that the Carmelites promised, and the values proclaimed by Salpointe, by which students were enjoined to live in and outside of school, were also their own values. Salpointe was orderly and seemed free of drugs and violence. While its enrollment was not much lower than competing public high schools, it was selective enough in admissions to ensure a more serious and effective learning environment, which they felt a deaf student required. They feared Jim would be lost and his needs neglected in a large urban high school, with what they believed to be a more impersonal social and learning environment. Jim was to continue to be mainstreamed, if his parents had their way, but in a setting in which mainstreaming is usually not anticipated—a private religious school, in which he would be surrounded, just as in public school, by hearing classmates. The situation was not unusual for children with physical or learning disabilities, although as a low-incidence disability, deafness and hearing impairments are necessarily relatively small in number in the total student population.

With all of these considerations in mind, the choice seemed fairly matter-of-fact to the Zobrests. Sandi Zobrest, who did most of the negotiating on Jim's behalf with schools and school systems throughout his childhood and adolescence while Larry dedicated himself to the conventional male role of provider, made a formal request to the Catalina Foothills School District in October 1987 asking that the assistive services, including sign language interpretation Jim required for a mainstreamed education, be provided by the district at Salpointe High School. She had been encouraged to believe, in an office conversation with Terry Downey, Jim's principal at Orange Grove Junior High School, who had been her main contact in facilitating Jim's education, that what she asked for was possible under the law, but, said Downey, she needed to make certain. Months passed, however, without any formal confirmation that her request would be granted. Finally, in the spring of 1988, not long before Jim's graduation from junior high school, a meeting with Sandi was scheduled by Downey and Robert Hetzel, the superintendent of schools of the Catalina Foothills District. It was the Zobrests' understanding that the EAHCA and the regulations it had generated entitled Jim to these resources and that they were portable from one school system to another. That was the expectation that Sandi brought to the meeting. The Zobrests were about to butt heads with the religion clauses of the First Amendment of the Constitution and ultimately to enter into the history of the Constitution.

Hetzel and Downey were prepared for this meeting with Sandi. After Downey's initial positive response, she began to have doubts about whether indeed what Sandi asked for was possible under law. As an education professional, what she knew of the EAHCA was that it was an option for public schools to take up such expenses, if they chose to, but what she understood of the state of constitutional law suggested to her that public resources could not be taken into a Catholic high school except under the most restricted circumstances.[18] It would be one thing for the district to continue to pay with public money for Jim's speech therapy, to which he was entitled under law, because that could be provided easily enough at a public school location. But his sign language interpreter, who would also be paid out of the taxes of local citizens, some Catholic and many not, would have to be employed in a classroom at Salpointe. Crucifixes adorned the walls of classrooms, and the curriculum was said by the Carmelites to be purposefully pervaded by religion. The sign interpreter would be translating courses that included requirements in theology and subjects, such as death and dying, seen from the perspective of Catholic doctrine throughout the full four years of every student's attendance. But what the exact state of the law was when Jim's disability was brought into the discussion remained a source of confusion for Downey and Hetzel. The school district's attorney, John Richardson, who would eventually argue its case in the Supreme Court, had recently confirmed their suspicions on the basis of his interpretation of four decades of Supreme Court rulings on the efforts of individual states to share public resources with religiously based and usually Catholic school systems. After Downey had contacted Richardson about her questions on the state of the law, opinions were solicited from first the Pima County Attorney's Office and then from the Arizona attorney general, both of whom confirmed the status of Arizona and federal constitutional doctrine.[19]

CHURCH-STATE LAW IN PRACTICE AND IN THE LAW COURTS

The Supreme Court had become more strictly separationist since World War II, in decision after decision drawing sharp lines between church and state in the name of preventing what the Constitution refers to as an "establishment" of religion, the Founding Fathers' term for government material subsidy and moral support of religion in general and of individual religions that failed to meet the test of absolute state neutrality and disengagement from religious matters. Thomas Jefferson's well-known statement in an 1802 letter to the Baptists of Danbury, Connecticut, about the benefits of having "a wall of separation between Church and State," may not be in the Constitution, but the working premise of decades of Supreme Court rulings was that such a wall, and preferably a high wall, was both desirable and required by its understanding of the meanings of the First Amendment.[20]

Here and there, of course, were exceptions. Every president since Eisenhower has taken part in the annual National Prayer Breakfast. The declaration of faith "In God We Trust" adorns American money, and students proclaim we are "One nation under God" every morning in public schools when they say the Pledge of Allegiance before the flag. The federal government pays for chaplains and religiously marked gravestones for military personnel. In matters of education, there have also been exceptions for the sake of assisting children and their parents. Reasoning from what has come to be known as "child benefit theory," the Supreme Court ruled constitutional in 1930, in its first decision on this issue, in *Cochran v. Louisiana State Board of Education*, state laws allowing public school systems to share textbooks in some secular subjects with parochial schools, a use of public resources it supported again in 1968 in a New York State case, *Board of Education v. Allen*, which involved lending textbooks on secular subjects to students in religiously affiliated schools. In 1947, a New Jersey case, *Everson v. Board of Education*, addressed state laws allowing public transportation subsidies to cover the expenses of students attending religiously affiliated day schools.[21] But these exceptions were expressed in decisions that carefully marked a concern for precedent and explained why such a narrow door in the wall was, in this one case or the other, constitutional. Indeed, Justice Hugo Black's majority opinion in *Everson* went to great lengths to define a long list of possible state actions that must be considered unconstitutional. The decision became known more for this statement than for enabling the transportation subsidy.

There have been distinct limits to benefiting children seeking education. In other decisions, in which the court shot down proposals friendly to the sharing of public resources across public-private boundaries, the majority spoke in clear and uncompromising terms about the necessity of maintaining a well-patrolled perimeter. Since a key decision in the case of *Lemon v. Kurtzman* (1971),[22] Richardson was well aware that the court often had been employing a demanding three-part test, the so-called Lemon Test, to decide the constitutionality of laws that proposed the sharing of resources: they must have a secular purpose; they must neither aid nor hinder religion; and they must not entangle government and religious institutions in an ongoing relationship that brought state officials and clerical authorities into formal and routine relationships. The test functioned in such a way that when state lawmakers struggled to meet its first two standards by setting up relations between the state and religious authorities to make certain that the first two standards were met, they fell afoul of the third by virtue of that very same oversight. It did not appear in the mid-1980s that the standards would change soon—and then, when they began to, only cautiously and incrementally, as the decision in the Zobrests' case would testify. The Arizona attorney general confirmed Richardson's understanding: what the Zobrests requested was not possible under law, and Jim's disability did not appear to make any difference in the matter.

THE ZOBRESTS' LAWSUIT ADVANCES

It was hardly clear in 1988 how the Supreme Court would read the EAHCA in this context of church-state doctrine, because it had yet to face a lawsuit that involved a disabled elementary or high school student going off to a parochial school and making claims to public resources through a direct challenge to Establishment Clause doctrine. But Richardson certainly had reason to believe that what the Zobrests asked for could never pass constitutional standards as they then existed. He told Hetzel and Downey this, and Hetzel was prepared to convey this message to Sandi Zobrest at that evening meeting in the spring of 1988, a few months before Jim graduated from junior high school. Hetzel is a kindly disposed and conciliatory man who seems the model of a tactful school superintendent accustomed to negotiating complicated and potentially emotionally explosive encounters with parents, school boards, politicians, and the community in general. He remembers inviting Sandi to reconsider the decision to send Jim to Salpointe. We have some fine public high schools, he told her, and we would be happy to continue working cooperatively with you, as we have over the last several years, to provide Jim with all of the assistance he needs to get an excellent education and prepare him for college. Just change your mind about sending Jim to Salpointe, Hetzel said, and we can move on to plan for providing him with the resources he will need to succeed in high school.[23]

Sandi, whom Larry refers to as "the PTA" for her fierce determination and tactical efficiency in fighting for Jim's welfare throughout his education from preschool through high school, proudly identifies herself as a type of "tiger mother" in her role as the interface between Jim and anybody standing in his way. She was not in the mood to be questioned, as if she and Larry had made a thoughtless decision and lacked enough knowledge to weigh the alternatives before them. To her mind, as a parent, she knew what was best for Jim. She herself had a graduate degree in education and wasn't intimidated by school authorities. She had been confronting his needs as a hearing impaired child all his life. Advocacy on his behalf had become the greatest single challenge and purpose of her life in the way that Andrew Solomon, the noted clinical psychologist and writer, has found common to parents, and especially mothers, of children with disabilities and chronic illnesses. Sandi is the sort of mother who populates the pages of Solomon's widely praised book *Far from the Tree: Parents, Children, and the Search for Identity*.[24] Moreover, Sandi reasoned, what about the freedom to act on their Catholic faith and see to their son's religious training? Aren't we supposed to enjoy religious liberty in the United States?

In a moment of impatience and irritation, she decided that evening that there was no sense in further discussion with Hetzel. She gathered together her notepad and purse, picked herself up, and left the room for the parking lot. But she is also as self-aware as she is cunning and strategic in negotiations. Sandi had brought a friend with her because she was apprehensive about losing her temper and in consequence forgetting the details of her conversation with Hetzel. Her friend eventually joined her in the parking lot and reported that Hetzel, who three decades later remembers Sandi's anger, had commented to her that Sandi's irritation had registered with him, but he didn't care how angry she was as long as she didn't sue him. Sandi remembers thinking to herself, "He doesn't know me, does he?"

Wherever they may be, Left or Right or Center on the political spectrum, Americans appreciate a "Frank Capra moment," the type of dramatic crescendo that occurs in the famous movie director's Great Depression–era films in which the little people, long forgotten and virtually friendless, rise up and demand what's rightfully theirs, as Americans, in the name of fairness. It's a moment of moral clarity, righteous and indignant. In Capra's films, it also conveys purposeful resolve, and it serves tentatively to bend the arc of justice slightly further in the direction of justice. The authors conjured with this metaphor as a narrative device for the story of the Zobrests, but Sandi Zobrest would have none of it. She reminded them of what she and Larry believed Jim was entitled to under the EAHCA and related that they had already, by the time of that evening meeting, considered consulting an attorney if it seemed that it would be necessary to obtain the resources Jim's education at Salpointe required. As soon as they were informed, before her meeting with Hetzel, that the school district had to make sure that what Sandi wanted was legal, she knew she had to prepare herself for disappointment and confrontation.[25]

Beyond the facts of that encounter with Superintendent Hetzel, whatever poetic drama that Capraesque moment might have possessed doesn't work to explain the Zobrests from a larger contextual perspective. Their search for justice, as they understood it—without having any grasp of the trail of constitutional law and court decisions that had to be traversed to build a case on Jim's behalf—involved much more than a simple spasm of righteous indignation. Though in talking about origins of their lawsuit the Zobrests do not refer explicitly to the civil rights movement of the disabled that was then going on around them, they surely were inspired to expect more in the way of opportunities and accommodations for Jim by the spirit of change it was evoking and the laws and policy changes growing out of protests and demonstrations. Moreover, even if they were not aware exactly what it entails in jurisprudential substance, like most Americans, they knew they possessed freedom of religion that gave them a choice about their son's schooling.

In addition, their lawsuit would mobilize not only their own expectations as Americans and their capacity for sacrifice and determination, the sources of which lay deep in their personal histories and their community of friends, but also the abilities, goodwill, and resolve of a unique team of attorneys, Thomas Berning and William Bentley Ball, representing both the Left and the Right of the contemporary political spectrum. They also became dependent on charitably inclined individuals and foundations, local and national and almost all Catholic, providing money to help support the Zobrests' legal team, as the lawsuit made its five-year way through the courts. Justice can be very expensive in the United States, and added to the expense of lawyers' fees and court costs in this case was the price of Jim's sign language interpreter at Salpointe over the course of four years, which was just about as long as the legal process that encompassed their lawsuit. Not until the Zobrests won their case by a narrow 5 to 4 vote announced in June 1993 did they get compensated by the Catalina Foothills School District for the costs, about $34,000, of Jim's interpreter. During the legal process, they hung on insecurely to a position in the middle class and often walked on the edge of a financial precipice. Business reversals led them into bankruptcy at the very time they had to assume these expenses. Without sufficient savings to fall back on and with their income insecure, they could not pay the costs of sign interpretation themselves and had to seek private donations to pay those costs. By the time of the decision, Jim had graduated from Salpointe, where the intellectually ambitious and athletic young man achieved a solid record as a student and played on the basketball team for four years. He was at the time enrolled at Pima Community College.

In place of that poetically dramatic moment, the authors present a social history of the lawsuit that seeks to address, among other questions: How do people like Sandi, Larry, and Jim Zobrest come to file lawsuits? What are the consequences for them and for society of their decision to do so? The answers to the first question have been found to be far more difficult to determine than the assertion that people, clear-eyed and single-minded, seek justice, as they understand it. The eminent legal anthropologist David Engel, who has done research both on disability education law and on personal injury law in the United States, has reminded us that Americans are actually not nearly as litigious as we often think, even when they are grievously harmed or wronged, such as in an accident or in experiencing a denial of rights they feel certain they possess under law. Americans, in fact, are reluctant to use the law to settle their problems with individuals, corporations, or the state and its agencies. They often do not trust the agents of justice, notably lawyers. Moreover, the processes of justice seem to be overwhelmingly complicated and impersonal. So far removed from their own daily struggles, neither these agents nor these processes seem to have an interest in them or in their troubles. They may also be intimidated by the people who wrong them, who often possess more knowledge and expertise than they possess, or who may be able to access the services of those who do. Even if wronged, many individuals don't like to appear in their communities as people who whine and complain or make claims to public resources while others around them struggle, without making such claims, to pay their bills and taxes and to support their families. Americans who are religious, moreover, sometimes feel that by depending on the law, they demonstrate a lack of faith in God and the willingness of a divine presence to bring justice to human affairs.[26]

Engel found in pioneering research in the 1980s on the involvement of parents of children with disabilities in the IEP process that even if wronged in negotiations, or treated with condescension and disrespect by heavily credentialed education professionals, or frustrated by a lack of positive results, these parents were often reluctant to resort to the law and retreated in the face of what they actually thought to be unjust and unfair. Eager to preserve relationships with those they will have to work with on their children's behalf and remain on good terms with people in the community, women in particular, Engel notes, often back off from confrontation and seek peaceful, face-to-face negotiations with school officials on behalf of their disabled children.[27] Seen from this perspective, not to mention the various financial and emotional costs of a long judicial process, the Zobrests had much in their own immediate cultural environment to overcome in waging their struggle for money to pay Jim's sign language interpreter and to assert their principled claim that they knew what was best for him. Much of this narrative will be devoted to explaining what they had to overcome and how they marshaled the emotional and material resources to do so in their search for justice as they conceived of it. This story winds its way from the origins of both Larry and Sandi in ethnic families in working-class western Pennsylvania in the 1950s through to the day in 1993 they received the news that after losing their lawsuit at every lower level, their appeal to the Supreme Court had been successful. That our detailed analytical narrative stops there should not be taken as an indication that they have ceased advocating on Jim's behalf even now, when Jim is in his forties and advocates for himself.

AN AMERICAN DILEMMA: A CLASH OF RIGHTS

When confronted by this narrative, many people of good will respond reflexively, "Good for the Zobrests!" It is not difficult to sympathize with their efforts on their son's behalf. Even if we have only the most remote understanding, far removed from personal experience, we can easily understand that deafness presents many obstacles to a mainstreamed education. But there is more involved in their claim to public resources than Jim's welfare, and the proof is that it required ultimately a decision by the nation's highest court to sort out the issues posed by one deaf boy's need for a sign language interpreter in a southern Arizona Catholic high school. On the other side of the lawsuit were plausible claims made in support of a fundamental operating premise of American political and social order, embedded deeply and increasingly throughout the twentieth century in the Constitution, that religion and the state should be kept separate from one another and that breaches in the wall of separation were a danger to individual liberty and to the stability of democratic political institutions. The Zobrests' lawsuit was accompanied through the courts by an unusually large number of friend of the court briefs filed by such large, well-respected public advocacy organizations as the American Civil Liberties Union (ACLU), the National School Boards Association, the American Jewish Committee, People for the American Way, the National PTA, Americans United for Separation of Church and State (Americans United), and the Council on Religious Freedom on behalf of the case presented by John Richardson for the Catalina Foothills School District.[28] Separation of church and state arguably represents one important formulation of the American Way, and for a good reason: it has assisted in maintaining unity in a greatly diverse society in which people do not want for reasons to be at one another's throats. For Americans concerned about religious liberty and anxious about the progressive secularization of American society, the high degree of church-state separation that came to exist in late twentieth-century America is a danger to social order and public morality. The ideological confrontation of secularists and believers and church-state separationists and accommodationists created a polarized public context for the weighing of the Zobrests' claims. In the Zobrests' lawsuit, the discourse of church-state separation was at the heart of the lawsuit from beginning to end, and because of its familiarity and the well-known controversies, such as those over school prayer or the teaching of evolution or creationism that were a part of it, that discourse mostly surpassed attention to just what rights are held by people with disabilities in Jim Zobrest's situation.

The authors struggled with themselves to find the exact place of their sympathies when thinking about the Zobrests' lawsuit, which seemed to them a struggle between two goods. Both authors are to one extent or another longtime partisans in defense of strict church-state separation. Whatever disagreements they may have with one another on the precise elevation of the barrier that answers the question "How high the wall of separation?" both believe in the claims made on behalf of the argument that preservation of a line of separation is a key to social peace and stability. But church-state conflicts never occur in a vacuum, and frequently those asserting needs that broach the wall have serious claims to justice, such as the education of a child with a disability, the right to which has been established in federal law. Both authors are separationists, but they are also partisans on behalf of the rights of those with disabilities. Like Jim Zobrest, Bruce Dierenfield has had a lifelong hearing impairment, though not to the same degree, and he, too, has experienced some of the misunderstanding, social isolation from, and impatience of the hearing majority that Jim has endured. At the same time, Dierenfield learned a great deal in the course of writing this book about Deaf culture and about signed languages, which he himself has not needed or mastered. In such conflicts between two equally compelling ideas of the good and the right, a balance has to be struck between not only which claim is more compelling in the present, but also which claim emerging triumphant is likely to guide us well (or poorly) in the future. The authors' enthusiasm for the Zobrests' lawsuit and for the court's decision in their favor is tempered by knowledge that the claims of both sides had merit. They share the anxieties of those who fear the dismantling of the wall of separation to which the *Zobrest* decision might contribute. Precedent must be taken seriously in constitutional interpretation.

Concern for precedent is a working assumption guiding the ordinary behaviors of prudent people and, not coincidentally, a judicial axiom guiding the decisions of judges and juries. Separationists were alarmed by the Zobrest lawsuit, as the large number of amicus briefs against their claim establishes. One of those friends of the court briefs was filed by Americans United, the oldest, largest, and the most ideologically consistent separationist organization in the country. Its then director of communications, Rob Boston, noted in response to an email inquiry in 2015 that the Zobrest case was "not an easy one for us," because Jim was both disabled and "academically gifted and a lot of people felt sympathy for him—and I can understand why."[29] But Americans United was also concerned with precedent.[30] Doubtless, its concerns grew with the understanding that the court seemed to be composed of justices increasingly eager to be more accommodating to religion and the knowledge that the senior counsel for the Zobrests was Pennsylvania attorney William Bentley Ball. Ball was a devout Catholic, staunch conservative politically since his anti–New Deal awakening in his teens in the 1930s and then in the Wendell Willkie presidential campaign of 1940, a long-time and articulate critic of strict separation of church and state, and one of the most prominent First Amendment litigators of the late twentieth century. For decades, he had been seeking strategies to bring down much of the wall of separation in the matter of educational resources.[31] But then, what might the partisans at Americans United have made of Thomas Berning, Ball's junior colleague in the Zobrests' struggle? Then in his early thirties, Berning came out of a grassroots, progressive legal advocacy background at the Arizona Center for Law in the Public Interest, and under most circumstances defined himself, as did his colleagues at the center, as a separationist in church-state conflicts.

Berning understands that his partnership with Ball looked odd on paper. Beyond his great admiration for Ball as a dedicated and principled attorney, and an understanding of what he might learn from him about constitutional litigation, Berning weighed the two sides of the issue and decided, as have the authors, that the claims on behalf of disability rights in the Zobrests' lawsuit were larger than the fears that could realistically grow from it about the height of the wall of separation.[32]

"We viewed," Rob Boston says by way of contrast, the Zobrests' case as "another slide, if you will on the slippery slope" that would hand public resources over to parochial schools.[33] Boston is correct. As doctrinal precedent, *Zobrest v. Catalina Foothills School District* has been invoked by the court in important decisions since 1993, and informally it has been a source of inspiration to parents with disabled children seeking public funds to send them to religiously affiliated schools to press their claims to public resources.[34] As becomes clear in our review of both the coming together of the views of the five-justice majority in the decision and the direction that the court at the time was taking toward a less strictly separationist stance, the decision in the Zobrests' lawsuit appears to have been conceived as one of a number of precedents for shifting the boundaries.[35] Ball sought ways to impress upon the court the sympathetic nature of the appellant as a serious and highly motivated, though profoundly deaf, student and of his financially struggling parents. (It was also made purposefully known that he had taken the case pro bono and had raised funds, alongside the Zobrests, to pay for his expenses and the court costs.) This compelling human detail was probably not irrelevant to the Supreme Court five-justice majority's sense that the case was a sympathetic one to help further a more general accommodationist stance.

But it also becomes clear, however sympathetic Jim and his struggling parents might have appeared, that the court majority did not inquire deeply into the disability aspects of the case. Its decision missed an opportunity to educate the public about disability rights and the practical, as well as legal, circumstances of people with hearing impairments. In consequence, the majority opinion assumed a position on the key problem of the role of sign language interpreters in schools that lacked intimate knowledge of the work that interpreters, including Jim Santeford, Jim Zobrest's principal sign interpreter while at Salpointe, actually did in the classroom and inside the school building more generally.[36] While students with disabilities certainly derived benefits from the decision, disability was the servant of a larger, more long-standing, and more intensely controversial agenda that was advancing on a broad front of practical issues. Religious voices were asserting themselves more aggressively in American electoral politics in the late twentieth century and called for friendlier laws and policies toward religious institutions and religions in their relations with government. Big hearted and full of sympathy for the underdog in confrontations with the state power, which his conservative instincts led him to deeply distrust, William Bentley Ball had a daughter, Virginia (Ginny), whose career is in speech therapy with hearing impaired children, and a deaf son-in-law, Sandy. He could certainly not be said to have cynically used the Zobrests to advance that larger agenda. He believed in their case because in fundamental ways, he saw the stakes in the case with the same attitudes toward equity and power as Thomas Berning did. But he was certainly conscious that the case he advanced was serving jurisprudential purposes that his life had been dedicated to pursuing.

The authors have presented their own individual views in the belief that with events as recent and as consequential as those related in this book, it would be disingenuous to leave the impression of a completely neutral stance. They are citizens of this time in history and teach the country's history from the distant past to the present moment. But they hope nonetheless to report objectively and accurately the claims of both sides of the dispute, with respect for the seriousness of purpose and sense of responsibility to advance the rule of law that they displayed throughout the course of the lawsuit. Ultimately, the claims of this book to make a contribution to the history of the United States in the late twentieth century and to capture the lives of ordinary Americans like the Zobrests, involved in extraordinary circumstances in that time, rest on that aspiration.

The book proceeds logically through a chronological narrative that combines the social history of the search for mainstream schooling with the legal history of the quest for justice, as the Zobrests have understood it. Chapter 1 traces Jim's life and early education from his pediatrician's diagnosis of his profound hearing loss through his schooling in Erie, Pennsylvania, and his parents' decision to move to Tucson to enroll him in ASDB. Chapter 2 traces Jim's years at ASDB, his enrollment in the public schools of suburban Catalina Foothills, and the decision to send him to Salpointe Catholic High School. Chapter 3 analyzes Jim's high school education and social experience at Salpointe and, among other matters, enquires into an issue, the role of the sign language interpreter in the mainstream classroom, which proved central to the Supreme Court pleadings and the court majority's decision. Chapter 4 discusses the origin to the lawsuit that became *Zobrest v. Catalina Foothills School District*, and chapter 5 analyzes the movement of the lawsuit before the Supreme Court and the court's June 1993 decision on the Zobrests' behalf. The final chapter, chapter 6, draws together the Zobrests' experience as successful litigants, Jim's adult life to this point in time, and the *Zobrest* decision's influence on court rulings since 1993.

1 PARENTING, TRAINING, AND SCHOOLING

The Zobrests Encounter Deafness

HEARING PARENTS, PARENTING A DEAF CHILD

Newborns, especially firstborns, are demanding strangers who enter their parents' lives as both a joy and a puzzle because their needs are incessant but can be only imperfectly understood.[1] Born on March 3, 1974, in Erie, Pennsylvania, Jim Zobrest soon constituted an especially perplexing puzzle and a slowly developing feeling of anxiety. The infant was in good health but seemed to be unresponsive to sound. "We could run a vacuum under his crib," Sandi Zobrest recalls, "and [he] never woke up." At an early checkup, the pediatrician assured Sandi and Larry that some babies are just that way and suggested that they be patient. As Jim approached a year old, their patience was wearing thin. They would occasionally bang pots and pans near his bed; sometimes he would awake, and they would convince themselves he could hear. At other times, however, there was no response. Finally, at one of their visits to the doctor, they raised the question more insistently. The pediatrician took out a whistle and blew it hard. When Jim didn't react, he called in a colleague from across the hall, an ear, nose, and throat specialist, who ran the standard tests. The little boy seemed to hear nothing. With that matter-of-fact tactlessness with which doctors steel themselves against yielding emotionally to news that parents are likely to take badly, the specialist announced, as Sandi paraphrases, "Oh, yeah, you're right, he's deaf, yeah.... But there's a real good school for deaf kiddies. He can go there."[2] Years later, as more came to be known about the heritability of deafness, the Zobrests learned Jim's deafness was a consequence of a genetic, autosomal recessive disorder found more commonly among people of southern European origin for which they, both with full or partial Calabrese Italian background, carried the contributive gene.[3] When the Zobrests tell the story of their discovery of Jim's deafness and its roots in group genetics, they reveal that in that knowledge there lay a key that not only explained their son's disability but also gave them a path they conceived for confronting it. Jim possessed a malady that had a medical explanation, and which, if it could not be cured, could be compensated for with the assistance of medical science.

Jim's sensorineural deafness affected both of his inner ears, resulting in a profound hearing loss at the level of all finer sounds, such as spoken language, because sound could not travel from his inner ears to be processed by the brain. His deafness was not progressive, but stable over time. His middle ears were healthy and functional at processing sound waves. As a result, with the assistance of hearing aids in both ears, with which he was fitted at a very early age, he could detect a wide frequency of sounds, mostly indistinct, but including with repetitive usage over time simple, familiar words. But Jim's comprehension of language would be largely independent of sound. Audiological examinations in 1985 and 1986 revealed that Jim possessed too little hearing, despite his hearing aids, to respond to even louder than normal conversation. After years of constant training in processing what sound he could detect and in speechreading (i.e., lipreading), by the time he was twelve, with visual cues provided through sign language interpretation, he could make sense of 80 to 90 percent of words in conversation.[4]

The doctor highlighted in that casual diagnosis and prescription what would become the central concern of the new parents' lives for the next two decades: Jim's deafness and the training and education that overcoming his disability would require. Jim's speechreading prowess, a measure of the effort to overcome his hearing impairment and integrate into the hearing majority that began at the Gertrude A. Barber Center in Erie—the school for deaf children and children with other disabilities the pediatrician referenced—is testimony to that concern and the struggles that grew out of it.

For the Zobrests, a brief period of grief and confusion followed the doctor's diagnosis. Sandi Zobrest recalls, "When I found out Jim was deaf, I was devastated. I had so many questions and so many doubts about my ability to deal with this. For two weeks I cried and mourned for his lack of hearing."[5] It is not difficult to understand her initial reaction. Congenital deafness is an invisible and low-incidence (approximately one in a thousand newborns) disability, but one with profound implications for the development of a child. Without hearing, the mastery of language is problematic, and without language, thinking becomes problematic. These are problems that have to be met head on and mastered in a timely way by parents of deaf infants, because the critical developmental moment for connecting meaning to sounds is the narrow window between eighteen and thirty-six months, and the foundations of language are sown by age five. By age twelve, our ability to learn a first language has significantly declined.[6]

Practical challenges aside—and they are many and constant—deafness has long been stigmatized. The representations of those born profoundly hearing impaired have been negative throughout the past, and they are often deeply aversive or pervaded by pity and fear. The profoundly deaf are not only unable to hear, but often they are also unable to speak intelligibly except with their hands, using a signed language.[7] Most hearing people do not appreciate what can be communicated with signed languages, nor the extent to which signed languages have their own complex structures and rich vocabularies. Unable to communicate in conventional ways, the deaf have been taken to be stupid, "deaf and dumb." Even those better informed, who know this is not so, find the investment of time and energy required to communicate with people who are hearing impaired too difficult to be worthwhile, which was often Jim Zobrest's experience with his classmates in the schools, public and parochial, in which he was mainstreamed.[8] So, the deaf are overlooked, and while they may enjoy the solidarity of their own community, with its history, language (American Sign Language [ASL]) and hard-won identity, they may easily become isolated from the hearing majority and from the larger society. Some deaf people come to prefer life that way and opt for a Deaf ethnicity, community, and identity, all of which have come to be symbolized by spelling *deaf* with a capital *D*, as if signifying peoplehood.[9] This position, being "culturally deaf," has intensified within the Deaf community in the last three decades, but it is not one that Jim Zobrest has ever embraced, in spite of his isolation from the hearing world. Throughout his life, as we shall see, Jim has remained suspended between the hearing and Deaf worlds, not completely at home in either one.

Seen in the conventionally ableist way, deafness is not a fate that the majority of hearing parents would choose for their children. That is not the only way to see the situation, because since the mid-twentieth century, changing attitudes toward disability, new assistive technologies, cochlear implants, and advances in the education of deaf students have come to make the possibilities for living a much fuller and productive life with a hearing impairment greater than ever before. But because 90 percent of those born deaf have hearing parents, who in all likelihood have no immediate family or social connection to deafness, the situation with which the Zobrests were presented was unprecedented for them and appeared a challenge at the most basic level of parenting, far beyond the inconveniences of middle-of-the-night feedings and diaper changes that deprive parents of newborns of sleep for months on end.

The doctor's diagnosis was the start of a long project of support, assistance, and advocacy for the Zobrests that continues to this day. Larry and Sandi Zobrest sought to become insiders to a condition of being that they, in effect, could only know from an existential position outside it. The practical and psychological burden of such a situation, all-consuming and constant, seems plainly apparent to those not sharing the challenges of being parents of a child with a disability, but aware themselves of what hard work responsible parenting is under the best of circumstances. Much more difficult to appreciate are the rewards involved, for they have been much slower to penetrate public consciousness.

For the Zobrests, and especially for Sandi Zobrest, Jim's deafness soon gave birth to an inspired, single-minded feeling of purpose that became a central force in the family's life. Larry played a role during the family's Erie years in activism on behalf of people who are hearing impaired but mostly defined his purpose as that of principal breadwinner. This often proved to be struggle enough in their up-and-down financial circumstances, especially during the years when Jim was at Salpointe Catholic High School—before they won their case and got compensated by the Catalina Foothills School District—and they were paying about $8,500 a year for his sign interpreter, out of pocket, with the assistance of donors. Larry has an extraordinary work ethic. (He was up on the roof of their home in the Tucson desert at three in the afternoon on a mid-July day, fixing the air conditioning condenser, the day the authors interviewed the family in 2015. It was 115 degrees.) He has been willing to go in different directions to make a living. He had always wanted to be in business for himself after years as a salesman for a large corporation. But a series of business reversals in the dry-cleaning business he owned in Tucson, in which Sandi also worked, and an arson fire in the central plant that did the dry cleaning, brought them ultimately to declare personal bankruptcy. Larry's brief engagement with advocacy and with intervening on Jim's behalf declined over the years, as the challenges of making a living became more difficult.[10]

Sandi grew quickly into the role she was to play seeking the means to achieve access to the hearing world for Jim. She recalls that after those two weeks of grieving, she said to herself finally, "Enough!" She began to understand that "it was my responsibility to be sure [Jim] was not denied anything because of his handicap."[11] Sandi also worked outside the home from time to time. She had the educational credentials for primary school teaching and was teaching first grade when Jim was born. After doing postgraduate work at both Edinboro State College and Mercyhurst College, she was able to teach methods of deaf communication to hearing people. She also proved a good office manager for engineering firms, and she worked as well as a real estate sales agent. Today, among other ways she earns money from time to time, she writes children's books. But it fell to her to mount the family's campaigns on Jim's behalf and to organize the family around Jim's needs. The same is true in many homes in which parents mobilize themselves around a disabled child's welfare, and mothers, as caregivers, negotiators, and facilitators, become the focus of those efforts, transforming the mother's traditional role into one of advocacy in public, the role that we see Sandi playing throughout Jim's education, from the Barber Center through his four years at Salpointe.[12] It would be Sandi who negotiated Jim's IEPs with school administrators over the years; and it would be Sandi who took the first steps that led to the lawsuit that brought the Zobrests to the Supreme Court in 1993.

Her practical guidance of Jim's education was intimately connected with another process of decision making regarding the course of his language development, which influenced his schooling but also was to lie at the heart of communications within the Zobrest family's own interrelationships. Choices were made early on over what sort of training in language Jim was to have. These choices were largely Sandi's to exercise, not only because of Larry's attention to making a living but also because Larry had trouble learning to sign. This is hardly uncommon in families with a deaf child. It is mothers who have most often been the ones who determine the family's mode of communication. Those choices vary with the parent's educational level, and they are exercised within the context of the availability of preschool training and the degree of the child's hearing loss. Mothers with a relatively high level of education, like Sandi, not only learn to sign, as Sandi did, but are likely to attempt to make a more or less careful study of the options for their deaf child's development and supplement the work of training and education at home. Larry played a role in these decisions, but without the ability to sign fluently and immersed in his efforts to make a living, he played a more limited role.[13]

Following the Zobrests' struggles and their unlikely path to the U.S. Supreme Court, which at that time heard only about 3 percent of the cases brought to it upon appeal, and to a successful outcome there, one cannot help but be impressed with Sandi Zobrest's dedication to and energy for the task she defined for herself. That task was never to concede an inch to popular wisdom about what Jim would not be able to do and to make certain he would enjoy every opportunity to have the mainstream life Americans typically aspired to—an education that prepared him for the workforce, a career at something worthy that he valued doing, and a place in the community, the community of hearing people. Expectations about what people with disabilities, the deaf and hearing impaired and others, too, with physical and cognitive disabilities, could do and the knowledge of their capacities for self-determination were rapidly changing in the United States in the late twentieth century, so Sandi's hopes were by no means outside a growing, progressive consensus.[14]

Interviews with two of Sandi Zobrest's longtime friends and one of her attorneys confirmed the authors' insights into her character. Both Ginny Ball Duncan and Mary Prus have known her since the Erie years, and both have long been involved to one extent or another in an active network of moral and practical support Sandi formed around her. If asked to characterize Sandi, they refer first to her energy and single-mindedness. In one of the first observations she made about Sandi, Ginny Ball Duncan, Jim's speech therapist at the Barber Center, who has been deeply involved for years in deaf education and in disability service work, called Sandi a "Queen Advocate." Ball Duncan observed that she is "a formidable force to reckon with."[15] Mary Prus, whose friendship with Larry began in childhood in Warren, Pennsylvania, and who was a classmate of Sandi's in college, stated that "her drive and determination know no bounds." "Sandi's way of dealing with something," Prus continued, "is to fight back. . . . The harder things get for Sandi, the more she digs in and is going to get through it and get past it. . . . If you told her that this was not the thing to do for Jim, and she thought it was, she would run right over you."[16] Those who have known her for a briefer period of time and solely professionally would agree. Thomas Berning, co-counsel in the Zobrests' lawsuit, has spoken of Sandi possessing "a laser-like focus" in getting what she believed was best for Jim and also what she thought was right for him.[17]

If Sandi Zobrest, as she explained her evolution out of grieving over the pediatrician's diagnosis, remembered "finding her voice" in resolving to become Jim's voice, she is quick to add that she did not come by challenging powerful institutions and authoritative individuals in the way common to many baby boomers—protesting the Vietnam War or for racial equality. She claims to have had a strong sense of right and wrong as a child, but to have been timid under most circumstances and to have been "terrified of public speaking" in school as an adolescent. Her sense of right and wrong did not lead her while in college during 1966–1970, at the height of the protests against the war, to oppose the war publicly. In fact, she assumed the opposite stance. "My brother was in the Navy patrolling the coast of Vietnam. My father received a Bronze Star for his service in World War II and my uncle was a [Navy] frogman. I felt it was an honor to fight for your country. . . . I thought it was extremely un-American [to protest against the war]. I spoke up in defense of our military in conversations with friends but stayed away from any organized movement."[18]

Nor did the disability rights movement of the late twentieth century appear as anything but a background inspiration for her single-minded pursuit of justice and opportunity for Jim. Aside from a brief period of public activism on behalf of deaf and hearing impaired children in Erie, the Zobrests have not united themselves with organized grassroots disability politics. Their struggles to keep up the middle-class standard of living to which they aspire, and toward which each of them has been variously employed, hardly gave them time for protests, demonstrations, and organizing. Sandi has certainly felt a sense of solidarity with other parents of deaf children struggling to find resources to assist in their education. But as was the case after the victory in the U.S. Supreme Court, when she was written or called for advice by those parents, the role she found most congenial was responding to individuals, as one by one they approached her. Furthermore, to the extent that late twentieth-century disability politics, especially among the deaf and hearing impaired, was also a politics of identity, community building, and culture, it was not of interest to the Zobrests, for ultimately their vision was one framed by access to the mainstream and individual opportunity, not collective disability identity and group solidarity. If she came to feel that deafness should not be mourned and should hold no one back, she was still not ready to celebrate it as the center of a culture and a new sort of ethnicity. It was still, for the Zobrests, a condition that required fixing, a deficit to be compensated for. Jim would come to share this understanding with his parents relatively early in his life. Ironically, had Sandi opted for the latter path in guiding Jim, the path into the Deaf world, judged from the perspective of contemporary disability politics the more radical alternative, she might not have been the effective agent for social change that she crafted herself into being. The need to challenge social institutions, educational experts, and the Constitution itself, in the quest to help her son advance against the resistance she often encountered, would have been less necessary, for Jim would have lived in the Deaf world and would not have sought the mainstream.[19]

However the Zobrests may actually vote, Sandi remains a person with conservative, traditional, and patriotic instincts. She regrets the shallow cultural roots and short historical memory she believes most Americans possess. She is proud of her Italian origins and wants to keep alive for her grandchildren the story of her family's emigration from southern Italy. She has a robust respect for the traditional work ethic she associates with her immigrant ancestors and is concerned that government welfare programs sap individual initiative. Her support for programs of assistance for people with disabilities is rooted in an understanding that most of them who are of employment age may need assistance to get to the point at which they can support themselves and stand on their own. The Zobrests' 2014 decision to begin preparations to relocate in North Carolina, they explained to the authors, was prompted by difficulties engaging Arizona's Vocational Rehabilitation Agency in the effort to help find employment for Jim, who has worked during his adult life at a variety of temporary and generally poorly paying jobs. Regardless of his substantial intelligence, he has had no career to follow.[20]

Tempting though it may be to cast the Zobrests' story as an overcoming narrative of pushing back effectively against hostile institutional power and heartless bureaucrats in the service of their son's welfare, it would not be an accurate picture from Sandi Zobrest's viewpoint. She has tended to explain the resistance she has encountered more to ignorance and the narrowed vision of public school administrators than to malice and prejudice. At the time, in many aspects of Jim's early training and of his education, they were pioneers, and neither they nor the people they had to negotiate with had a great deal of experience in fitting deaf children into the world on equal terms with their hearing peers. She could be scrupulously fair in stating the views of those who opposed her to the extent that John Richardson, the Catalina Foothill's School District's attorney, expressed gratitude for the generosity with which she characterized the position of the school district in a television interview a few days after the Zobrests' disappointing result in Federal District Court in Tucson.[21] She is aware that her single-mindedness and matter-of-fact way of expressing herself could be off-putting, if not simply counterproductive. Besides, it is exhausting to be constantly in an oppositional stance. It places a particular burden on a woman, for cultural expectations, even in the post-feminist late twentieth century, remained inclined to find nonaggressive and conciliatory complaint behavior desirable in women, and women themselves might be likely to act accordingly.[22] Women like Sandi were invited to try to fulfill those expectations, no matter how counterproductive they might be.

The tensions in the situation are tellingly revealed in a conversation with Sandi that Mary Prus recalls. She remembers Sandi saying to her, with apparent frustration and annoyance in the midst of the family's legal struggles, something like, "'Why does it have to be this hard? When is the day going to come when I will not have to be pushing and shoving and coming off as the bitch mother in the room . . . in order for my child to have what he deserves to have?'" Prus came to feel that Sandi, in fact, had no choice but to assume the demanding stance she assumed, precisely because the Zobrests were pioneers in mainstreaming a deaf child. They chose to raise

Jim in a hearing world that needed to be shaken up before it was ready to extend itself to understand his needs.[23] Whatever ambivalence she might have felt, the authors found that most of the time when she felt she had to, Sandi Zobrest did indeed run over those who stood in her way, and she didn't look back.

THE ERIE YEARS

Both Larry and Sandi Zobrest are deeply rooted in the world of mid-twentieth-century ethnic Catholic working people and in western Pennsylvania, one of the heartlands of that American experience. Their backgrounds stand out only for how representative they are of that broad strand of Middle America. Larry was born in 1947 in the small industrial city of Warren, Pennsylvania, to parents of Polish and Italian background who divorced when he was twelve. He lived with his father and mostly shifted for himself. He got used to being independent and self-sufficient. The Polish surname *Zobrest* was hardly Italian, but if you grew up on the west side of Warren in the 1950s, you were more or less Italian, and Larry was half Italian. Prus remembers Larry as one of a group of "goombahs," regular neighborhood guys, who wore their "West End Boys" social club jackets, had a camp in the woods where they hung out and drank beer, and attended the Italian parish Catholic Church and the city's Catholic high school, where Larry played football. Larry's mother was a nurse, and his father owned and operated a truck service.[24] Sandi Mangone was born in Pittsburgh in 1948. Her parents were both descended from southern Italian immigrants. They resided in one of the city's ethnic enclaves, and, like Larry, she was raised with a deep sense of Italian Americanness and given a Catholic education. Her mother worked for the Social Security Administration in Pittsburgh, while her father was director of recreation at a correctional facility.[25]

While before World War II adolescents of their background might not have gone on to college but directly into marriage and the workforce, the United States was flush with prosperity and opportunities for social mobility when they left high school in the mid-1960s, and increasingly a college education was not only financially possible but also seemed necessary for work in a changing economy. Both went on to college at Erie's two Catholic schools, Gannon for men and Mercyhurst for women. Sandi developed a tight circle of friends, including Mary Prus, among her suite mates who would follow her through life. She and Larry met at a party, began dating, and married in 1972.[26]

In the 1970s, before wholesale deindustrialization had begun to damage its economy and to lead to the decline of its older neighborhoods, Erie, with

With their son, Jim, Larry and Sandi Zobrest in front of a highway sign they had petitioned the Pennsylvania Department of Transportation to post, Erie, Pennsylvania, winter 1977. (Reprinted with permission from Times Publishing Company, Erie, PA. Copyright 2019)

a population near 130,000, was a congenial, scenic, and prosperous place for young couples like the Zobrests. The job market was still buoyant and a magnet for newcomers, good housing was affordable, and Presque Isle State Park and the Lake Erie shore offered possibilities for recreation. It had the prestige of its two Catholic institutions of higher education, while only twenty miles away a public teachers' college had been expanded at Edinboro in 1960 to become a branch of the state university system. New shopping malls were bringing the contemporary consumer economy to residents. Ginny Ball Duncan remembers, too, that Erie was familiarly Roman Catholic and working class, and she characterizes it in the early 1970s as a city with a parish church and a bar on every corner.[27]

It was the sort of city that invited young people to stay and look for work after graduating, or to come from elsewhere in search of a job, and that is how the cohort of post–bachelor's degree young adults who became the Zobrests' friends and Sandi's network of support took form. When Larry graduated in 1970 with a BA in business administration, he took a local job with the 3M Corporation selling business machines and copiers, a lucrative and popular new technology.[28] Sandi lacked strong direction in her own studies and freely confessed to her friend Mary that, like many young women at Mercyhurst at the time, she was in college in pursuit of a "MRS. Degree," seeking a husband. But she had a practical side and knew she would probably have to work after she left college. Her mother had a longtime job, so she certainly had models of working women immediately around her. She had to pick a major, which was originally domesticity-related home economics, but when she proved poor at sewing, she was encouraged to switch to elementary education. She got a job after graduating, teaching in the Erie public schools. Though she would drop out of full-time employment after Jim was born in 1974, a decision enhanced by the birth of their second child, Sam, in 1976, Sandi saw the value of deepening her credentials to raise her teacher's pay grade. She got a master's degree at Edinboro State in the late 1970s. By that time, the value of being skillful in signed language was already well apparent to her as a parent, and she took courses in deaf communication and in audiology, which augmented what she had already learned to assist Jim and helped fulfill her MA requirements.[29]

The Zobrests remember their years in Erie fondly. They were both to find a sense of purpose in parenting a disabled child, who might have been deaf, but who was cute, clever, smart, and stubborn, and hence an unending surprise and delight. Just as his parents hoped in quickly planning a second child after Jim's birth, Jim and his brother bonded firmly early in life, a bond that continued through their Salpointe years and has never lessened in adulthood. Though Sam is not hearing impaired, his first language was ASL, which his mother taught him. One of his earliest explicit conversations with his mother was to inform her in sign, at a bit less than a year old, that his new booties were too tight. "Shoes off, hurt!" he signed.[30] The brothers quickly became a conspiracy of two, pulling pranks that were successful in proportion to the cluelessness of the outside world about what they were up to and its ignorance of the language, complete with many of their own private signs, by which they expressed themselves to one another. They regularly fooled babysitters. Years later, in crowded, noisy corridors in high school between classes, they could conveniently speak to each other from a distance.[31]

The family's life in Erie was comfortable and communal. Larry did well as a salesman, and within a few years, they were able to buy a much larger house on open land in an attractive neighborhood.[32] Their home became the center of a network of friendships, largely directed by Sandi and her female friends, among former college classmates and newcomers to Erie and their spouses.[33] This network contained overlapping connections to the extent it also served as a support network for childcare and training for Sandi. Ginny Ball Duncan, who was Jim's first speech therapist, and her husband were participants, as was Mary Prus, then a daycare teacher, and her husband. Mary and Sandi often merged care of their children, and their families socialized frequently. Mary interacted with Jim often enough that she decided to learn to sign. Her children became Jim's lifelong friends.

THE GERTRUDE A. BARBER CENTER

The "school for deaf kiddies" Jim's pediatrician referenced was the Gertrude A. Barber Center (now the Barber National Institute), a uniquely progressive facility for its time that was dedicated to the training and education of children with disabilities. Its existence was one of those resources, public and private, the Zobrests discovered and developed in themselves, in their friends, and in their local community, that supported their efforts to raise Jim and helped them settle more confidently into their role as parents of a deaf child. The Barber Center was not dedicated exclusively to deaf children but did have a Deaf and Hard of Hearing Division.

The center was the vision of Gertrude A. Barber (1911–2000), an Erie native and Penn State graduate. As assistant superintendent for elementary education in the Erie Public Schools, she developed an interest in the education of children with disabilities. Dr. Barber's post–World War II vision of special education was progressive, but not because it anticipated the idea of mainstreaming disabled children as much as possible in classrooms with their nondisabled peers. Segregation was less the problem for Barber than the fact that there was no provision for children with developmental disabilities in the public schools. To the extent they were educated at all, they were being sent away from their families and their communities to distant state and private educational facilities. Others were kept at home, without benefit of any schooling and in isolation from their peers. She wanted all these children schooled where they lived, not institutionalized or neglected, and she believed early in her career that that should be a public responsibility undertaken by educated professionals. In 1952 she established the first local classroom for developmentally disabled children within Erie's public school system. Barber left the Erie public schools and the uncertainties involved in making claims for the relatively small population of children she wanted to serve out of public school budgets in the 1960s. Through the aggressive pursuit of private funds, grants, and state funding, she built an educational center with a vision of service that came to encompass a wide variety of disabilities and a large staff of professionals. The children in the early years were mostly local, though there were some who came from outside Erie. Eventually in the early twenty-first century the institution Barber founded would serve over five thousand children and adults and become one of the largest employers in the region. The center was an obvious resource for the Zobrests, and they took full advantage of it.[34]

Just as the Barber Center was engaged in cutting-edge efforts to draw children with disabilities into school, it would also take part in the new trends in the training and education of deaf children through its emerging commitment to Total Communication. This was a new methodology of deaf pedagogy that had emerged in the late 1960s and made claims to surmount limitations imposed by past approaches. For a century, partisans of *oralism*, teaching the deaf language through lipreading and speech, and *manualism*, teaching the deaf language by building on ASL, as it had been developed historically by deaf people themselves, had fought a bitter, polemical battle. ASL became the language of instruction in 1817 when the American School for the Deaf, the nation's first school for the deaf, opened at Hartford, Connecticut, and its influence spread thereafter. It would become the language of instruction at what became Gallaudet University, the world's first institution of higher education for the deaf, when it was founded in Washington, D.C., in 1864. But the oralists came to have the advantage in the argument from the late nineteenth century on for two reasons. They enjoyed both the possession of superior resources through support of Alexander Graham Bell, the wealthy inventor of the telephone whose wife was deaf, and the support of most hearing parents of deaf children, who possessed the desire for conventional communication with their children and for imparting skills that would prepare children to live in their world, the hearing world. A prominent argument they employed against the manualists was that ASL was not a language, but merely a rude gestural vernacular that served not to enlighten, but to isolate and hence to keep deaf people ignorant. Under the hegemony of oralism, most deaf children henceforth were to be educated in an oral-only setting, and signed language would serve as their vernacular outside the classroom, where it was enthusiastically employed in ordinary conversation. To the extent that speechreading and articulation were difficult for a profoundly hearing impaired child who was born deaf, the results for imparting orally based language were very uneven. With a tenuous hold on language, most deaf children were poorly educated.[35]

Yet by the mid-twentieth century the language of the American Deaf, ASL, was being seriously studied and regarded as the basis for pedagogy. The research of the Gallaudet University English professor and linguist William Stokoe Jr., published in the 1960s, was at the time beginning to establish ASL as a true language with a syntax, structure, and grammar, expressed not through the methods of oral language, but by location of hands relative to the body, handshaping, orientation of the signer's body, facial expression, and motion in space. Stokoe's dramatic findings were being digested among educators in the early 1970s, but even so, it continued to be unclear to parents and to deaf educators focused on mainstream opportunities whether ASL was an effective foundation for a traditional, English-language education.[36]

Total Communication, in contrast, made two very compelling claims on the attention of parents like the Zobrests and those who would educate and train their children. It broke through the old polemic of signed language versus speech and advanced the claim of both of them, acting together as part of a total package of skills. It would employ signing, speechreading, speech and speech therapy, and fingerspelling, and use of whatever hearing a child possessed, enhanced by powerful new hearing aids. It advanced individual communication through speech and signing performed simultaneously. Instead of ASL, however, most proponents offered Signed Exact English (SEE). SEE is not a language and does not possess a vocabulary, but is instead a visual coding system. Introduced around 1971, SEE takes ASL and translates it into a type of English by adopting English word order and adding English word endings and tenses. SEE advances the structure of English, like ASL, through handshaping, the direction of the palm, location, and movement. In the classroom setting, SEE serves to provide a signed interpretation of what a teacher says, while simultaneously a teacher pronounces English words, and students also use both speechreading and whatever hearing they possess to understand it. Students have the benefit simultaneously of the teacher and the interpreter. Students are encouraged to speak, both to communicate with those who can hear, and as an aid in their own development of speechreading. SEE and Total Communication seemed to offer hearing impaired Americans the claims of the language of the powerful hearing majority, which was a compelling accompaniment to the emerging ideology of mainstreaming.[37]

Certainly for hearing parents like the Zobrests, who never envisioned that Jim's community would be, nor should it necessarily be, other deaf people, and who wanted their son to participate in the hearing world, the claims of Total Communication and SEE advanced by the Barber Center could not have been more attractive. Under any circumstance, Total Communication and SEE provided the prospect of a more effective pedagogy than oral-only methods, though ultimately it certainly depended on orality. To that extent, as the situation was explained to them by educators, the Zobrests appeared to have positive choices the parents of deaf children had lacked in the past.

The experience of the first generations of mainstreamed deaf children, however, did not suggest that Total Communication and SEE in a mainstreamed environment of the type to which the Zobrests aspired offered an uncomplicated triumph over the limitations imposed by deafness in schools dominated by the hearing majority. Students still might lose a good deal of content, depending on their individual speechreading abilities and hearing comprehension and on the skills of their instructors and interpreters. Moreover, even if the relatively few deaf students in that hearing environment were able to get a good education from the standpoint of learning the

English-language curriculum, they could not necessarily share equally in the culture of the school nor of their peer group, which might have its effects on self-esteem and self-confidence, and hence ultimately on learning itself. Socialization, both at the instructional and peer group levels, is a vital part of the larger experience of being in K–12 schools, as are the informal interactions over course work that take place daily among students.[38]

In consequence, it has been observed that young deaf children may be among the only students with disabilities for whom the mainstreamed educational situation is not necessarily the best way to get educated, at least until they have a good command of language and relatively strong identities that breed self-confidence. When ASL is the early language of instruction and is taught as the language of the deaf and as integral to a unique and historical culture, with its own poetry or song or drama, it imparts an identity that lends itself to confidence, pride, and participation in a community of learners. Speechreading and learning conventional articulation, a major part of Total Communication, while not irrelevant for those who can make use of them, may well be a distraction from the perspective of effective early language learning. Moreover, as the relatively high level of educational achievement of deaf children of ASL-using deaf parents has suggested, ASL has proven to be an effective foundation for learning English.[39]

But these polarities had not yet been widely or publicly formed at the time the Zobrests encountered SEE and Total Communication. A pragmatic synthesis—a bicultural (hearing and Deaf) approach formed out of SEE, Total Communication, and ASL—would be formed years later but was not an option for the Zobrests at the time. Like other parents of deaf children, they had to make decisions in a situation that was unstable. The results of research on the consequences of SEE and Total Communication in a mainstreamed environment would not be known for some time, until the experience of Jim and other deaf students who were pioneers of this pedagogy was known.

The Zobrests could not know the extent to which the course they had begun to choose for Jim brought with it being isolated in a mainstreamed environment and would not solve all the learning problems he would encounter. What they did already know was that they were reluctant to see him become tracked in a different direction—into what they regarded as the much more restricted Deaf environment. But the path they personally had embarked on was by no means an even one, and their choices about Jim's education would continue to be made, sometimes seemingly contradictorily and without sufficient information to guide them, over the next decade. Eventually, too, in adolescence, as Jim began to examine his own identity and think about the future he wanted for himself, he would have a definite say in those choices. When he spoke to the media during the course of the lawsuit, Jim made strong public claims in defense of getting the resources to go into the mainstream environment offered at Salpointe, where he would be the only deaf student in the four years he attended the high school.

Jim Zobrest was somewhat less than two years old when he began to attend preschool at the Barber Center. He was a student there more or less continually until 1979, when he was five, and he was briefly enrolled in kindergarten at Grover Cleveland Elementary School in Erie. At the Barber Center there were at that moment too few deaf students to have an early childhood deaf program; Jim's classroom of eight to ten little children was also composed of those with autism and developmental disabilities. His preschool teacher, Mary Rita Weschler, then a recent graduate of Kent State University with a special education and deaf studies bachelor's degree, describes the purposes of the early childhood program for deaf children as preparing them "to have a basic understanding and facility with language . . . in order to promote normal communication as well as optimal emotional and social development."[40] Practically speaking, the program was also oriented toward preparing the children to enter the self-contained classroom for beginning learners with disabilities in Erie's public schools. Weschler and Jim's speech therapist, Ginny Ball Duncan, who had recently graduated with a bachelor's degree from Carlow College in Pittsburgh and was working on her master's degree at Edinboro State College at the time, both instructed him. They introduced him to language, largely through drills presented as games, that helped him understand things had names and characteristics that could be described. A round object, for example, was a ball, and it could be brown, or red, or blue. While in class Jim wore a phonic ear, the outsized sound processing box attached to big earphones then characteristic of auditory training, and was addressed by his teachers using a microphone. Though Ball Duncan found that Jim possessed insufficient hearing—eventually, with training, he would vaguely hear sounds and voices but no distinct words—to profit much from the phonic ear, these exercises were nonetheless supplemented by speechreading and articulation, as Total Communication required.[41] Both Ball Duncan and Weschler found young Jim to be highly intelligent and a quick, eager learner, who was active and curious in the classroom. But, Weschler recalls, he would have "profited from a more homogeneous mix of students," that is, a deaf classroom—as opposed to one with children with a variety of disabilities—where he could converse in signed language with the other children.[42] Though shy, he was, Ball Duncan recalls, "very headstrong," and in the manner of deaf children he would close his eyes when he did not want to cooperate.[43] Perhaps he was sometimes bored, outpacing the program for his training in language.

Both Ball Duncan and Weschler remember their experience with Jim as especially rewarding, because of active, cooperative involvement of the Zobrests in the work being done with Jim at the Barber Center and in the Erie deaf community.[44] The Zobrests enthusiastically assisted in Jim's education and in advocacy for local people with hearing impairments. Like other mothers, Sandi helped out as a teacher's aide in the classroom and on field trips, but the Zobrests went beyond that sort of typical assistance. The Barber Center encouraged parents to observe their children's school day training from a room off their classroom and continue the teachers' work at home, which Sandi quickly took up.

The first assignment for both parents was learning to sign through the methods Jim was learning. They committed themselves not only to help further his language abilities, but out of a feeling that he should not be left out of family conversations in familiar environments such as the dinner table. It has also become clearer, as the authors have already noted, through research on deaf children of deaf parents, that the educational attainment of those who learn signed language at a very early point is higher than deaf children who do not learn to sign early on, so Sandi's intuitive understanding of Jim's needs was of significant pedagogical help. Sandi learned SEE in coordination with the methods of Total Communication, and she took readily enough to this method of communication that after several years of study she would eventually teach it at Pima Community College in Tucson.[45] To this day, in all conversations with hearing people who do not sign, Sandi interprets constantly for Jim, while also keeping up her end of the oral conversation. It's exhausting work, as professional interpreters are quick to observe.

Relative to women, many adult men are lacking in fine small motor coordination that facilitates skill in sign. Early on, Larry found learning and practicing signed language much more difficult than Sandi did. He could fingerspell English words with some facility, but that is no way to have a conversation. He came to depend on Jim's abilities at speechreading to be understood by his son, or on Sandi or Sam to be his translators, and when all else failed, out of frustration he spoke loudly. In contrast, Sandi, Sam, and Jim (and eventually Jim's maternal grandmother, too) shared SEE and the methods of Total Communication and their own improvisations in vocabulary and shortcuts around grammar and punctuation—a "home sign"—that are common to creating a shared family idiom.[46]

Ginny Ball Duncan would send the little boy home with a "speech badge" taped to his coat, instructing the Zobrests on how to build upon what he had done in class that day. This was Ball Duncan's first job in what would be a long career working with deaf people, and Sandi's communication activities with Jim, not only following up what was being done in the classroom but also involving him in family conversations, made a deep impression on her. She learned how important it was for families to play a role in language development and in combating the isolation of deaf children, whose hearing parents often lacked the ability to communicate with them. She found Jim an above average communicator, because of the presence of Total Communication in his family and Sandi's willingness to instruct him at home. Sandi also discovered the oralist John Tracy Clinic in California, which provided parents, through the mail, with a step program of exercises in encouraging speech, and she used those materials, too, for a time.[47]

Beyond the Barber Center, the Zobrests were engaged in the Erie community. The young special educators and parents of deaf children found the deaf community in Erie too poorly organized to advance children's interests and isolated from the hearing world, a situation that many deaf people may well have preferred but that was not in line with the aspirations of these hearing parents to gain access and opportunity to the hearing world for their children and to sensitize the hearing world to their children's needs to facilitate that path. While certainly not hostile to the deaf community, they were hardly a part of it. A social club for the deaf did exist, but it was not advocacy oriented and catered only to adults seeking recreation and companionship. The Zobrests, Ginny Ball Duncan, and other members of their network founded the Erie County Speech and Hearing Association, a descendant of which continues to exist, within a few years of Jim's birth. In 1976, as a measure of its rootedness in hearing parents and its isolation from the adult deaf community, Sandi and Larry served as co-presidents. One of their first activities, with the support of elected township supervisors, was to convince Pennsylvania highway authorities to place two "Deaf Child Area" signs as a caution to drivers on a well-traveled state road near the Zobrests' home. They advocated for more of these signs in locations near schools attended by deaf children. They had "deaf awareness" cards, with relevant signs printed on them, for circulation among local emergency workers who might encounter deaf people in their work. Larry also worked with the Lions Club to get the service organization to subsidize the distribution of telephone linked telecommunications devices for the deaf and hearing impaired.[48]

LEAVING ERIE

While they appeared to be settling into the Erie community comfortably and purposefully, they nonetheless soon faced important decisions about Jim's schooling that would ultimately lead to their move to Tucson, Arizona.

Jim was about to exhaust the Barber Center's ability to assist him, and it was logical for him to now enter the Erie public schools. But the Erie schools were not yet set up to provide much in the way of early childhood education to approximately thirty deaf and hearing impaired students living in the school district. All hearing impaired young learners were congregated in a consolidated classroom, which comprised at once four grades, including kindergarten. After some years of trying to effect change, in 1978, a year before Jim was to enter kindergarten, a group of parents of deaf children in Erie filed a complaint with the Center for Law and the Deaf in Washington, which then presented it to the Office for Civil Rights of the U.S. Department of Education. Parents complained about the four grade levels in one classroom under the direction of one teacher, the absence of a coherent curriculum, and the fact that many of the teachers and school administrators, including school nurses, speech therapists, psychologists, and school bus drivers, who interacted daily with the children, did not know signed language. It was time, the parents thought, to begin to apply the terms of the new EAHCA, as they understood them, to the Erie schools. The school district argued that it was attempting to institute positive changes, and it was buying new equipment and hiring new, appropriately trained staff. It was mainstreaming those students, mostly those with some useful hearing, who could profit from integration into regular classrooms. It pointed out proudly that, in a reversal of the usual relations between urban and suburban school districts, the latter were sending deaf and hearing impaired students into Erie for their education rather than starting their own programs. But these Erie parents were not optimistic that the situation would change fast enough to benefit their children.[49]

The Zobrests agreed. Though Jim was only about three, they began to plan his education. Kindergarten at age five and then first grade at age six would be a turning point in Jim's education, at which they hoped to see formal, conventional schooling introduced into his education. They began to investigate alternatives to the Erie public schools. They quickly rejected sending such a young child to one of the tuition-free state boarding schools for the deaf, which were located in Pittsburgh and Philadelphia. He would spend so much time in a distant institutional environment that he would not know his family when he came home on weekends. Besides, he was too young to do that commuting. Sandi remembers thinking, "I didn't have children to put them on a bus, and not see them." Moreover, they had developed such strong habits of vigilance over his education that they wanted to be cognizant of his progress more than occasionally. Sandi was a hands-on parent, and a loss of that control was not something she could accept.[50]

The Zobrest Family, 1988. (Courtesy of Sandi Zobrest)

They felt at home in Erie. They were prosperous and were surrounded by new and longtime friends with whom they socialized and who were also part of a support network that assisted them in caring for and training their deaf son. But they seemed to have no choice at this point other than finding a school outside Erie and relocating. There was St. Mary's School for the Deaf in Buffalo, New York, a venerable Catholic institution founded in 1853 by the Sisters of St. Joseph, which had embraced Total Communication in 1972.[51] Nearby in Pittsburgh was the Western Pennsylvania School for the Deaf, which the family toured, one of Jim's earliest childhood memories.[52] But Sandi did not want to live in Pittsburgh, where she had grown up, while Buffalo, with winters in the Lake Erie Snowbelt similar to Erie's, held even fewer attractions. As long as they had to move, they reasoned, why not at least find a more congenial climate?

Always conscious of family support networks, the Zobrests turned to family connections as they contemplated their alternatives. With its expanding economy, its mild winters, and the increasing ubiquity of air conditioning, the Southwest seemed attractive. Larry had an uncle and aunt who lived in Tucson. They could be of assistance in the family's resettlement. Larry contemplated eventually realizing his dream of having his own business and being his own boss. But most important of all in the decision to establish residence in Tucson was their discovery of the Arizona School for the Deaf and the Blind (ASDB), which appeared to offer a positive resolution to the search for options for Jim's education. Sandi had done some research on the school to find out more about it. She telephoned an organization with which she was unfamiliar, but that came highly recommended, the National Association of the Deaf (NAD), the oldest and the principal deaf advocacy organization in the country. She made inquiries to NAD and was told the ASDB was an excellent school.[53]

The ASDB is a state agency, headquartered in Tucson with branches around the state, and has the legal status of a regular public school. It represents Arizona's historic commitment to the education of children with disabilities. It was established by the state's first legislature in 1912, the year Arizona became a state.[54] It has an attractive and extensive landscaped campus on the city's West Side. At the time it opened, it was virtually in the country, not far from the mountain passes overlooking the desert plains that extend westward toward California. Over the years, as the city has expanded, it came to have a more urban feeling.

As in a conventional public school, a comprehensive IEP is negotiated between parents and the school's Department of Hearing Impairment, and the precise implementation of the IEP is worked out by parents in consultation and cooperation among the audiologists, speech therapists, learning specialists, and subject teachers who worked with the individual student. The student's cognitive and skills development and subject knowledge were frequently tested. Each year, too, students had a comprehensive audiological workup to track changes, if any, in their hearing. Vision was also tested annually, because of the importance of visual cues in both signed language and speechreading, and students like Jim, who was soon found to be both astigmatic and myopic, were fitted with glasses or contact lenses integral to their learning process.[55]

What it offered Jim in terms of pedagogy was complicated, certainly more complicated than Sandi knew in accepting the recommendation from the people at NAD whom she had consulted. On paper, the school certainly presented a comprehensive curriculum, with mandates not only in basic subjects, especially written and oral language training, but also auditory training and speechreading, and each semester a vocational course in a subject such as cooking, typing, or fabrics that seemed fitted for the deaf. Above all perhaps, the Zobrests were relieved that they were not going to have to deal with the curricular inadequacies of what they had found in the Erie public schools. No one could question the school's longstanding record of efforts in the work of education of the deaf and the blind.[56]

The ASDB seems nonetheless a deviation from the path the Zobrests chose in embracing mainstreaming. ASDB is a segregated environment not strongly geared to immersion in the hearing world. Sandi did not know that NAD was a defender of ASL, and that it was thoughtfully capital *D* Deaf in its assumptions.[57] The old battle between manualists and oralists might have been played out, and new public conflicts then arising between degrees of preparation for the hearing and for the deaf worlds were still gathering form. With the passage of the EAHCA and the appearance of Total Communication, deliberate paths into the mainstream seemed the order of the day. Or at least Sandi thought so, for what she expected seemed logical to her in light of her own values.[58]

The inexact fit between what Sandi desired and what ASDB offered was in evidence in each of the three years Jim was at ASDB in Sandi's response, as part of the IEP process, to stipulating "a justification for placement at ASDB." Among the choices available, Sandi checked off only the desire for "a self-contained program for the hearing impaired" on one occasion but checked off "educational program needs for hearing handicap" for each of the three years she completed the form. She may have been resisting the logic of a segregated environment that suggested to her preparation for the Deaf world, not for integration into the general population. What she wanted most was a supportive, small classroom environment where Jim might experience an education of the type available at a regular public school. She would gradually come to regret the decision to place Jim there.[59]

ASDB was Total Communication oriented at the time, but in nuanced ways that Sandi would come to understand and question, the program tilted away from immersion in the hearing world and toward socialization in the Deaf world. ASDB did emphasize speechreading and speech therapy. But ASDB also anticipated the bicultural-bilingual (Bi-Bi) approach to deaf education that would begin to take form in the mid-1980s, as educational research in the United States and Europe revealed limitations of SEE and Total Communication as a foundation for language learning. It sought to combine, through a method referred to as "pairing," ASL as a first language and SEE presented in relation to one another.[60] To that extent, ASDB attempted to prepare its students for both the hearing world and the community of Deaf people. The identities and languages of its teachers also suggested that. Sandi recalls that in personal communications with students and others, the hearing teachers used SEE, while the Deaf teachers used ASL. ASDB was Jim's first systematic exposure to ASL, which he had previously acquired here and there, but not formally. Jim, however, would never become comfortably bilingual. To this day, his brother, Sam, who never had formal training in SEE and picked up more or less colloquial ASL, is said to sign more like an ASL Deaf individual than Jim does.[61]

This commitment to the Deaf community was present, too, in the school's concern for the development of the whole child within a world in which children with hearing impairments, like people with disabilities in general, were devalued. Through individual and group counseling, the school promised to help its deaf and its blind students "learn to deal with personal issues that are of importance to the self." Later, as a ten-year-old, Jim entered into a counseling process alongside his hearing impaired peers to put him at ease with himself.[62]

Practical issues soon interrupted Jim's education at ASDB. The Zobrests first moved to Tucson in 1977. They lived with Larry's aunt and uncle for the first month. Larry got a job with Hughes-Callahan, a 3M franchise in Tucson, and was going to sell the same products he had been selling in Erie. They bought a small house. But they had put their home in Erie on the market just as the real estate market in the city took a sharp turn downward alongside the city's declining industrial economy. They were unable to sell their Erie property, so they found themselves with two mortgages and another painful choice. It proved financially more beneficial to rent the Tucson house and, after only five months, to move back to Erie and back into their unsold home. They resumed life pretty much where they had left off. Larry got his old job back with 3M, and Jim returned to the Barber Center, and then briefly attended an Erie public school for kindergarten. Not until 1980 did they finally sell the Erie house; they returned to their Tucson home and placed Jim in ASDB, where he would start first grade in the fall of 1980.[63]

Parenting is a never-ending task, a second career that seems to grow only more demanding and complicated as children get older. It is not difficult to understand the wisdom of Tolstoy's observation that Utopia is a place in which all children are babies and all parents are young. But parenting is especially complicated when a child has a disability, because the world is shaped around people without disabilities by people who, no matter how well-meaning they may be, often are unthinking in their ableist assumptions about how everything relevant to the most ordinary aspects of life should be organized. At the time the Zobrests were making decisions about Jim's future, American society had begun a process of introspection about the marginalization of people with disabilities, and especially of children with disabilities. Deaf education itself, both in terms of pedagogy and in its understanding of its ultimate purposes, was in a state of flux. At that moment, for parents like the Zobrests, the prospects for a child with a disability for equality of opportunity and integration into the life of the hearing community seemed more promising than ever before. Within that new framework of possibilities, the Zobrests took on the responsibility for a degree of parental strategizing over the most basic aspects of their son's future that required their constant attention. Their task would grow more complicated in the next decade. The ASDB proved not to be the answer to their questions about how Jim could be best educated for the life they wished for him. Jim would eventually leave the ASDB for the district public schools in the area of their new home in the foothills immediately to the north of Tucson. New challenges awaited them in negotiations with the public schools, and those challenges would eventually lead to the U.S. Supreme Court.

2 INTO THE MAINSTREAM

SETTLING IN TUCSON

When the Zobrest family settled permanently in Tucson in 1980, the city was riding the crest of the postwar economic expansion then transforming the nation's Sunbelt. The population of Arizona's second city had grown from 45,000 in 1950 to 330,000 in 1980, buoyed by the migrations of northern retirees and of those of employment age attracted by an expanding local job market, anchored in defense and aerospace contracting, the University of Arizona, the Davis–Monthan Air Force Base, and the recent appearance of IBM. Local people did not see Tucson as just another metropolis in the making. They were conscious of the city's distinctiveness, which emerged as a point of pride when comparing it to Phoenix, the state capital located 120 miles away. The state university, comprehensive in its undergraduate, graduate, and professional programs and rapidly expanding, stood not in a new suburb but in the middle of Tucson, where it had been located since 1885. While Phoenix would host professional teams in all four major sports, the university's sports teams inspired fanatic local loyalty. Under legendary coach Robert "Lute" Olson, the men's basketball teams went to the NCAA playoffs for twenty-five consecutive years between 1985 and 2009, and young Jim Zobrest, who quickly took to basketball as he reached adolescence, came to aspire to play for Olson. Locals believed that Tucsonans made conscious efforts to fit into their desert environment rather than struggle to subdue it. They didn't plant the elm trees and grass found in parks in Phoenix but used native succulents for their yards, and they laid out stones and boulders rather than sod and grass. They took pride in successful historical preservation campaigns that featured neighborhoods with nineteenth- and early twentieth-century Mexican and Anglo-American colonial or cottage-style adobe buildings, while Phoenix seemed preoccupied with creating skyscrapers on the model of midtown Manhattan. Tucson adopted the name "the Old Pueblo" in recognition of its Mexican and then American frontier history. The city's politics were historically liberal, in contrast increasingly to northern Arizona, and voters routinely, and in the Arizona context unusually, sent Democrats to the state legislature.[1]

Tucson seemed to many locals to be the kinder, gentler Arizona. Local people fondly believed that even as the city grew greatly beyond its prewar population and expanded out into the desert to fill the bowl that the mountains surrounding it formed, Tucson preserved somehow the feel of a smaller place, where public networks rested on familiarity, and where personal relations, courtesy, and neighborliness counted. Rose Daly-Rooney, a lawyer interviewed for this study, speaks of the sense of professional propriety and the general good manners thought characteristic of members of the Tucson bar, relative to their Phoenix colleagues, whose style was more strategic and aggressively confrontational. Growing up there in the 1980s and 1990s, Chris Koester, a friend of Sam and Jim Zobrest's, fondly recalls Tucson at the time as possessing something approaching "a big small town feel, or a small big town feel."[2] It seemed to many residents an ideal and hopeful place to live.

The foundations of a larger and more metropolitan, polluted, and congested region of the twenty-first century were nonetheless emerging. Evidence lay, for example, in the rapid emergence of suburbanization. One of the city's first suburban municipalities, Catalina Foothills, where the Zobrests would ultimately reside, lay just over the north-central border of Tucson on the edge of the Santa Catalina Mountains. The suburb became known for its white-collar, professional, and well-educated residents and the high prices of its homes, which were not tract houses fashioned in bulk by developers but instead designed to the requirements of their individual owners. The attractiveness of Catalina Foothills lay not only in the ease with which suburbanites could drive into the city. Though it would not have a high school until the 1990s, its primary schools and its junior high school were arguably the best in Pima County. The district's standardized test scores were the highest in Arizona. Sam Zobrest would thrive in these schools, skipping a grade early in his education. Jim would enter them in the sixth grade. In spite of the Zobrests' legal struggle against the school board, Sandi continues to praise the school district for the education her sons got in the district's schools.[3]

The foothills elevation offered some relief from the heat of the desert basin that the city occupied, where the temperature averages over 90 degrees five months a year, and over 100 degrees in July, and asphalt paving in parking lots melts under one's feet. The suburb's new residences, zoned for one-acre lots, sat in a desert landscape that was relatively pristine and commanded at various levels impressive views of the urban landscape in the basin below. A private golf course and four resort hotels would be located in Catalina Foothills. Nearby was Coronado National Park, and up a twenty-five-mile road, Mt. Lemmon, at 6,700 feet the tallest of the Santa Catalinas and the southernmost ski resort in the United States, offered a retreat from the boiling desert temperatures in the summer.[4]

The Zobrests were pioneers in the settlement of Catalina Foothills and hopeful about starting a new life there. They were optimistic about their future in the expanding local economy. Larry got a job with Hughes-Callahan, a 3M affiliate that allowed him to sell the familiar business machines he had sold in Erie. Soon he would leave that job, and they would invest in a dry-cleaning enterprise of their own. Sandi would be employed part-time, teaching in the public schools as a substitute or at the community college, working in the dry-cleaning business, and at times working in their relatives' real estate business or for a collection agency. While living with their relatives briefly after their arrival in 1980 and establishing legal residency so that Jim could attend the Arizona School for the Deaf and the Blind (ASDB) tuition-free, they planned a large, comfortable home of their own. Theirs was the second house on the street. They were not in a position to put a large amount of money into building, and they were wary of debt. They saved a great deal of money on its construction because Larry and one hired worker did much of the building themselves.[5]

The Zobrests settled into the community developing around them in the desert that was largely composed of retirees, "snowbirds," who were seasonal residents from northern states, and local baby boomers with growing families. They affiliated with the Roman Catholic parish, named for Pope Pius XII, and, believing their sons' religious formation was important, Larry and Sandi took them to Mass on Sundays. Networks of friendship and support grew around them in Catalina Foothills. Sam and Jim and their friends and classmates remember a neighborhood full of children, with frequent visiting and mothers overseeing the children's social life, as the children rode their bikes to one another's houses. Most families had swimming pools in their backyards. Like most of their friends, too, Sam and Jim had a basketball hoop of their own, but they also went to a nearby elementary school to play.[6]

Restarting family life in a new, dynamic region of the country that offered an escape from winter and an exotic landscape was not the primary reason the Zobrests relocated. Their goal was to see Jim properly educated and put on the path toward integration into the hearing majority. Over the three years that Jim was in attendance at ASDB, they came gradually to question their choice of schools. After fifth grade, Jim transferred to Sunrise Elementary School in the Catalina Foothills public school system. It is hard to see how it could have gone any other way, given Sandi Zobrest's overall thinking about the ultimate purposes of Jim's education and the philosophy and methodologies governing ASDB, about which Sandi was not well versed when the decision was made to send Jim there.

Problems ultimately lay not only in contrasting approaches to deaf education, as important as that would prove for the Zobrests, but also, in their minds, in the quality of education and in classroom and institutional discipline. The ASDB drew children from all over the state, including Native American reservations, small Hispanic hamlets, and remote rural school districts that lacked resources for offering much in the way of the preparatory training for a deaf or a blind child of the sort Jim had had at the Barber Center. In deference to its democratic and inclusive values and its interest in building disability identity and community, the school wished to place all children in the same classes, teaching to the level of those less prepared. Allowance would be made, however, for the fact that Jim was prepared for a more advanced curriculum. In the battery of standardized intelligence and achievement tests to which Jim and other students were subjected as their specific Individualized Education Programs (IEPs) were developed, Jim's formal intelligence and his academic learning were already in evidence when he entered the ASDB and would remain pronounced. While standardized test scores from the time of his entrance at ASDB are not available, his performance on the Stanford Achievement Test at the close of his three years at ASDB may be suggestive of his native abilities. It showed him performing considerably above grade level in three subjects, at grade level in three, and below grade level in only one (language). Language was likely to be a problem for a deaf student, to be sure, but other standardized tests showed that within that broad category, Jim had both pronounced strengths and a few weaknesses. Other language tests revealed that he was especially skilled at deriving meanings from context, and this probably helped to account for the fact that he showed strength in reading and grammar.[7]

In third grade at ASDB, Jim and four classmates were placed in a separate, more advanced class. But the general subject curriculum was not as advanced as the regular public schools, which was evident in the fact that Jim's performance in science and social studies was evaluated by the same teacher, as if they were being presented to students in some conglomerate subject setting, or by a generalist rather than a specialist.[8] Jim came to resent the fact that although Sam was two years younger and one grade behind him, he was nonetheless doing more advanced work in math and science. Feeling competitive and hurt, Jim complained to his parents. He felt he was being treated at school as if he were stupid. He admitted to being bored much of the time in class, and his teacher's comments on his classroom behavior occasionally made reference to a failure to stay on task. Sandi remembers that he was increasingly unhappy at school and wanted the same opportunities, both social and educational, as his brother enjoyed at the neighborhood public school.[9]

Meanwhile, Sandi visited ASDB and, in anticipation of Jim's future there, sat in on a high school class in which she found the classroom behavior a poor model for his development. She remembers that the students pounded on their desks to get the teacher's attention and vocalized in a way she thought rude, both of which assaulted her ideas of proper classroom decorum. Instructors, in contrast, might well have seen such attention-getting behavior as a sign of their students' enthusiasm within the framework of their options for communicating.[10] Sandi did not see it that way. She was conscious of the comments of Jim's teachers that in spite of his substantial abilities, he sometimes seemed indifferent in class and goofed around.[11] It was not too much to believe that the classroom environment contributed to those behaviors, although how different Jim actually was from large numbers of young boys in this regard is certainly debatable.

A matter of discipline proved the basis for the Zobrests' final confrontation with the school. As Sandi tells it, it came in fifth grade when Jim complained to his parents of repeated physical harassment on the school bus by an older student who was preying on the younger ones. Sandi made an appointment to talk to the superintendent about the situation, and when he sent an assistant to the appointment, this was unacceptable to her. The situation was significant enough to her mind that she also talked to the police. She felt that she was not being taken seriously. Throughout the years of her advocacy for Jim with school officials, she always resented being brushed aside, taken for just another angry, meddling, and overbearing mother who wouldn't allow the professionals to do the job for which they were educated and had acquired years of experience. While her style of advocacy was strong and single-minded, she also knew the value of restraint and civility, and she understood the difficulties she would create for herself if she came on too strongly.[12]

Yet, for all for Sandi's complaints about ASDB, it needs to be emphasized that the high level of thoughtful engagement it brought to the intellectual and psychological development of its students was reflected in the progress

Jim made in his three years there. He left in the spring of 1985 functioning at a high intellectual level, prepared for the demanding Catalina Foothills public schools. His grades at ASDB were in the very good to excellent range, and his last evaluation consisted of a combination of grades in the B to A+ range. His standardized test scores indicated a strong foundation of intellectual abilities.[13]

For a number a reasons, then, the decision was made to send Jim to public school beginning in sixth grade. Children transfer from one school to another frequently, but this was no ordinary transfer, because it was not simply a change in a physical setting. It was also a change of identity and community that touched at the core of who Jim was to be. Jim was going from a school in which he was surrounded by other deaf children and taught by instructors, both deaf and hearing, who were especially sensitive to and knowledgeable about deafness, to one in which he was destined to be the only deaf student on the campus and in which both teachers and administrators had no experience in instructing deaf students. This would, in fact, be his fate not only for the remaining year of elementary school, but also thereafter, both at Orange Grove Junior High School and Salpointe Catholic High School.

ASDB was Jim's last experience of immersion in a Deaf institutional setting. He left it feeling resentment at the limitations of that environment and with little sense of community with deaf people, which might have been the basis for a judgment of counselors around the time he left ASDB that Jim was "not accepting of his deafness," and "bluffed" his way through some encounters with others, as if he were hearing, hardly an uncommon behavior among people with hearing impairment.[14] Both observations touched centrally at Jim's preparation for the world, as it had been conditioned at home and in school, even prior to entering ASDB. The effectiveness of Signed Exact English (SEE) and Total Communication ultimately depended on an element of bluff, because even with an interpreter nearby, at any given moment and depending where his attention was focused, there were certainly likely to be gaps between what Jim could actually hear and speech-read and the oral communications directed at him. Moreover, Jim had been told at home not to be accepting of his deafness if the measure of that acceptance meant narrowing his ambitions and believing himself somehow not to be good enough for the hearing world.

Like other adolescents, but under the most challenging of individual circumstances, Jim was crafting his own identity and making sense of the world on his own terms, coming to his own conclusions. The conclusions he was reaching about his deaf identity have remained with him more or less throughout his life. He has strongly shared with people who are deaf resentment at the prejudices, dehumanizing stereotypes, and discrimination they suffer. A proud moment that Sandi recalls speaks to this, because it marks Jim's assertiveness as a deaf individual on his own behalf. One day at public school a few years after he left ASDB, Jim's interpreter failed to show up because of illness, and the teacher asked him to stand outside rather than sit in class on the premise that he could not derive any benefit from attending. Jim challenged the teacher, whom he accused, in an impassioned, in his mother's words, "speech," of discrimination against him. Jim deeply resents the presumption he associates with many hearing people that the deaf are necessarily unintelligent and can't make decisions on their own behalf, and he is wary in anticipation of such attitudes. But a sense of solidarity—of peoplehood and common identity, as opposed to a shared stake in a fairer world—is largely absent. He does not share the culture of the capital *D* in deaf, and he is not a fluent American Sign Language (ASL) signer. Animated ASL signing by deaf people in public that calls attention to them he finds off-putting. For the next seven years of his education, in both public and Catholic schools, he would be immersed in the hearing world, a more or less enthusiastic pioneer in a larger social project—the mainstreaming of deaf students and disabled students more generally, among their peers who were not disabled.[15]

INTO THE MAINSTREAM

Sandi Zobrest might have ultimately rejected ASDB, but she never had to convince the administration there that deaf students were educable and that it was within the institutional abilities of the school in which they worked to educate them. When she approached the Catalina Foothills School District about her plans to enroll Jim at Sunrise Elementary School in the fall of 1985 and requested provision be made for daily auditory training, speech training, and signed language interpretation so that Jim could be educated alongside his hearing peers, that was exactly what she had the right to do under the EAHCA. The Catalina Foothills School District resisted enrolling Jim and attempted to persuade the Zobrests to find another public school, for example, somewhere in the large Tucson school system where there might be separate classes for disabled students. The alternatives proposed were not at all practical, largely because of distance, nor were they viable from Larry and Sandi Zobrest's educational perspective. Eventually, the Catalina Foothills School District relented and cooperated fully in creating a plan to integrate Jim into Sunrise Elementary, but the brief impasse is illustrative, in this formative period of the application of the mainstreaming principle, of a process of defining what mainstreaming actually meant at the most local level of public education.[16]

After sending her letter of intention, Sandi dealt directly with Robert Hetzel, the superintendent of schools, and Terry Downey, the district's head of counseling who worked out of Orange Grove Junior High School and would soon become its principal. Downey, a specialist in counselor education (which is essentially a human relations portfolio in many school districts) with graduate degrees from the University of Virginia and Northeastern University, was in an excellent position to observe Jim's progress through the three grades. Throughout her four decades with the school district, Downey took particular interest in middle school–age students, because the transition from childhood to adolescence seemed to occur daily before the eyes of the adults who interacted with them. As the district's counselor and then as a school principal, Downey was the liaison between the school district and the Zobrests, not only as far as guiding his education in the district but also later, during the discussions about what public resources might accompany Jim to Salpointe. She was sensitive, too, to the quality of Jim's experience at school, as he daily lived it.[17]

While Hetzel and Downey both plausibly emphasize the positive outcomes of Jim's three years in the Catalina Foothills schools, they forget their initial lack of enthusiasm about mainstreaming Jim. The response of the school district, Sandi recalls, was at first to inform her that the district "did not have a program" that could accommodate Jim.[18] It was then that Sandi was invited to seek out alternatives that might exist for hearing impaired students elsewhere, although, as it soon turned out, there were no programs that could accommodate Jim, especially to the extent his parents rejected the type of educational process that the school district advanced for him.

The model for compliance with the EAHCA the Catalina Foothills School District administrators had in mind that led to these suggestions was one that the district had developed for educating learning disabled students. These students were put into separate classrooms for basic instruction and given the assistance in learning their disabilities required. But in the name of providing the least restrictive environment within the school for them, which EAHCA mandated must be the ultimate goal of the public schools, they were typically mainstreamed, albeit on a limited basis, into such common activities as physical education, lunchroom, art and music, and assemblies. The law allowed for these accommodations, which took into account a disabled student's singular learning needs, as these were determined in consultation between parents, teachers, and administrators and by standardized testing through the IEP process. Students might be educated in isolation, but they were brought as much as possible (and often in quite limited ways) into the work and life of the school.[19] Sandi was invited to find this kind of program for the hearing impaired somewhere, and the district offered to help her in that search.

This was hardly the type of program the Zobrests had in mind. Their goal was preparation for life in the hearing world, and thus, they had reached the conclusion that mainstreaming Jim had no value unless he was integrated completely into the life of a traditional classroom with students who were not disabled. Jim was not learning disabled but had a strong natural intelligence and proven abilities as a student. He simply needed a translator, Sandi told Downey, because he possessed a different way of receiving English. Provide him with an interpreter and let the classroom teacher make whatever minimal accommodations were needed for the interpreter's presence and for Jim's need for unimpeded visual access to the teacher at the front of the room, and nothing more would be required. On the basis of what was best for Jim's education, as she understood it, Sandi rejected the invitation to find an alternative. Besides, the Zobrests lived in Catalina Foothills, paid taxes there, and had no desire to place Jim on a bus to commute miles to school when a school in their own neighborhood, where Sam was already enrolled, was a mile away.[20]

Because of the clear intentions of the law to mainstream students with disabilities and the larger professional and moral disposition of both Hetzel and Downey to provide a quality education to all of the residents of the district, the school district soon accepted its responsibilities for Jim's education. Having prevailed, however, Sandi knew that the details had to be worked out. Those details would involve matters more complicated than the law, as written, recognized and provided a process for realizing. When today, even after the five-year legal struggle, she praises the Catalina Foothills School District, she is thinking more than anything else of those three years in Jim's schooling and of the close and positive cooperation she achieved in working with Downey, other administrative staff, and Jim's teachers.[21] The school administration officials she dealt with accepted the role she played in advocating for Jim. They accommodated his needs in consultation with her, and they gave her and Jim virtual veto power over the hiring and retention of Jim's classroom sign language interpreters, who were the pivotal element in his mainstreamed educational experience. Whatever they may have privately felt about her sometimes uncompromising nature, they no doubt saw that Sandi was knowledgeable about deaf education, was articulate in her presentation of Jim's needs, and spoke their language as a teacher with graduate degree credentials. They themselves had no immediate experience of dealing with the needs of deaf students, and Sandi's advice and her interventions took the pressure off them to make decisions that they may not have felt wholly confident to make.

Working out the details must have been reassuring for the Zobrests because in the months before Jim started Sunrise Elementary School, the terms not only of his individual education but also of his integration into the life of the school were cooperatively spelled out. In regard to the latter, a nine-point program for bringing Jim into the school community and creating an accepting environment was developed. At Sandi's suggestion, faculty and students were given the opportunity for collective instruction about deafness and sign language interpretation. (A counselor was assigned to answer the questions of individual hearing students.) Sandi herself was invited to come into the school and talk to the students about deafness, and she made the point in her talks that the deaf students were not lacking in intelligence but in need of assistance, such as a classroom interpreter, to learn. Moreover, the school district eventually sponsored afterschool enrichment courses in sign language for faculty, staff, and students in the hope that Jim would have more people to converse with on his own terms. One or two students were to be assigned to be "special friends" who could assist Jim in practical ways to get to know the building, the routines of the school day, and other students. These students were to have TTYs (teletypewriters) in order to communicate with Jim after school.[22]

Jim himself was not left out of the responsibilities outlined in this nine-point plan. The plan rested on the assumption not only that hearing students would get to know Jim and would have opportunities to learn to communicate with him, but also that he would attempt to get to know them as much as possible on their terms. A "behavior modification program" was proposed "to encourage clear articulation from Jimmy." It consisted of identification of a list of common words that were employed in ordinary contexts, which he could then say with clarity—for example, "Mommy." He was to be made "aware of these words" and receive unspecified rewards for new additions to the list.[23] The terms of such assimilation into the hearing world could not have been more different from the more nuanced, Deaf-inclined approach to language and identity at ASBD. Moreover, in the understanding of the give-and-take between Jim's obligations and those of his hearing peers, there was no doubt the burden was placed on Jim.

Simultaneously, within the framework of the EAHCA, Jim's educational needs needed to be determined, and an IEP needed to be drawn up to create a basic framework for his education. The work was done in this district by the school psychologist in consultation with parents. Jim's ASBD records were accessed and backed up by another hearing evaluation, to provide formal justification for the expense of an interpreter. The IEP left it clear that however well Jim's ability to speech-read might evolve, he could not profit in the mainstream classroom without an interpreter. Additional methods for assisting him were outlined. The specific targets regarding, for example, speech therapy, remedial academic assistance, or speechreading changed from year to year, but mostly the template for compensating for his hearing loss and extending his communication skills remained the same.[24] It would accompany Jim when he went to Salpointe to guide Salpointe teachers, and because the public schools retained responsibility for his speech therapy in a public school location even after he transferred to the Catholic high school, it remained a relevant guide for public school administrators. It was the extent of the responsibility of the public school district in regard to his academic education in the high school classroom that remained the point at law leading to the Zobrests' lawsuit.

To compensate for the gap between ASDB and the Catalina Foothills schools in some basic subjects, Jim was to receive tutoring for his academic work. He would have more speech therapy than in the past. In the interests of preparing Jim for communication in the hearing world without sign language interpretation and to supplement the practical incentivized program for expanding his vocabulary, over time little or no sign was used in speech therapy. Speech work was to be done orally as much possible but utilizing as supplements writing and gesture and speechreading, the tools of Total Communication.[25] Jim and his family drew so close to Mary Hodgson, the district's speech therapist, that she eventually took over Jim's semi-annual reviews and negotiating the annual IEP from the school psychologist, an adaptation that the school district embraced without resistance, though it bent its methods in a new direction. Jim regarded Hodgson as a friend and was resentful when in the midst of the lawsuit, although his speech therapy continued, she herself was instructed by the administration for legal reasons to withdraw from providing him with it.[26]

The modes of assisting Jim outlined in the IEP soon had positive outcomes of the sort the Zobrests desired. Robin Konrad, the teacher with the responsibility of overseeing Jim's progress through the curriculum, noted in her final evaluation of the year that it had been a "very demanding year for him" intellectually and socially and that he had done "very well." He had five grades in the A range and four in the B range.[27] By the middle of eighth grade, the gap between Jim and the public schools was closed in all subjects but mathematics, and he no longer needed to go to the resource room for tutoring. He had been in two remedial classes, math and English, in seventh grade but now was only in the former, which seemed to owe more to the bent of his mind away from mathematics, in which he was skilled at computation and application but not at more abstract thinking, than to his deafness. When he graduated from junior high school with his good to excellent grades in every one of his subjects, it marked an accomplishment the significance of which can only be appreciated when the challenges that he faced in an exclusively hearing environment are considered. An updated IEP appraising his level of attainment and his continuing needs at the end of eighth grade that accompanied him to Salpointe noted that his oral language was "very advanced," with respect to both English grammar and syntax, which was a strength SEE was intended to provide. His vocabulary was not quite as advanced, and while he needed continuing work in some of the social aspects of language (for example, how to attract attention to what he wished to say in conversation and how to draw a teacher's attention in class), his classroom participation was nonetheless "excellent," both frequent and positive. (Jim had been praised the previous year for giving a "speech," perhaps an oral book report, in English class.) His classroom interpreter during eighth grade, Hodgson noted, "insisted that Jim sign/speak [simultaneously] at all times in class. This has resulted in considerable improvement in intelligibility, since it forces him to speak more slowly and to fingerspell/speak words that [may be] difficult to understand." In general, in and outside of class, his oral interactions were noted to have grown over the three years he had been in the public schools. For the Zobrests, nothing could have been a better outcome from the standpoint of Jim's formal education and his preparation for the adult world. For Jim himself, as for many deaf people, speaking is a physical chore, and it presents the risk of being stigmatized, so it is testimony to his comfort level at school and with his peers and to his self-confidence in asserting himself at this point in his young life that he did so enthusiastically.[28]

A great deal of daily effort was required on the part of Sandi, Mary Hodgson, and Terry Downey, his classroom teachers and sign interpreters, and, above all, Jim himself to bring about these positive results. The formal evaluation masked a crucial behind-the-classroom-scenes aspect of the processes of Jim's education. His instruction depended on having a sign interpreter with him throughout the day, and it was of critical importance that a method be created, where one did not then exist in the school district's experience, to find candidates for that position, to interview them, and to develop criteria for determining their competence and monitoring their performance in the classroom, which depended not only on their rapport with Jim but also with the classroom teacher who was speaking as they were interpreting. The sign interpreter turned out to be the principal point of ongoing cooperation between Sandi Zobrest and Terry Downey. Jim was involved as well, because without his point of view and evaluation of the interpreter, the exercise of hiring and retaining a sign interpreter was worthless. For the district at the time, involving Jim in the process was a singular innovation, a tribute to Downey's understanding of what was required to create arrangements that worked to Jim's advantage. In later years, perhaps building on this experience, students with disabilities in the district were themselves drawn routinely into the district's IEP process.[29] It is noteworthy that instructional matters not relevant to hearing students (or worked out completely for them within the pedagogy of the school) became part of Jim's daily responsibilities at school. This process of schooling invited a level of judgment and personal responsibility in the process of his education that demanded more maturity than was required of his nondisabled adolescent peers.

Because the school district had the legal responsibility for paying for Jim's signed language interpreter, who became a district employee, Terry Downey searched for candidates to interview for the position and hired them, but the evaluation of their performance was ultimately subject to review by Sandi and Jim. The use of signed language in the traditional public school classroom was new for the Zobrests, the school district, and the interpreters themselves. Over time, the criteria for evaluation, ranging from proficiency in the classroom to dependability, coordination with teachers, and rapport with Jim, emerged. Sign interpreters came and went with regularity, based on their individual employment options and their performance in the task, to the extent that the names of a few are not remembered today. Some, like his sixth-grade interpreter, worked out well, but others proved problematic. At least three of the interpreters in junior high school stand out as posing difficulties because they lacked rapport with Jim, had irregular work habits, or failed to know the limits of their role in the classroom. (One of them assigned Jim to detention for an offense he denies to this day, though it was hardly her responsibility to do so.) That Sandi had the power, never actually formalized in an IEP, to terminate the employment of interpreters who were not effective in their work is clear when she recalls having "fired" one of them not only because she was late one morning but also because she took offense when Jim asked her where she had been when she finally showed up, and she walked out, leaving him without any classroom support.[30]

The interpreters' individual skills and personal habits aside, their role in the classroom had to be defined and made understandable and acceptable to teachers, and above all else, they had to be effective in furthering Jim's learning. Teachers and students alike needed to accept the presence of, and not be distracted by, another adult in the classroom. Facilitating this were the facts that Jim sat off to the side of the room facing the teacher while the interpreters stood nearby him, and that the interpreters did their work in silence. Moreover, Downey recalls that it was a frequent practice in the district for principals, assistant and associate principals, and counselors to visit classrooms and observe teaching in the Catalina Foothills system and that teachers were accustomed to the presence of other adults in their classrooms. Downey did not get very far in her own efforts at learning fingerspelling, let alone sign. Though she herself lacked the technical knowledge for evaluating interpreters, she remembers seeking at intervals to observe and to evaluate Jim's interpreters at work in visits to his classes.[31]

Teachers were obviously concerned about the effectiveness of the situation. Because in the Catalina Foothills public schools (and later, too, at Salpointe) there was no formal, systematic effort to prepare teachers for the instruction of hearing impaired students, teachers had to learn, sometimes in awkward and certainly ad hoc ways, to make adjustments in their teaching, including coordination with the interpreter. Two telling examples suggest how the need for these accommodations might come to be recognized. A teacher complained that Jim was not always concentrating on the interpreter's signing and appeared to drift. The interpreter continued to sign, though Jim was quietly looking away, lost for the moment in his own thoughts. The concerned instructor made her observations known to Sandi, who reminded her that all students tune out periodically and that it was just more obvious in Jim's case because his gaze was targeted elsewhere. Hearing students, in contrast, could daydream while appearing to be virtuously paying attention. Allowance needed to be made for the wandering adolescent mind in all students. In general, however, over the course of the three years, as Hodgson's final IEP noted, Jim was increasingly known for being alert and attentive in class. He enthusiastically asked and answered questions, requesting clarification of things he did not understand, and he took part in classroom discussions. Whatever occasional lapses that that were noted in his behavior over those three years were never ascribed to his deafness or to a judgment about his lack of fitness for the regular public schools. The assumption was universally shared, at least as far as the formal record is concerned, that as a student Jim was where he belonged.[32]

The other example concerns a poor fit between sign and conventional oral instruction of the type that only seems embarrassingly obvious after it has been experienced. Sandi observed a considerable gap at one point between Jim's spelling test grades, which were uniformly one hundreds, and his written compositions, which were full of spelling errors. Inquiry revealed that, in line with the logic and methods of Total Communication and SEE, his

Sandi Zobrest signs with her son Jim in their Tucson home, February 25, 1993. (Courtesy of Rick Wiley/Tucson Citizen)

sign interpreter was fingerspelling in English the spelling test words that the teacher was announcing orally from the front of the class. Of course, the inadvertent error in test procedure gave Jim the ultimate competitive advantage, probably one of the few his deafness ever afforded him in a mainstreamed classroom. On the other hand, arguably, it also provided him with some of the enhanced spelling instruction he appeared to need.[33]

Formal instruction marks one of two principal purposes of K–12 schools. Schools are also places in which students are socialized into a community of peers and learn the habits of civil and cooperative, formal and informal interaction with others. Testimonies of those hearing impaired students who, like Jim Zobrest, were pioneers of mainstreaming, often testify to how problematic a mainstream education could be from this perspective. Thankful for the quality of the education they received, they nonetheless record experiencing social isolation and marginalization amid the hearing majority. Not unexpectedly, this is especially burdensome in adolescence, a vulnerable time of life in which children are especially in need of friends and peer acceptance. Gina Oliva, a hearing impaired, though not profoundly deaf, Gallaudet University professor, had a mainstream schooling experience a generation before Jim's in a political and cultural environment considerably less willing to be attuned to the needs of students with disabilities. But she captures a typical appraisal of the social situation of deaf students—then, in Jim's time, and now—in the title of her memoir, *Alone in the Mainstream: A*

Deaf Woman Remembers Public School, which is a record of both her experience and the experience of other mainstreamed students, whose testimonies about their school experience often begin with the statement, "I was the only one." Typically, these memoirs do not record repeated instances of bullying or mocking, which under any circumstance are experienced by many students, whether disabled or not, as a matter of course in school settings. Hearing impairment itself might at times protect deaf students from knowing what his or her peers were saying about them. Often recalled instead is the combination of a very good education and the grinding social experience of isolation. This was the experience of knowing there was a world of communication and activity, both in and out of the classroom, beyond that to which one was admitted to participate. Jim's experience may have been in a different era than Oliva's, but he, too, as the solitary deaf person surrounded by hundreds of students who inevitably took their ability to hear for granted, recalls the difficulty of making friends. The school-supervised buddy system that was part of the nine-point program for integrating him into the life of the school in sixth grade was of limited value in the longer run to the extent that adolescents are not likely to take to adult-supervised friendships. Many classmates, he recalls when characterizing his high school experience, did not want to take the time and expend the energy to find ways to communicate with him, and some of them were too embarrassed at the prospects of the likely initial awkwardness of the exchange to try.[34]

Yet junior high school was not just a time of constant social trials for Jim. There were points of successful integration, mostly on the terms of the hearing majority, among his peers in school, and some carried over beyond the school day into the community. Jim's confidence in his ability to function in a hearing environment grew considerably over time. In her 1988 IEP, Mary Hodgson noted that Jim's casual and classroom oral interactions, without the assistance of signed language interpretation, had "increased markedly over the three years [he] has been in the Catalina Foothills School District. . . . He enters conversations, maintains/changes topics, adds information and asks questions—both academically and socially."[35]

Jim's agency in communicating with teachers and peers was not without its limits. If he departed for high school a more confident young man than he was when he entered the public schools, his transformation did not occur quickly or evenly. There were a variety of influences that worked to assist in his effort to free himself from marginalization. One of these was certainly the male friendships that he formed at school and in the community. In retrospect, the Zobrests recall, these years were richer in such relationships than high school at Salpointe would be, perhaps because early adolescent peer groups are not as strictly bounded as ones in the more advanced teenage years. His circle of friends began with his brother Sam. Downey recalls that while Jim's first year in junior high school was not always easy academically or socially, when Sam, a grade behind Jim, appeared in school as Jim entered eighth grade, it lessened Jim's isolation. Sam's presence reliably gave him someone to converse with off and on during the school day. The schools used Sam advantageously to assist in accommodating Jim's needs. The school system did not provide Jim with sign interpretation for organized sports in seventh grade, when he played both baseball and basketball. He had to use his own Total Communication skills to communicate with coaches and teammates. This might at times prove cumbersome in competitive circumstances. In eighth grade, to accommodate Jim's needs and because of his prominent place on the basketball team, the coach appointed Sam team manager/interpreter.[36]

Close as the brothers were, and remain to this day, Jim had already reached the point in life at which he felt as burdened by having his younger brother around, acting as if he were Jim's peer, as he felt comforted by Sam's presence. Jim was developing his own interests and his own set of friends. As with many adolescent males at the time, a principal source for the development of those friendships was sports. As Jim made the transition to adolescence, he grew tall and strong, with the speed and the seamless hand-eye coordination of an athlete. (In high school, he would reach 6'4".) He had the body and natural abilities for basketball and had begun to demonstrate his abilities at ASDB, where he won a medal in the sport.[37] He would play basketball as a team sport for the next six years, throughout junior high and high school, and it provided him with his most inspired aspirations. His best friend in junior high school, Terek Amin, a teammate, remembers Jim as excelling at all aspects of the game; he had "amazing ball handling skills," his significant height advantage enabled him to be a "great rebounder," and he had a reliable shot from both the middle distance and close in to the basket. He was a generous and cooperative teammate. Basketball provided Jim with peers with whom he could regularly interact and with a round of activities that united the school day with after-school time and vacations. He began to attend summer basketball camps, including the prestigious one in Tucson organized by University of Arizona coach, Lute Olson.[38]

Basketball also provided Jim with teammates, but whether they were close friends is another matter. It's telling that Terek Amin was also an outsider, but one whose own distance from the culture of their peers was a consequence not of disability but of nationality and partly of religion. Amin's father is Egyptian and a Muslim, and his mother an American and a Christian. He spent the first decade of his life going to Christian schools in Egypt, but his parents relocated to the United States in 1984 for economic reasons. In seventh grade he and Jim were in remedial math and English classes together at Orange Grove Junior High School. Amin had a place throughout his childhood, even as he attended Christian schools, in both Islam and Christianity. That and his childhood in Egypt provided him with a unique vantage point on America and a singular ability, even at a young age, to come by his own standards and craft his own identity.[39]

Amin (then called "Terry," to fit in better in school) came to possess only rudimentary abilities in signed language. He tried fingerspelling without much confidence in his abilities. Yet the two boys nonetheless developed what Amin remembers to be completely comfortable interactions. Whatever self-consciousness Jim might have about his speaking voice in informal social relations, his discomfort outside the classroom with his peers was less the case when in the company of Amin. The boys, Amin recalls, conversed easily. Their interactions were facilitated by the fact that the Zobrests, whom he remembers as "a very decent family [and] lovely people," accepted him generously and facilitated the boys getting together and their ability to communicate with one another. As with some of Jim's other friends, they provided him with a telecommunications device so that the boys could use the telephone together. Beyond basketball and just hanging out, they also shared a passion for movies, a lifelong source of fascination for Jim, who began to dream about a career in some aspect of film. As he does today, even with the contemporary benefit of closed captioning, Jim preferred action and horror films in which the visual more than the aural enables grasping the plot. He began to develop an impressive knowledge of film and Hollywood lore.[40]

Although their friendship does not seem to have contained a conscious element of defensive solidarity against peers who refused to accept their differences from the majority, Amin has strong memories of the casual cruelties that thoughtless peers sometimes engaged in at Jim's expense. He recalls overhearing another boy make fun of Jim as Jim and Terek passed him in the hall in school. Terek pushed him, and a fight ensued. Jim did not know of the immediate situation, and to that extent, on this and other occasions, he was protected by his deafness from mockery. His family attempted to protect him as well. Occasionally, Sandi would answer the telephone to find someone mimicking deaf speech, but she would not inform Jim of such incidents. To that extent, Amin's memory of Jim hiding in his encounters with others whatever frustrations he might have felt and never whining or being depressed, or expressing a view of himself as a victim, may well have mirrored a complicated reflection of Jim's state of mind. On the one hand, there was what Jim was able to accomplish to make life in the mainstream work for him by consciously attempting to pay as little attention as possible to rejection and mockery; on the other hand, there was what Jim could not completely grasp about the world around him. In this way, though still a child, he was making the life he had been given work for him, in school and outside of it.[41]

CHANGING SCHOOLS AGAIN

The Catalina Foothills School District did not have a high school until 1992. A number of explanations have been offered: taxpayers' reluctance to fund an expensive construction project; parents' reluctance to seal their children off in an elite enclave in which they could not know the diverse and less privileged world around them across the town line in Tucson; and the apprehension that the district's sports teams could not be competitive with bigger high schools, and its athletes would have less chance to develop their potentials than if they were able to attend schools with established, competitive sports programs. Regardless of what the reasons were, in the late 1980s at the start of eighth grade, parents in the district had to begin the process of deciding where to send their children to high school.[42] The origins of the Zobrests' lawsuit lies in this fateful decision. The decision involved calculation of what was best for their child for all parents in the district, but it was obviously especially complex and weighty for the Zobrests, because Jim was just not any student. He needed uncommon, costly resources to succeed, and he was vulnerable to neglect and marginalization. Larry and Sandi Zobrest, and Jim, too, had to make their decision on what high school to attend with more factors in mind than most parents and students. In the end, they not only choose Salpointe but also rejected the public schools, so explanations are needed on both sides of the decision. The reasons were academic, cultural, and social and were grounded not only in Jim's deafness and his educational goals but also in both the Zobrests' criticisms of American society in the 1980s and the evaluation of their own experiences of schooling.

The nearest public high school to Catalina Foothills, Amphitheater High School ("Amphi"), lay in the Tucson School District. Opened in 1939, it was extensive in its physical layout. Its enrollment peaked at around 1,200 students, and it had a diverse student population in terms of class, race, and ethnicity. It does not provide a feeling of intimacy or community but rather seems more like a southwestern corporate business park, with a series of detached one-story buildings spread out over extensive space. While upholding strong academic standards, it was also subject to some of the same social problems that plagued other urban high schools. How pervasive drugs, alcohol, weapons, and gangs were at the time is hardly easy to know. Certainly, parental anxieties prompted by rumors and the occasional news story, which easily came to represent what was typical in some parents' minds, played a role in building this aspect of the school's reputation. Another choice was Sabino High School, a Tucson school farther away from Catalina Foothills, which opened in 1972 and also accommodated just over a thousand students. It is located on the city's ever-expanding northeast side in an affluent neighborhood, but one in the 1980s in which, Sam Zobrest recalled, "there was too much money and too little supervision of the kids." Today the Zobrests remember rejecting Sabino High School because it was said to have a drug problem.[43]

Neither Amphi nor Sabino seems to have been a "blackboard jungle" in the late 1980s, but if one believed the national media at the time, more or less every urban public high school was suffering from, or could imminently suffer from, a moral crisis, prompted by drugs, disrespect for authority, and violence, that did not lend itself to providing an environment conducive to learning. Students who were serious about preparing for college could certainly do so at both schools, but nonetheless their parents might worry about the temptations that would shift their attention to less productive pursuits.

That is certainly the way the Zobrests came to understand Amphitheater, the public high school most convenient to them and the one most likely to attract Jim's hearing classmates at Orange Grove Junior High School. Sandi's insistence on self-discipline, responsible behavior firmly grounded in an explicit understanding of right and wrong, and respect for legitimate authority did not allow her to be indifferent to what she took to be a lax moral environment present in society or in the public high schools. "Too many people today," she says, "think rules are for everyone else . . . and that's just wrong." While not necessarily rigid about such matters nor unrealistic about the need for adolescents to experiment with ways of being themselves, she certainly could agree with the criticisms of "permissiveness" that were widely heard at the time in reference to public high schools and, in general, to the ways many Americans seemed to be raising their children. Religious liberty was not an argument that entered explicitly into the claims made in the Zobrests' lawsuit because, for reasons that will eventually be made clear, William Bentley Ball chose to argue the case with reference to the Establishment Clause of the First Amendment. But uppermost in the Zobrests' minds as they contemplated their decision about where Jim would go to high school was the linkage between their religious liberty to choose a Catholic school, their own Catholic faith—palpable enough, if not greatly devotional in practice—and their belief that Catholicism as it was institutionalized at Salpointe provided a firm foundation for combatting the insidious cultural influences that Larry and Sandi believed were compromising public education.[44]

Though at approximately one thousand students Salpointe was not much smaller than the public high schools, the Zobrests felt that Jim would too easily be neglected in a big and impersonal public high school, where they believed class sizes were larger than at Salpointe. If Jim were to be prepared for college, he would need a more intimate, sustaining environment where the guidance he required was not an afterthought of a school administration that was preoccupied with keeping order. There also was some concern about finding a school where Jim's basketball ability, which had made him a star in junior high school and hence was a great morale booster and a source for inspiration for him, could continue to thrive rather than be overwhelmed by the competition around him. The students who constituted Jim's competition did not have to enter into the struggle for a roster spot by first proving that a hearing impairment would not be a problem on the basketball court. Sabino and Amphi were both high schools that took great pride in the competitiveness of their big-sport teams and regularly featured players who went on to college and, in a few cases, to professional careers as athletes.[45]

The public high schools were quickly dismissed in the process of deciding Jim's future. In contrast to Sandi's past experience of seeking information about and engaging in consultations with the ASDB and with the Catalina Foothills School District, she does not appear to have had any sustained discussion in either of these public high schools about mainstreaming Jim in the school. By the point at which she talked to Robert Hetzel and Terry Downey at an evening meeting in the spring of 1988, all that she requested was assurance that the school district was prepared to pay the costs of Jim's sign interpreter at Salpointe. Superintendent Hetzel's warm-hearted invitation at their fateful evening meeting to reconsider what the public high schools could do for Jim was not something she had any interest in pursuing.[46]

The reason for Sandi's reluctance is clear, and it goes beyond her criticism of the public high schools too. From the beginning of the process of choosing a high school for Jim, what proved attractive to the Zobrests about Salpointe was that it looked like and presented itself as a traditional Catholic high school of the type both she and Larry had attended in Pennsylvania. There was a chapel, there was religious symbolism displayed, priests and nuns were among the teachers and staff, and the banner on the wall, near the main entrance, proudly proclaimed Salpointe's *Lancers Values*—**L**ove of Justice and Peace; **A**cademic Excellence, **N**urturing the Whole Person; **C**ommunity; **E**vangelization; **R**esponsibility and Respect; **S**olidarity. Salpointe was unapologetically Catholic, and there was no doubt that Lancer values were

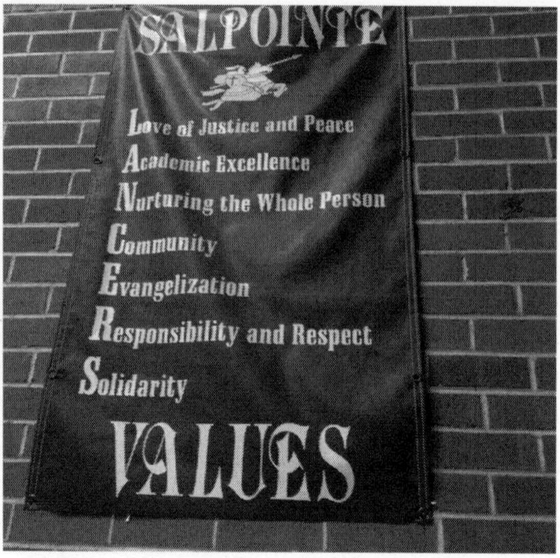

A lobby banner proclaiming the values Salpointe Roman Catholic High School has sought to inculcate in its students. (Photo taken by David A. Gerber, 2015)

rooted in its Catholicism. It seemed an ideal place to extend the religious formation of both of their sons beyond what they might absorb at Mass on Sundays.

Salpointe also offered a number of social and academic benefits. It was diverse racially and ethnically, and it had its share of poorer scholarship students; it looked increasingly like the larger Tucson community. Yet it also had a reputation for being the elite address in choosing a high school for the city's higher socioeconomic groups, independent of religious faith. It carried some prestige in Tucson, largely the result of its reputation for academic excellence and deliberate preparation of students for college. In 1987, a year before Jim matriculated there, Salpointe became Tucson's first formally recognized college preparatory high school when it was certified as such by the North Central Association of Colleges and Schools. There were no advanced placement courses at Salpointe; every student was prepared for college work at an advanced level. The curriculum consisted of a narrow range of challenging, traditional courses in basic subjects. Graduates would remember their first year in college as easier than other students found it, because of the high level of preparation for higher education at Salpointe. It was also known for pushing students in the direction of developing a mature understanding of their responsibility for themselves and for contributing to the world around them. There was insistence on student self-discipline, responsible behavior, and membership in a moral community that bound students, teachers, staff, and administrators in common understanding and common purposes.[47]

In embracing Salpointe, the Zobrests were not only thinking as the parents of a deaf child making choices within the limited framework of the Tucson community. They were also representative of an opinion about Catholic education that had come to be shared by many American parents, Catholic and non-Catholic alike. That change of mind had led Catholic school systems around the country to be transformed from being thought of as unprogressive, mediocre, and, in the common historic usage Americans had developed for describing them, "parochial," to being choice locations for educating American children, and especially American adolescents.[48] Sandi Zobrest today explains her preference for sending Jim to Salpointe partly by saying that she herself had been a product of Roman Catholic education from K–12 through college at Mercyhurst. While she acknowledges disliking that education intensely for its constant surveillance of student behavior when she was enrolled, its virtues appeared much clearer to her when she became a parent, especially in the context of the unraveling of moral values she and Larry associated with America in the 1980s.

The Catholic education available to Jim, however, was not the same as that which had been available to his parents. Much had changed over the course of a quarter of a century. The evolution both of Catholic education and of a national reevaluation of Catholic schools in the late twentieth century represented complex developments on both sides, Catholic and non-Catholic, of the religious divide. Catholic education in America had evolved in the nineteenth century with a defensive solidarity born of Protestant anti-Catholic nativism, on the one hand, and on the other hand, and relatedly, a fear that without deliberate institutional efforts, the millions of Catholic European immigrants to the United States would find it convenient to lose their faith or would be pressured into doing so. In the decades after World War II, anti-Catholic prejudice greatly abated, and Catholicism alongside Judaism and Protestantism became one of the three faiths that symbolized American religiosity.[49] At the same time, Roman Catholic intellectuals, such as the eminent Jesuit theologian John Courtney Murray, and clergy were making their own tentative peace with American religious pluralism. They accepted occupying a space that required negotiating the distance between being the one true faith, with a monopoly on truth, and being one religion among a number, within a social order in which guarantees of religious liberty enabled an open competition for souls.[50] The anxieties about vulnerable European immigrants losing their faith declined as European immigration collapsed after the 1940s because of the successful economic reconstruction of Western Europe and the rise of the Iron Curtain in Central and Eastern Europe. Nor did assimilation prove disastrous for religious faith. As was also the case for America's Jews, assimilation was a spur to the development of new religious forms and understandings within historical faiths that were increasingly at home with American life. Far from leaving the religion of their parents, in the immediate postwar decades the immigrants' children and grandchildren, like Larry and Sandi Zobrest, helped transform it into a more Americanized Catholic faith.[51]

Then came the changes within the global Roman Catholic Church that eventuated from the Second Vatican Ecumenical Council (1962–65), an epic of renewal and transformation of Catholic religious forms and understandings that produced a less austere and rigid and more colloquial Catholicism. Vatican II had a profound influence on American Catholic education. While the effects are certainly uneven throughout a complex faith-based system of Catholic educational institutions—some affiliated with regional and local diocesan authorities through their clerical leadership and others through religious orders, such as the Carmelites, who founded and govern Salpointe—in general, Catholic schools became more open to a fuller scope of general philosophical and theological instruction and less focused on the teaching of Catholic dogma absorbed through memorization. Yet these schools did not compromise their serious intellectual aspirations that evolved out of Catholic scholasticism. While the curriculum might be narrower than a well-funded public high school, Catholic high schools focused intently on preparing students for a traditional college or university education. While once they had also offered a range of practical vocational subjects approved of by practical, working-class immigrant parents, with increasing socioeconomic mobility of Catholics into the middle class the emphasis changed toward the liberal arts. Vocational tracks remained a significant option within the public schools. Subtly the message was reinforced that the Catholic schools were representative of intellectualism, and the public schools were a supermarket in ideas and programs.[52]

The trend toward the cosmopolitan and the diverse in Catholic secondary schools was reinforced by the changing composition of the ranks of teachers and of students. There was a rapid decline in the numbers of priests and of members of religious orders, and as a result, teachers from clerical ranks were increasingly replaced by laymen and laywomen. Between 1967 and 1990, clerical instructors declined from nearly 60 percent in Catholic schools to 15 percent. The composition of the student body was influenced by complex pressures. The necessity of paying tuition at Catholic schools and the attractiveness of the varied programs at public schools led to significant numbers of Catholic parents sending their children to public schools. Enrollments declined by three million students between 1965 and 1990. This was compensated for somewhat by the enrollment of non-Catholic students in Catholic schools, which opened themselves up, as was certainly the case at Salpointe by the mid-1980s, to a diverse student body because it made good business sense and because of an ecumenical feeling that Catholicism had something to offer everyone, including non-Catholics. Among them were many scholarship minority students who sought refuge from especially troubled inner-city schools.[53]

It remains a puzzle from the standpoint of conventional labor market theory why lay teachers in Catholic schools in the United States would be willing to work for less money than they would make if working in public schools and do without the job rights and many of the generous benefits that come with unionization and formal collective bargaining. Moreover, they work under circumstances in which more can be and routinely is asked of them beyond classroom obligations, such as coaching athletic teams or offering remedial instruction, which lengthen their working hours after school and spill over into weekends. The answer is not difficult to seek: their job satisfaction is connected to the qualitative experience of teaching in a Catholic institution. What is attractive is the type of moral community that Catholic schools explicitly seek to form. Growing out of the Catholic doctrine of personalism, Catholic schools have placed emphasis on mutual respect and caring among students, faculty, and staff and on forming a concern for social justice and habits of civility as foundations for a moralized community. These understandings ultimately grow, too, out of the traditional Catholic principle of *subsidiarity*, which argues that the formation of a just and humane world must begin at intimate and local levels of social life and only then ascend beyond them to the societal. If community is to be built and mutual caring is to be inspired, it must begin in the lives of children and adolescents in the context of schools and in the classroom and in the interactions of teacher and student.[54] The school as moral community is not simply founded on good feelings, however, but on a stated disciplinary code that governs student conduct. At Salpointe that code, a specification of Lancers Values including instructions on dress and on personal grooming, was known suggestively as "JUG," *Justice under God*—as the dean of men and the dean of women were given to understand what God intended for the lives of American adolescents.[55]

In the late twentieth century, as many American parents contemplated critically what was wrong with public secondary education, they found in

Catholic schools an answer to the problems they had identified. It was hardly the case that public schools rejected the values that the Catholic schools proclaimed and with which teachers at those schools identified. Though the Deweyan idiom of the Progressive Era extolling public education for citizenship might have been in decline by the late twentieth century, the public schools, too, expressed concern for the moral community, civil discourse, preparation for democratic citizenship, and inculcating habits of responsible behavior. But they had many mandates to fulfill, and they did not have the luxury of selective admissions, as did schools such as Salpointe, where Jim had to take a written admissions test in order to be enrolled. The public schools have to admit everyone and hope for the best regarding how the mix of students will work out. Mirroring trends on the larger culture, moreover, public schools tended to abandon the principle of in loco parentis, embracing instead codes of student rights and a less harsh disciplinary order. Bound by those codes in imposing order within the school, school administrators were also responsible to elected officials, who were themselves swayed this way and that by a democratic electorate wanting good schools that were also somehow low in cost, and to the union contracts and collective bargaining rights governing relations with unionized faculty. Administering a large urban high school in the second half of the twentieth century was nothing less than governing a complex public bureaucracy in which sensitivity to multiple centers of power and authority was constantly demanded.[56]

To be sure, this is a stark portrait of an institutional complex that encompassed thousands of public school districts, many of them deeply influenced by varying ethnicities, races, income levels, and religious faiths, and tens of thousands of K–12 public schools. But, whatever its exaggerations, it is the way the Zobrests and many other parents of adolescents came to understand public secondary education in the 1980s, when Sandi and Larry had to make a decision about where Jim was to go to high school.

In a comprehensive 1993 ethnography and analysis of the revitalization of Catholic secondary education and its growing reputation in the American community, sociologists Anthony Bryk, Valerie Lee, and Peter Holland identified four characteristics that defined at the time for many parents, such as the Zobrests, the perception of the promise of the Catholic secondary school: a core curriculum focused on preparation for a traditional liberal arts college education; a desire to create and to sustain the school as a community engaged in a common endeavor; decentralized governance that gave administrators of each school more power over decisions and fewer distractions in making them; and an inspirational ideology at the juncture of personalism and subsidiarity. Paired with the belief that these schools offered relief from the social problems of the public schools, their promise was overwhelming for many parents searching for an institution to guide their children through adolescence.[57]

The Zobrests' decision-making process on the choice of Jim's high school was embedded in a matrix of choices that did not necessarily relate directly to his disability. It immersed them in the general concerns of rank-and-file late twentieth-century parents of all adolescents. They did not understand their choices as limited only by the polarity of *hearing v. deafness*. Of necessity, their idea of responsible parenting led them to a broader range of considerations than whether Jim was to be hearing or Deaf. It made their lives no less complicated to have opted for the former over the latter.

ADMISSION TO SALPOINTE

For all the hopefulness that Catholic education inspired in the Zobrests, the initial response of the Salpointe administration to their expression of interest in enrolling Jim there for high school was not much different from that which Sandi had encountered three years before when she presented the Catalina Foothills School District with the desire to enroll Jim at Sunrise Elementary School. In principle, Catholic schools had opened themselves up to everyone, but they still needed to be convinced to mainstream hearing impaired students. The Roman Catholic Church had a long tradition of educating the hearing impaired, to be sure, but that was in separate institutional settings. As Sandi recalls, she and Larry were given the same response of "We don't have a program" for educating deaf students from the otherwise affable Principal Father (Fr.) Leo McCarthy. While there were a few students at Salpointe with physical disabilities, there were none with conditions that might impact as directly on learning as Jim's deafness. Salpointe's administrators wondered if they were equal to the task. Sandi found herself in the familiar position of instructing school administrators, in appointments with both Fr. Leo and Assistant Principal Michele Brubaker, about how Jim's academic education could be organized for success. Jim required an interpreter who would be paid for, as she understood the law, by the Catalina Foothills School District under the terms of the EAHCA. His speech therapy would be provided at a public school campus, and it, too, would be paid for with public resources. All that was required was the willingness of Salpointe's teachers to accommodate the sign interpreter in their classrooms.[58]

McCarthy and Brubaker were ultimately persuaded. It helped, of course, that what Sandi was proposing required little of Salpointe in the way of resources or special preparations. Furthermore, McCarthy came to the position that integration on terms of equality was the right course for a hearing impaired student. According to Charlotte Harris, a longtime director of development at Salpointe, McCarthy also concluded that Jim should have "as normal an experience as possible and not have any special attention."[59] What this meant in practice was that in contrast to the Catalina Foothills primary and junior high schools, there was no systematic effort requiring reorganizing the school's resources to prepare faculty for the problems of a hearing impaired student or, beyond conventional testing of the sort used for all students, to monitor Jim's progress.[60] Sandi was given permission to speak to the teachers to prepare them, if and when Jim passed the standard admissions test required of all applicants. In her well-practiced role as explainer of deafness, she brought a recording of speech that demonstrated what hearing impaired people were able to hear at various degrees of impairment, and she explained how signed language interpretation might easily be integrated into the classroom.[61]

Pending the outcome of that test, Jim had to get in a queue in which as a transfer student from a public school, he would be prioritized behind students who were graduates of Catholic junior high schools. What Sandi then learned, in a singular variation on the confusion surrounding spelling tests a few years before, was that instruction of teachers, staff, and administrators on the methodology of interpretation in the classroom would need to be ongoing. Jim and Sandi, who accompanied him to interpret the test instructions, came into the room where the written test was being given, and the religious sister administering it strenuously ordered her out of the room in the belief that she would be giving Jim the answers. After a heated exchange, the sister got the permission she felt she needed to have Sandi involved in signing the test directions. Jim's four years at Salpointe had a number of such moments, but for the most part in the classroom, his education there would go more smoothly than an observer might have predicted on the basis of this exchange. An incident of this type perhaps served as a prompt to the administration at Salpointe that teachers had to be prepared to meet Jim's singular needs, and in the months prior to the start of the school year, teachers were alerted to the need to accommodate the presence of a sign interpreter in the classroom and to the fact that Jim might need some help negotiating the changes in activities and events prompted by sound alerts, such as the ubiquitous bell announcing the end of one instructional period and the need to proceed to the next classroom. Without a practical model for or experience in mainstreaming, Salpointe found its path to accommodating Jim through a series of improvisations. So, too, had the Catalina Foothills

School District a few years before, but however much Terry Downey had found it necessary to develop practical improvisations for accommodating Jim's needs, the public schools were also ultimately bound by the strictures of the law. Catholic parochial schools and other nonpublic schools were not.[62]

As for Jim himself, after learning he passed the test and would be admitted, he recalls that he was filled with anticipation and hopefulness about entering Salpointe, where he would be the only deaf student during the period of his enrollment there. It was one more step in the direction of filling his dawning ambitions to enter the hearing world.[63]

3 MAINSTREAMING IN A CATHOLIC SCHOOL

WHO'S TO PAY FOR THE INTERPRETER?

After Jim Zobrest enrolled in Tucson's Salpointe Catholic High School in 1988, a dispute over the meaning of the Constitution's First Amendment would take place that involved the degree to which church and state should be separated. The battle was not one the Zobrests sought, for they simply wanted what their public school district had provided for their deaf son in junior high school—an interpreter—in a school of their choosing. The Zobrests chose not to segregate Jim in a deaf classroom or a deaf school in the hope he would be better served by adjusting to the hearing world. The issue for the Zobrests was to secure what they regarded as legally mandated help for Jim and his disability. Federal law, after all, required a "free appropriate public education" for every child, including those who were "handicapped," to use the phrase embedded in the statute. The law also provided financial assistance to states and localities obliged to offer this service. What the Zobrests overlooked was the law's stipulation that such aid was contingent upon the kind of school students with disabilities attended, and the contingency was that eligible students had to attend a public school unless no public school nearby offered needed services. Under the law, it was the state government or the "appropriate local educational agency," not the parents of a disabled child, who would make the determination as to the suitability of a given public school for, say, a deaf child.[1]

When officials in the Catalina Foothills School District refused on constitutional grounds to provide the interpreter, the Zobrests paid for their son's interpreter themselves, a sum that more than quadrupled the $1,875 annual cost of tuition. The Zobrests believed so strongly in helping Jim adjust more fully to the hearing world that they endured considerable financial pressure for four years so that he could attend the best school in the Tucson area. The Zobrests came to feel that the cost of paying for an interpreter infringed upon their right to practice their religious convictions, and so the issue of disability in the Zobrests' dispute came to be joined with the family's insistence upon their right to practice the religion they professed. It would take five years to sort out the competing constitutional claims asserted on the one hand by a disabled child's parents and on the other by the school district's refusal to recognize these claims.[2]

ENTERING SALPOINTE CATHOLIC HIGH SCHOOL

Jim Zobrest and his peers—the Class of 1992—entered Salpointe High at the end of the Reagan era, a time of considerable geopolitical change. During the next four years, a series of dramatic world events captured newspaper headlines, which Salpointe's yearbook duly noted. "Freedom bells rang" out when Germany's Berlin Wall was demolished, marking the de facto end of Soviet control of Eastern Europe, and South Africa's Nelson Mandela was finally freed from prison after a lifetime of opposing apartheid. After the United States launched Operation Desert Storm to repel Iraq's invasion of Kuwait, Salpointe officials held a Mass for peace, which filled the chapel to the point of overflowing, handed out white ribbons for all to wear to remember the soldiers fighting halfway around the globe, said prayers for their safe return, and organized a seminar titled "The Challenge for Peace," which informed students about the Roman Catholic Church's view on war. Thanks to a videotape recording, Salpointe students also learned about the brutal beating of an unarmed black motorist named Rodney King in Los Angeles, the first of many such racial incidents involving the police that would be transmitted by national television. These remarkable events seemed far removed from the lives of Salpointe students in the desert of southern Arizona. Like most teenagers, including Jim, they were more interested in dating, music, and sports than in political crises elsewhere.[3]

When Jim enrolled in 1988 as the only deaf student, Salpointe officials welcomed the new arrivals and returning students with a message of "love and service" during the Holy Spirit Mass, which was held in the gymnasium. Students from each class put on a skit that emphasized the importance of Christian commitment to society. Fr. Roy Conry, a priest who often presided at the Mass, observed, "Salpointe is dedicated to more than education. It is important to have an expression of faith to start the year." One of Jim's freshman classmates remarked, "I think it is important to show that there is a bond between our lives at school and our religious lives. After a summer of goofing off, it was important to remember our commitment to God." Once the Mass ended, first-year students were treated to a frosh/senior picnic, during which each senior painted his or her "little" brother or sister with happy faces and short sayings, such as "My big sister loves me." The fun continued with the game of "red rover," a water-balloon fight, and a free-for-all mud war on a wet football field.[4]

Salpointe offered an abundant variety of clubs, events, and activities that were typical of the better private schools. Salpointe's diversions included dances, a forty-member band, a drama club that put on theatrical plays, a debate team, a bowling club, a Nintendo club, and Students for Earth Survival. Salpointe also organized high school staples, such as Homecoming, with its royal court and parade before the football game, and Spirit Week, which permitted students to ignore the school's dress code as they wore cowboy hats and bolo ties, hippie beads and peace signs, or grass skirts and birds of paradise. There were other events as well, including Valentine's Day, with chocolate roses, a women's sports lunch, and a walk-a-thon, which called for each student to raise $50 by walking ten miles in order to help with various school expenses, including new blinds for classrooms, a new telephone system, and student trips to Peru. There was also a consortium for high school journalists; separate summer camps for cheerleaders, girl basketball players, and minority pre-engineering students; and Spanish language study in Guadalajara, Mexico. The net effect, the yearbook reported, was that "every day was busy and someone, somewhere was doing something unusual," with plenty of "confusion, excitement, enthusiasm, or laughter." Salpointe alumni remembered the friendly atmosphere at the school, a place where everyone—students and teachers alike—knew everyone else.[5]

Jim Zobrest had a somewhat different experience. His deafness set him apart from his classmates because of his inability to communicate easily and the fact that they typically made little attempt to communicate with him. It was also true that besides basketball, Jim did not join a single school team or club in his four years at Salpointe, a decision that further isolated him. Such isolation could take its toll on a deaf student's self-esteem, as one study of deaf students in schools with a hearing majority demonstrated. A number of participants in the study recalled that their isolation led to alienation and, for some, anger and regret at not having at least one other deaf student to bond with. Certainly, Jim's parents, especially his mother, provided unconditional support and encouragement for their oldest son at home, but the experience of navigating a hearing environment at Salpointe remained challenging. For Sandi Zobrest, the obstacles her deaf son faced every day in adjusting to Salpointe would be worth it in the end. As she explained to the school newspaper, "In order for Jim to live his life 'normally,' he had to be around 'normal' hearing children."[6]

To a large extent, the social whirl of Salpointe revolved around cliques, and Jim Zobrest, as the only deaf student in the school, was mostly confined to the periphery. He was, to use the terminology of deaf memoirist Gina Oliva, a "solitaire" in a hearing environment. The behind-the-ear hearing aids he wore marked him as "different" and yet were of little help beyond hearing the school bell and indistinct sounds, such as laughter or boom box music. Jim was trim and handsome, with "an engaging smile and a facile wit," but he had few friends. Typically, deaf students in hearing-dominated schools make and retain one friend at a time. Jim had the services of an interpreter who accompanied him in most situations, and from what the interpreter could see over four years on the job, Jim was a typical teenager who wanted to "fit in with his peers." In the sensitive period of adolescence, however, few of Jim's high school classmates were interested in—or could be bothered to—communicate with a deaf peer. Jim got along well with his younger brother, Sam, who was a competent interpreter. When Sam entered Salpointe a year after Jim, he translated when Jim and their classmates saw each other outside of class. Although Jim had a more active social life in junior high than he did at Salpointe, there were still aspects of his high school years that he enjoyed, such as attending parties at friends' homes, watching sporting events, and eating at popular restaurants in downtown Tucson. When Jim did attend social functions with his brother, he did have one advantage over his hearing classmates. Because Jim and Sam could sign to each other, they could communicate silently across noisy spaces and during performances of various kinds.[7]

Communication for Jim with hearing classmates, teachers, coaches, and administrators was difficult without his brother or his interpreter. Jim certainly went the extra mile in trying to communicate, as he asserted himself verbally in a way deemed awkward by the hearing majority. Jim was, by most accounts, a good speechreader, and he insisted on speaking as part of his continuing effort to function within—and thereby gain acceptance from—the hearing community. In so doing, Jim realized he risked stigmatization from his peers. Many deaf people refrain from speaking altogether, because the risk of ridicule is too painful to contemplate or to repeat. In Sam's recollection, Jim could speak "pretty good" in those days when he felt comfortable and "when he was really trying his best," but Sam had the advantage of being intimately familiar with Jim's speaking style. Much, if not most, of the time,

Jim could not consistently produce speech that was intelligible to listeners beyond family and a few friends, and none of his teachers, coaches, or other classmates knew signed language.[8]

Because mainstreaming in school usually referred to the classroom, little attention was paid to the deaf student in the hallway, lunchroom, or after-school activities. The all-too-often result was that the deaf student felt "fear, confusion, neglect, and fragmentation." At a time when the convenience of texting and social media did not exist, Salpointe classmates who wanted or needed to speak to Jim usually had to go through his interpreter. The mere existence of an interpreter—an "artificial third party"—inhibited informal conversation that is characteristic of the high school experience. The all-too-common result was that Jim was socially isolated beyond a perfunctory greeting, such as "Hey, how's it going?" Jim knew exactly why few classmates approached him. As he told the yearbook editor, "Some people here have had a hard time accepting that I'm deaf, so they just avoid conversation." This candid comment well expressed the ongoing problem of mainstreaming in education. It should be remembered Jim came from a public school, not one of Salpointe's Catholic feeder schools, and so he had few existing friends to draw upon. Terek Amin, Jim's closest friend in junior high, had enrolled in Flowing Wells High School. Jim dated occasionally at Salpointe but went to the senior prom with someone he knew from junior high. One classmate recalled Jim as a loner but never heard of Salpointe students consciously excluding Jim. The truth was that Jim did not want to be a loner; deafness was a disability that isolated him. A related truth was that too few people at Salpointe went to enough trouble to smooth the path of mainstreaming for Jim. The same could be said of any other school with a hearing majority. It was easier to think Jim chose his isolation—his loneliness—rather than trying to include him into the life of the school community. The cost of differentness was considerable for a deaf student being mainstreamed.[9]

Others had different perspectives on Jim's network of friends. A theology teacher described Jim as "so normal." She saw Jim on the freshman patio, getting along well with his classmates. "He was all kid . . . and he just bumped along with everybody else and talking with everybody." From her vantage point, Jim was not a lonely student. "He was just in it with everybody." The chemistry teacher never taught Jim, but when she saw him in the hallways, she thought he was "as happy and as well-adjusted as the typical Salpointe student." The librarian saw Jim come into the library frequently, often with his class. "He'd have everybody laughing," the librarian recalled, "because he was a good joke-teller." The librarian regarded Jim as "a popular kid." Such observations were likely to be superficial, because of the distance between teacher or staff member and student. In addition, positive observations of Jim's adjustment to Salpointe obviated the need for the school to do more to assist him.[10]

Throughout his high school career, Jim's parents remained committed to helping Jim enter and remain in the hearing world, where he was a minority of one at Salpointe. There was his interpreter, of course, but beyond that no one. The Zobrests bought a couple of teletypewriters (TTYs) and loaned one to a friend of Jim's in the hope that friendships could be nurtured or maintained mechanically. The state of Arizona also gave a free TTY to the Zobrests, and Jim's maternal grandmother bought a machine for herself. For whatever reason, Jim used his device infrequently, and when he did often had trouble understanding what was meant in the flow of words. When Jim was not in school, he took advantage of a new government-funded service for the deaf. The Zobrests signed up with the Arizona Relay Service for the hearing impaired. Ever since the Americans with Disabilities Act of 1990, states have had to provide this service without cost to users. The TTY procedure required Jim to dial a toll-free 711 telephone number in order to reach a human relay operator. The operator then called the person to whom Jim wanted to speak and read the messages to Jim's friend. The operator then typed messages to and from Jim. The advantage of this service was that only Jim needed to have access to a TTY because the operator communicated orally with the other party. The service was "slow and frustrating," and according to Jim's mother, no one ever called him through it. Some teenagers remained hesitant about discussing sensitive matters with a complete stranger—and an adult at that.[11]

Although Jim could not process most sounds, his life as a teenager mirrored the lives of hearing adolescents in several ways. Because the state of Arizona had no restrictions on deaf drivers—deaf drivers have significantly better peripheral vision than hearing drivers and their rates of accidents are comparable—Jim learned how to drive a car at age sixteen along with his classmates. His parents bought him a 1963 Chevy Impala—dubbed the "Blue Beast"—which he drove to early morning basketball practice and to part-time jobs he held at Blockbuster Video and Fry's Food and Drug. A basketball junkie, Jim shot hoops for hours on the family's outdoor basketball court and at a floating net in their swimming pool. Jim also spent much of his leisure time reading Stephen King novels, watching television shows, and listening to the Australian hard-rock band AC/DC, which he appreciated largely by the vibrations of the music. Besides sporting contests, Jim enjoyed following the Sunday evening antics of *In Living Color*, an offbeat sketch comedy starring the Wayans brothers, and *Parker Lewis Can't Lose*, a teen sitcom in which the title character is preoccupied with being popular and overcomes all obstacles. Perhaps Jim's greatest passion, aside from sports, was watching all kinds of movies, particularly *Poltergeist* and other horror films, at the theater and then renting videos of the films to watch them again at home. In that way, he could read the dialogue in the closed captioning that appeared at the bottom of the television screen, a development that became available to the deaf and hard of hearing community in the early 1980s.[12]

ADAPTING TO THE MAINSTREAM

In one sense, Salpointe had prepared for a differently abled student for years before Jim Zobrest matriculated. Under the Elementary and Secondary Education Act of 1965—the most far-reaching federal law ever passed concerning education—Salpointe had formed a working partnership with Amphitheater and Tucson United High Schools in the mid-1970s to provide assistance to students with "special learning needs," as assistant principal Michele Brubaker put it. Amphitheater sent a resource teacher to advise Salpointe instructors, as well as various kinds of instructional materials, including audiovisual aids for students with different levels of sensory ability. Salpointe alerted its teachers and staff members that a deaf student was coming, but it did little else to help Jim succeed beyond permitting his sign interpreter to enter classes, the gym, and religious services; situating Jim in a suitable seat at the rear of the class where he could see the teacher and his interpreter; and allowing his mother to speak periodically to Jim's teachers about his progress. The administration explained to Salpointe teachers who were unfamiliar with the languages of the deaf that Jim's interpreter was permitted to sign what was said in class, which did not mean that Jim was cheating on tests or other assignments. Individual teachers recalled they were unaware of any accommodations Jim would receive, beyond what was indispensable—an omnipresent sign interpreter. Jim's math teacher remembers no special instructions or coaching concerning Jim: "I pretty much just taught him the way I would anybody." As far as Jim was concerned, Salpointe provided "adequate" accommodation of his disability. In trying to help Jim learn, neither the public schools nor Salpointe intended to pay for the interpreter that he needed, and the refusal of his own school district to do so on constitutional grounds became the basis for the Zobrests' lawsuit.[13]

To determine his readiness for high school, Jim Zobrest received an Individualized Education Plan (IEP) in line with the Education for All Handicapped Children Act. The evaluator, Mary Hodgson, a speech therapist and counselor who worked for the Catalina Foothills School District, endeavored to see where Jim stood with respect to speech, language, and hearing norms.

She described Jim as a "profoundly deaf" boy who relied chiefly on signing and speechreading to succeed in school. The IEP report briefly reviewed his public schooling history for the three years prior to enrolling at Salpointe. The school district had provided him with a "mainstream program," which included "resource room assistance for academics," speech and language therapy, and an interpreter in all classes. Jim did well in junior high by relying on signed language "almost exclusively," which he supplemented with speechreading and two behind-the-ear hearing aids for the extremely limited hearing he had. The one exception to Jim's reliance on signed language came in speech class, where he agreed to perform all classwork using Total Communication, meaning a combination of oral speech, sign, gesture, and writing.[14]

As part of preparing Jim's IEP, Hodgson administered a one-hundred-word vocabulary list, and his results were typical of someone with his disability. He relied on his speechreading skill in an attempt to repeat the words said to him. He managed to produce intelligibly all consonant and vowel sounds except for words with "poor visibility," words with /d/, /t/, /k/, and /g/. He used /h/ instead of those sounds. In conversation testing, Jim could be understood 40 percent of the time when the listener knew the content. It should be noted that when Jim was with people who knew him and his speech pattern, he did much better in oral communication. After a review of Jim's oral speech, the school district's long-term goals for Jim called for his speech, receptive/expressive language, and articulation to reach a level "appropriate for his age."[15]

An analysis of some deaf students who were successfully mainstreamed in an integrated educational learning environment shows that Jim Zobrest shared several key characteristics with them. Successful deaf students had high expectations of themselves, displayed a strong inner drive, and were prepared to speak up for themselves, disability and all. They were outgoing, possessed high self-esteem, and had good social skills. They also participated in athletics or other extra-curricular activities, their families strongly supported them, and they had effective sign language interpreters.[16]

To succeed in a hearing environment—to be mainstreamed, in other words—Jim Zobrest needed continuing assistance in the form of a good interpreter and student note-takers. As he freely admitted, "Without an interpreter, I could not have succeeded." According to the code for interpreters, an interpreter functions like a machine that merely translates what is said into a language the deaf can understand. In practice, such a mechanical comparison collided head on with the complicated realities of signing for three-dimensional human beings. Interpreters would invariably discover that their diligent efforts to sign entailed opportunities, obstacles, and costs that they had not always anticipated or experienced. For one thing, signing does not occur in a vacuum, and interpreters must recognize and analyze different conditions for signing to help clients understand the world of speech. The language of a deaf person might require subtle adjustment by the interpreter, perhaps, as in Jim's case, when the client uses Total Communication. When a teacher inadvertently impeded Jim's learning, the interpreter was obligated to explain a more suitable means of instruction. In the sometimes volatile sporting environment, a coach would yell at the players, and the interpreter was hardly an innocent bystander. Jim's interpreters had to deflect such abuse in order to concentrate on their obligation to serve their client.[17]

The attributes or qualities interpreters should possess include stamina, a long attention span, considerable intelligence, a sense of humor, good interpersonal skills, and a strong sense of responsibility, especially for being on time to all assignments. In facilitating and shaping interactive discourse, interpreters require space that will permit good communication—meaning clear sightlines and reasonably close proximity to the deaf client—a necessity that is overlooked sometimes. To communicate effectively, interpreters must be bilingual and bicultural, as they serve as intermediaries between the deaf and hearing communities. Interpreters are also obliged to ask their clients about the appropriateness and effectiveness of the signed language and the manner of interpretation. Further, interpreters must recognize that they have at least two audiences, with one being the client and the other a hearing person. The styles of communication are not only idiosyncratic for each person, but they are also affected by the larger community that deaf and hearing people inhabit. Interpreters must assess every linguistic situation in which they work and make adjustments accordingly. In a school, for example, each teacher has a distinctive teaching and speaking style, and interpreters must become familiar with both styles and communicate effectively with their client. As significant, if not more so, interpreters must familiarize themselves with the subject matter and the vocabulary typically used in a given course. Even so, interpreters must be ready for unusual or unexpected ideas, words, or concepts that cannot be anticipated. When signed interpretation is negatively affected, interpreters must reflect on the problem and must negotiate with the speaker in order to reach an acceptable solution. At bottom, sign interpreters must do what other foreign language interpreters do, which is to "convey what is *meant* by what is said." Moreover, as Anne McIntosh, a deaf professor of communication studies, argues, interpreters should intervene in social situations to help deaf students address the core problem of social isolation. In so doing, interpreters can help increase opportunities for social interaction and thereby make the school experience a more pleasant time. In all of these ways, interpreters must make subtle adjustments that a machine cannot.[18]

As strained as socializing is for a deaf student in a hearing environment, academic work under a teacher's direction can be even more demanding. Deaf students face barriers that can affect their performance and their interaction with hearing students and teachers. The lag time between a teacher's spoken message and a signer's interpreted message may prevent deaf students from responding appropriately or at all. The rapidity with which a lively discussion usually takes place sometimes means that deaf students relying on speechreading cannot follow what is said. Signers and deaf students may be unable to look at each speaker who participates because their words keep coming in a kind of jumble, and there is little to no time to associate thoughts expressed with a specific speaker. Such interaction occurs in a spatial configuration that may interfere with the mainstreaming scheme. Deaf students must sit so they can see the instructor, the blackboard or screen, and their interpreters, all at the same time. When instructors move around the classroom, deaf students must choose between watching them for revealing facial expressions and body language and looking at their interpreters for the words the instructors are saying. Even highly skilled interpreters invariably cannot communicate a host of sounds and speech, including noise, group reaction, plays on words, specialized vocabulary that has no sign equivalent, laughter, teacher comments to other students, and comments between students. In addition, deaf students usually miss out on lighthearted joking or teasing done by hearing students that can contribute to a comfortable learning environment.[19]

RELIGION AT SALPOINTE CATHOLIC HIGH SCHOOL

When the Zobrests went to court to have their public school district pay for Jim's interpreter, district officials denied the request, noting that Salpointe was a parochial school. There was no doubt that Salpointe's environment was pervasively Catholic. Salpointe's annual report stated frankly: "We will forever proclaim the fact that Salpointe is a religious school, proud of our heritage and the moral values that influence our actions." The sectarian purpose of Salpointe was stated explicitly in its annual report for 1988: "Salpointe Catholic High School is a community of parents, faculty, staff, and students dedicated to living and perpetuating the mission of Jesus Christ, serving the young people of the Tucson metropolitan area who desire a Catholic education. . . . It also nurtures the ability to make moral choices, instills a sense of

Christian values, and engenders friendliness and understanding among students of diverse temperaments and backgrounds. As an "educational vehicle for the Church," as the Salpointe faculty handbook put it, Catholic principles and priorities were visible at many points. According to school expectations, Salpointe "encourages its faculty to assist students in experiencing how the presence of God is manifest in nature, human history, in the struggles for economic and political justice, and other secular areas of the curriculum." Three of Salpointe's goals called for school officials to work with students to (1) "develop their moral and academic ability to make responsible decisions as informed Christians," (2) "understand the need to interact with society in a realistic, productive, and Christian manner," and (3) "develop the spirit of Christian sportsmanship."[20]

Certainly, Salpointe went to considerable lengths to promote Catholic ideology and practices but refrained from proselytizing its students. Salpointe's goal was "to turn every child into the best person they can become," not to recruit young men for the priesthood or young women to become nuns. There was a noticeable presence on campus of several Catholic orders, including the principal, Fr. Leo McCarthy, a Carmelite priest who actively promoted the school's ministries program. Salpointe had always made worship services available to—though not required for—students and staff alike, especially the daily half-hour Mass or Eucharist, which began at 7:55 a.m. Prayers at Salpointe were said at the start of the school day, along with the Pledge of Allegiance, and before general assemblies and athletic contests. Students often composed the prayers, which were characteristically "short and sweet," such as "Pray Me Our Father," or particular petitions for divine favor, as in the case of bodily injury suffered by a Salpointe family member. Some teachers recited prayers before beginning the day's academic lesson, and all instructors regarded their teaching duties as their ministry. Students heard and said prayers in classrooms with crucifixes, and they saw other religious iconography as they walked around the campus.[21]

Salpointe students, faculty, and staff expressed their religious convictions in other ways, too. The Salpointe Singers sang for the Masses on campus, as well as for funerals and at the nursing home operated by the Carondelet Holy Family Center. The school put on the rock musical *Godspell*, which recounts the parables of Jesus of Nazareth as recorded in the Gospel of Matthew, with music chosen from the Catholic Church's hymnody. "*Godspell* was not like any other play," one senior declared. "With the clown outfits and the junkyard scenery, it showed that Jesus loved everybody, no matter who or where, and we should love ourselves for that." Fr. Joe Fitzgerald took students on four-day retreats in order to reflect on their relationships with others, in what was described as an exercise in "personal discovery." A delighted Salpointe senior said of the retreat, "It's an unexplainable event that you shouldn't miss. It's a chance to get to know yourself, your friends, and God." Fitzgerald also formed the Liturgy Club to plan more creative liturgies during chapel services. At Christmastime, each Salpointe homeroom adopted a family and donated clothing, toys, and cash for their needs.[22]

In order to promote a common value system, the Salpointe curriculum required all students, including the 20 percent of the students who were non-Catholics, to complete four years of coursework in Catholic theology. "You don't have to believe it," Father Leo often remarked, "but you've got to pass it." The theology courses included Understanding Catholic Christianity and Jesus in the Gospels, as well as electives such as Comparative World Religions, Death and Dying, Christian Lifestyles, and Social Justice and Social Action. All of these courses were conducted from a Catholic point of view, which, as Salpointe theology teacher Denise Jensen put it, rejected the "fairly medieval stance" of traditional Catholic doctrinal thinking in favor of Pope John XXIII's modernizing approach of the Second Vatican Council. A former Salpointe student herself who sent her children there as well, Jensen encouraged her students to express themselves freely in order to develop a logical basis for their actions. "People learn by thinking things through for themselves," so she told her students to say whatever was on their minds. "You're thinking it," she said, "so why can't you say it?"[23]

In line with the school's religious mission, all Salpointe students had to perform some sort of service to society. The school required community service in its Moral Decisions course, and the students in it worked either at the Tucson AIDS Project or the Primavera shelter for homeless men. There were volunteer service opportunities as well. The school's Key Club organized blood drives and fund-raising activities, such as car washes and graduation roses, to raise money for others, including disabled children and families "in crisis" who were assisted by Casa de los Niños, one of the city's oldest social welfare organizations. A group called Assisteens gave teenage girls, largely from Salpointe, opportunities to donate money from charity balls or fashion shows to worthy causes, such as a children's research center.[24]

Salpointe's emphasis on religion and good conduct influenced many parents to send their children there. For the students, however, the constant emphasis on behaving in a moral fashion elicited some resentment. Some students complained that the faculty acted more like parents than teachers, especially by promoting and enforcing conservative values that allegedly stifled their creativity. Given this resistance, the Salpointe staff found it gratifying when their charges made wise choices. In one case, a young woman decided not to drink alcohol at a backyard pool party in order to drive the inebriated home safely. "Mom," she reported later with a sense of amazement in her voice, "I made a moral decision." One example of Salpointe's emphasis on discipline was a detention program that required students who violated school policy to report to the school on Saturday morning to do manual labor, such as painting or cleaning. Sandi Zobrest "love[d]" that policy, which she saw as an unmistakable sign that at Salpointe students were "held accountable for everything. I thought that was excellent training for college, when you were not held accountable for anything."[25]

Although religion was an important part of Salpointe's educational scheme, the Zobrest brothers did not think the school's atmosphere was pervasively sectarian. Jim remarked, "there wasn't much difference . . . between [Salpointe and] a public school, except the religion class—and you would see priests and nuns," which, he said, took some getting used to. Despite the efforts of Jim's parents to instill religion, he had never been particularly religious, found the concept of a divine being incomprehensible, and never attended Mass at Salpointe. Jim's younger brother, Sam, echoed the idea that religion did not suffuse the school day at Salpointe. He thought Salpointe "felt like a normal high school, except for those small parts of the day" where a teacher taught theology or religion. These comments by the Zobrest brothers about the minimal presence of religion appear to underestimate the extent to which Catholic values permeated Salpointe's environment, so much so that some students became largely oblivious to this pervasive emphasis. Whether or not the Zobrest brothers noticed or acknowledged the extent of religion at Salpointe, the school's religious mission, curriculum, and worship services raised the constitutional question of who would pay for Jim's sign interpreter.[26]

JIM'S EDUCATION AT SALPOINTE

Salpointe's strategy in assisting students with "special needs" was to remove administrative obstacles that might come between parents and their children's teachers. Assistant principal Michele Brubaker made sure, for example, that Sandi Zobrest could speak to Jim's teachers directly, and she kept a close watch on how her disabled son was doing at Salpointe. One teacher recalled Sandi as an "incredible" advocate for her older son. Adopting a matter-of-fact approach, Sandi refused to identify Jim as "at risk," saying, "This is who he is. This is what he needs. Don't treat him special. Just make sure that he can see his interpreter." She did not want Jim's disability to make him stand out in the ways the school responded to him. Sandi simply encouraged Jim's teachers to work with him: "What can we do to make sure that you and Jim are successful?" Such parental concern did not mean the Zobrests marched down to the school's office frequently. Brubaker and the dean of men saw the Zobrests only twice yearly, when the school convened its well-attended parent-teacher conferences.[27]

The Zobrests did not need to check on Jim frequently because he was a generally diligent and capable student. The librarian believed he was "smart as a whip," and he made the school's honor roll in his sophomore year. Although Jim struggled mightily with geometry and advanced algebra, his math teacher described him as "a hard worker, very attentive . . . very intelligent." Another teacher recalled Jim as being "very engaged" and "real good" as a student, with fine penmanship. His native intelligence meant he did not spend much time on homework in order to earn good marks. When motivated, as in the case of the class with his American history teacher, Tom Joseph, Jim found schooling "enjoyable," even entertaining. As a football coach, Joseph was a fellow jock—one of the guys—who laced his lectures with humor and references to popular culture that compelled Jim to pay attention to "every word that came out of his mouth, which was next to impossible to achieve." Denise Jensen, the theology teacher with a master's degree in special education, pointed out that Salpointe had a clear policy to "birddog" kids who were struggling academically, and she was unaware of any academic difficulty Jim experienced.[28]

Indeed, Jim received good grades except in mathematics, which had always given him trouble. Studies show that most deaf students lag well behind hearing students in mathematics, often because of a lack of familiarity with numbers, language obstacles, teacher-dominated pedagogy, and insufficient emphasis on real-world problem solving. Salpointe provided help for students like Jim who struggled with certain subjects, including meetings with the school counselor and review sessions held by teachers before and after school. Sometimes Jim felt he received a grade that was unwarranted, and on those occasions, he was ready to challenge the mark. Jim's biology teacher, Mark Brunenkant, observed that Jim "wanted to make sure that he got a fair shake" if his grades slipped. Brunenkant recalled Jim could be "very sensitive" when he did not do well, and teachers "better have your ducks in line" if Jim or his mother challenged low marks. Except for occasional tardiness to class, Jim Zobrest was a serious student who avoided trouble in school. He never received detention or was assigned to a Saturday morning work detail, as his brother once was.[29]

THE TASK OF INTERPRETATION

On the recommendation of his interpreter, Jim typically sat in the rear of class and off to the side in order not to disrupt the proceedings. Jim's math teacher, who was right-handed, suggested that Jim sit in the back-left side of the room (from the teacher's perspective) so he could see the teacher and read his lips as he wrote problems on the blackboard at the front of the class. Denise Jensen commented that when she called on students to answer her questions about religion, she "didn't ever notice anything odd or different with the way the kids treated him or the way Jim interacted in his group." At least in theology class, Jim never asked questions of the teacher, because he did not want to draw attention to himself, and never spoke in front of his classmates, though he did so after class ended, when he could approach the teacher privately. On such occasions, Jim kept on talking until Jensen understood what he said. Jensen had a "hard time" communicating with Jim without his interpreter, but "we just hung in there," she said, "'til I got what he was telling me." In class, it helped Jim that some teachers at Salpointe wrote out key ideas and terms on plastic sheets, which were projected on screens at the front of the room. They understood "the best way to reach everybody is to speak it and write it, so that they can hear and see."[30]

Jim's success in the classroom depended most of all on the help of a skilled and dedicated interpreter. When possible, Jim tried to speech-read, but sometimes that was impossible, as in the case with his math teacher. For most of his Salpointe career, Jim worked with James Santeford, a likeable, conscientious, and "very mild-mannered" twenty-three-year-old with dirty blond hair who habitually carried a backpack. A native of Illinois, Santeford had earned an associate of applied arts degree in interpreter training from Pima Community College in Tucson, and Sandi Zobrest came across Santeford's name by contacting that school's Office of Disabled Student Resources. She was insistent the interpreter be male, because Jim would play basketball and the interpreter would need access to the locker room. After interviewing Santeford, the Zobrests agreed to pay him a modest hourly rate that amounted to as much as $8,500 a year in a time of accelerating inflation. Santeford accepted the offer because he could pay his expenses by living at home with his newly widowed mother and because he did additional interpreting work for an institution of higher learning. Once the arrangement to interpret for Jim was made, Santeford saw little of Jim's parents except at Salpointe events, most often at basketball games. Jim Zobrest and Jim Santeford got along famously because they were both young and enjoyed sports. Santeford was also Jim's first male interpreter.[31]

The task of interpreting at Salpointe was in some ways challenging because Santeford had not signed in a classroom previously. In addition, Santeford had mastered ASL, while Jim had learned SEE and developed some mutually crafted signs with his brother, Sam. Although Jim never felt comfortable with ASL, according to his mother, and did not sign "like a Deaf person," he and Santeford devised their own vernacular, one that combined ASL and SEE. Further, Santeford was on call from early morning until late afternoon, interpreting freshman and junior varsity basketball practice at 6:00 a.m. and then all of Jim's classes. Jim and his interpreter usually walked together from class to class, and in that interval discussed what the teacher had just said. Salpointe did permit Santeford to relax in the teachers' lounge and eat in the faculty dining area. When Jim had a test in class, Santeford could catch his breath and divert his attention, usually by reading a book or gazing out a window.[32]

Santeford handled interpreting unobtrusively from the front of the classroom. It was his understanding that the interpreter should be as "invisible" as possible, because "the conversation is and should be between the hearing person and the Deaf person." Santeford explained to teachers, "the interpreter is there for their client and therefore all interactions are to be done between themselves and the client."[33] The interpreter in this view is "simply a communication tool between two or more persons." It was thus no surprise that Santeford regarded his interpretive work as "mechanical," something that a technician does, rather than possessing artistic qualities. Every teacher at Salpointe accepted Santeford's interpretive role without difficulty. Santeford "just seemed like he was another person that was in the classroom," Denise Jensen recalled, though she admitted it took a while to adjust to another adult in the classroom. It took further adjustment not to look at the interpreter when Jim answered questions. It helped enormously that the consensus among teachers was that Santeford was "a very, very nice guy . . . very friendly, very easy to work with." When a teacher went to groups of students to ask them for questions, Santeford went to Jim's group to interpret any questions Jim had. On rare occasions and in private, Santeford made suggestions to teachers about how to reach Jim more effectively, which contradicted his claim that he was merely a human machine rather than part of an instructional team.

An important part of Santeford's task as Jim's interpreter concerned the subject of religion. Because Salpointe was, as its name said, a Catholic school, the atmosphere and some of the academic requirements were steeped in Catholicism. For Jim Santeford, the religiosity of Salpointe was predictable; it was to "be expected that a Catholic worldview would permeate the curriculum." This plain fact did not pose a difficulty for Santeford because he had been raised in the Christian Reformed Church, a Calvinist variant of Christianity, and has had an intellectual interest in religion all of his life. He was certainly familiar with the Bible. Nevertheless, Santeford did confess he was puzzled by Catholic rituals because he "did not understand them." His job was to communicate what was said to his young client, whether that was an academic subject or a religious exercise. As a sign interpretation professional, the content of the matter to be translated was immaterial to Santeford.[34]

Sometimes Santeford found himself in what seemed like an awkward situation not of his making. Like other students, Jim Zobrest sometimes fell asleep in class, especially in theology, which had no appeal to him. The theology class was scheduled after Jim had physical education and had eaten lunch, and it was held in a room with cinderblock walls that faced the searing afternoon sun without an adequate air conditioner. Denise Jensen, the theology teacher who saw Jim (and others) occasionally succumb to exhaustion in the warm classroom, witnessed something far more unusual at these times. When Jim fell asleep, Jim Santeford kept translating every word and thought the teacher expressed verbally. Jensen thought this practice was odd, and when she had a moment alone with Santeford, she inquired as to the rationale for continuing to sign when Jim was asleep. Santeford replied, "Look, I am a machine. If you could have an interpreting machine, that's what I am. Just because he fell asleep does not mean that I stop interpreting." Jensen, who was becoming aware of disability issues, in part because of the new Americans with Disabilities Act, and who would become the special education staff member at Salpointe after Jim graduated, was "flabbergasted" by this explanation, thinking it was a pointless waste of energy because the deaf student was asleep.[35]

By Jim Zobrest's senior year, the Zobrests agreed to reduce Santeford's nonstop translation schedule to morning classes, followed by late afternoon basketball practices, leaving him with several hours of "free time" after lunch to resume his education. Jim had grown accustomed to Santeford's easy-going personality and signing style, so he had to adjust to the interpreters who replaced him. On occasion, when Jim Santeford was ill or had an off-school appointment, a substitute interpreter would take his place. After school, Jim's mother quizzed her son about the suitability of each new interpreter: "Did you like this interpreter?" "Were they good?" "Did you understand them?" Such questions were ones that Sandi had always asked about Jim's new interpreters, because the skill and commitment of interpreters could vary considerably and because there had to be a good "fit" between a particular interpreter and a particular deaf person. This fit was all the more imperative because the standard deaf language of interpreters was ASL, and Jim's competency was in SEE and Total Communication.[36]

Although Jim Santeford spent long hours translating for Jim in class and in the gym, he remained on the job in the evening, too, much to his unhappiness. The obvious truth was that Santeford was a human being, not a machine, who had finite limits as to how much work he could bear, whether physically or psychologically. At the same time, his client naturally had questions about the day's events or homework he had been given, and his interpreter was the most logical person to communicate with through his TTY. Santeford readily admitted he "wanted to be there to answer Jim's questions" but also felt strongly his "personal time" was "being invaded and that there was a lack of boundaries." Still, out of a strong and continuing sense of obligation to his likeable client, Santeford never told Jim such evening calls were either unwelcome or forbidden. Unsurprisingly, the calls kept coming.[37]

BASKETBALL

For Jim Zobrest, schoolwork was mostly a chore to get through to be eligible for his passion—playing sports. While Jim played soccer and baseball and watched televised games of the National Football League, he enjoyed playing basketball as much as doing anything else in life, perhaps more so. A lot of Jim's self-regard was wrapped up in basketball, a fast-paced and action-packed sport he played well. He was tall, at 6'4", and athletic, with an excellent feel for the ball and a good outside shooting touch—all prime qualities for success on the hardcourt. In addition, Jim had gone to summer basketball camp at the University of Arizona several times. The weeklong camp drew many local boys ages nine to seventeen, chiefly because the Arizona Wildcats men's basketball team was coached by Lute Olson. Olson was well on his way to making Arizona a perennial national powerhouse with dozens of his players, including Steve Kerr, Sean Elliott, and Mike Bibby, going on to successful careers in the National Basketball Association. Word had spread among Salpointe athletes that Jim had attended Olson's camp regularly, which stirred envy in some circles.[38]

Deafness still created many challenges for athletes like Jim. Deaf basketball players could not always—and sometimes never—hear whistles that stopped play or assigned fouls. They could not hear coaches calling for sudden changes in offensive or defensive schemes during games, and they could not hear teammates warn them of blindside screens while on defense or hear teammates call for the ball while on offense. There were ways to adjust to such limitations, especially by playing farther away from the opponent whom a deaf player was to guard in order to gain a wider field of vision and movement. On offense, a deaf player often depends on learning the distinctive style of basketball that each teammate uses. As for Jim, he tried mightily to bridge the deaf and hearing worlds by communicating through speechreading and turning to his interpreter when he could not understand what was being said. One of Jim's teammates thought "a lot of times" Jim did "pick up on" what the coach and his teammates told him.[39]

There are some advantages for basketball players who are deaf. In a sport as fast-paced as basketball with few stoppages, good vision matters far more than hearing, and deaf players generally pay close attention to visual cues and body language to guide their performance. In consequence, when a coach diagrams a play or demonstrates a drill, a deaf player may pick it up more quickly than a hearing player would. Most deaf players work as hard, if not harder, than hearing players, because they must compensate for their inability to hear most sounds. For deaf players, practicing hard is not anathema but a task in the normal course of events, as they have had to work through significant difficulties their entire lives. For the Salpointe basketball coach, there was an additional advantage in one of his players being deaf. When the game's outcome hung in the balance, a deaf player who was fouled and was awarded free throw attempts would not hear taunts and jeers of opposing fans.[40]

Deafness, then, is not an insurmountable barrier to excelling in basketball, especially at the high school level. Most secondary school basketball coaches devise one offensive and one defensive scheme for a given opponent, and they organize practices that introduce and drill their teams into adopting these schemes before the game is played. Any changes in these schemes seldom come during the game itself, unless a team is behind as time is running out, when a standard pressing defense might be employed. Generally speaking, changes in offense and defense patterns are made during halftime in the locker room or during time-outs in the second half. Changes in these areas, which occur during a noisy game, are typically made by hand signal, not voice command. Such practices accommodated deaf players such as Jim Zobrest. Moreover, players on a given team become accustomed to each other's manner of playing, making speech largely superfluous.[41]

To make sure he understood what the coaching staff called for, Jim Zobrest wore behind-the-ear hearing aids, as usual, though they were of minimal use insofar as spoken English was concerned. More helpfully, Jim's interpreter was always available during practices and games, as he sat quietly at the far end of the bench and waited until his services were needed. During time-outs, Jim Santeford was "like a shadow" to the basketball coach, kneeling next to him and interpreting what the coach said, word for word. Santeford "really helped Jim out," the varsity coach recalled, especially when changes were made in practice drills or game-time planning. Communication still remained an issue and was, on occasion, a source of some tension on the team, though the coach never noticed any squabbling involving Jim.[42]

At times, Jim's deafness created an awkward situation for all three parties involved—the coach, the player, and the interpreter. In Jim's sophomore year, when he was on the junior varsity boys' basketball team, the coach had a difficult time communicating directly to Jim, preferring, instead, to speak to the interpreter. That was a clear violation of the norms of communicating with deaf people. Another problem was that the coach's manner of communication was sometimes abusive, as he often screamed obscenities at Jim Santeford. After the coach's emotional outburst had subsided, he would explain to the interpreter, "you know I am not yelling at you, but at Jim." It was a distinction without a difference, as far as Santeford was concerned. Santeford later regretted not speaking up for himself on those disturbing occasions.[43]

At the start of his high school career in basketball, Jim's hopes of becoming a star player appeared to be well on track. His freshman coach recognized both Jim's ability in basketball and his disability regarding hearing and found ways for Jim—and the team—to perform well on the court with Jim as a starting player. The JV coach also appreciated Jim's abilities and put his talent on the floor. Jim's teammate Derek Hersha thought Jim had a "really nice touch" in shooting the ball from ten to fifteen feet away from the basket and considered him one of the "better players" on the freshman and junior varsity teams. Richard McBride, who was Jim's math teacher and a former basketball coach who played pickup games with Jim after school, regarded Jim as a "very good" player. Jim started on the freshman team and, according to his interpreter, "dominated" the other centers in the league. One freshman game stands out in Jim Zobrest's memory. His team was headed to defeat in the waning minutes when a combination of personal fouls and technical fouls sent Jim to the foul line for six straight free throws. He sank all of them, and Salpointe won that contest. Jim's greatest game came in his sophomore year, when he scored 26 points. Overall, Jim averaged about 10 points per game as a freshman and junior varsity player. It was not just Jim who played well. The freshman team achieved a 15–1 record, the best in school history. Expectations soared in the belief these players would perform equally well when they joined the varsity team.[44]

The Salpointe boys' varsity basketball coach was Jim Flannery, a 1966 Salpointe graduate who had twice been named as Tucson's basketball coach of the year. The mustachioed Flannery was an "old-school" coach with the ironic nickname "Smiling Jim," because he seldom smiled. One of his fellow coaches at Salpointe remembered Flannery as both "tough" and "mean . . .

Basketball Team Photo, Salpointe Catholic High School Lancers, 1990–91. Front row: Coach Jim Flannery, kneeling; Back row: Jim Santeford, far left in street clothes, Sean Flannery, #32, Jim Zobrest, #42, the eighth person from the left. (Courtesy of Salpointe Catholic High School)

a screamer, a Bobby Knight," a reference to the tempestuous basketball hall of fame coach at Indiana University. To make the varsity basketball team, Coach Flannery had tryouts. There were several "cuts," with the first one being the requirement that would-be players run a mile in less than six minutes. A failure to break that demanding time limit meant an automatic dismissal. Flannery scouted his team's opponents, prepped his team for certain tendencies he observed, and orchestrated team drills to get them ready for the games. In the games themselves, Flannery's intensity sometimes turned his face red and led him to yell at his players to "play tougher, be stronger." The coach's intention was purely to motivate his team to perform at a higher level on the court in order to win the game. No one—not his son Sean Flannery, not Jim Zobrest—was spared from the coach's emotional outbursts. Interpreter Jim Santeford found such anger and use of epithets distasteful.[45]

When Jim Zobrest reached the varsity team as a junior, he did not start but was one of the top reserves off the bench. Even so, Jim played little, primarily when the game was no longer in doubt. The Zobrests recall some opposing coaches questioning why Jim was consigned to riding the bench and declaring Jim would have started on their teams. The fun Jim had always had in playing basketball quickly dissipated. At some point, Jim questioned his limited playing time, which prompted Coach Flannery to belittle Jim as a disabled person. Jim recalls Flannery saying to him, "You're lucky even to be on [the team] here because you're deaf." Jim's mother thought the blunt comment was his "first taste of the 'real world,'" an observation that was meant to emphasize Jim's bitter disappointment but could not be literally true. The Zobrests came to suspect the coach gave preferential treatment to his talented 6'5" son Sean—the first Salpointe player ever to start on the varsity team as a freshman—as he barked out commands for other players to "throw the ball to Sean, throw the ball to Sean." To be fair, Sean Flannery was a prolific scorer, finishing his career as one of the state's all-time scorers. Moreover, there were times in the heat of the moment when Coach Flannery shouted out changes in the defense or offense, which Jim did not hear because his back prevented him from seeing the coach's lips or his interpreter signing to him. The speed of the game and its shifting fortunes did not permit Flannery to wait for Jim's attention.[46]

In his senior year at Salpointe, Jim became ever more disenchanted with his high school experience, a feeling that arose from growing frustration over not playing much basketball on the team. He was in the coach's "doghouse," as Jim put it, and played hardly at all. The Zobrests complained to the athletic director about Jim's minimal playing time, but they were told that Coach Flannery was an institution at the school and was therefore untouchable. "There's nothing I can do," the athletic director reportedly said. Reflecting years later on Jim's disappointing basketball career at Salpointe, Coach Flannery thought Jim did "an incredible job" despite his deafness. Flannery's remark would seem either to be a glowing retrospective on a player with a notable disability who had little opportunity to take the court or an attitude that deaf athletes in team sports were largely incapable of excelling. In addition, few Salpointe teammates befriended Jim, and he was not close to any of them. Jim's deafness and what one teammate dubbed as Jim's aura of self-confidence about his playing ability, in spite of the obstacles he faced, made close friendships almost impossible on the Salpointe varsity boys' basketball team. It seems plain that Jim's coaches and teammates not only ignored Jim but, by and large, did not help him overcome his disability. As a result of all these factors, Jim became increasingly disenchanted with the sport he loved and with the school itself.[47]

For deaf students in hearing schools, the quality of their extracurricular experiences is the major reason for their level of satisfaction about their entire educational experience. When Jim Zobrest's dreams of athletic success went up in smoke, he lost his best chance to make close friends with a common interest. Jim's inability to break into the varsity basketball team's starting lineup also limited his opportunities to display his creativity and skills in school. Sports or other such pastimes that required little verbal communication were usually more suitable activities for deaf students than the academic classes that hearing and deaf students alike were required to complete. At the same time, sport participation could give the false appearance that a deaf student was getting along fine at the school, even in sports themselves, when he or she may have missed out on team jokes, coaching instructions, and teammate comments during competition itself. Busyness could mask isolation and alienation in sport, as onlookers, even coaches, were given to what has been described as the "but he looks like he is participating just fine" syndrome. Successful integration of deaf students in sports requires more than simple participation in organized physical activity.[48]

After Jim finished playing basketball competitively, societal awareness grew about the capabilities of deaf athletes, a change in attitude that occurred with the appearance of other deaf pioneers in this popular sport. One example was Lance Allred of the Cleveland Cavaliers, the only deaf athlete ever to play in the National Basketball Association. Tamika Catchings of the Indiana Fever of the Women's NBA was an outstanding defender, rebounder, and scorer, who was named an All-Star a record number of times. Michael Lizarraga, who played at Cal State Northridge College, averaged 20 points a game as a junior. More recently, Luke Adams ran the offense for the Texas Tech Red Raiders as a point guard and has coaching ambitions in the sport. "My whole story is you can't take 'no' for an answer," Adams told an audience of young deaf students. Using an interpreter, Adams recalled that doctors once told his parents he would never advance beyond the second grade. Friends laughed at him when he spent countless hours perfecting his basketball skills, dismissing his ambition of playing Division I basketball as a pipe dream. Unfortunately, all of these players competed a decade or more after Jim Zobrest did, so Jim had no role models as a deaf person in playing basketball on a hearing team. Whether Jim would have benefited from a basketball role model who was deaf is impossible to say. Another way to look at the lack of deaf players is to note that neither Jim's teammates nor his coaches were familiar with this disability, in part because they did not know and had never heard of a deaf basketball player. This lack of familiarity with, or bias against, deaf basketball players may well have made it more difficult for Jim to be given enough opportunities to develop his basketball skills and thereby play more during games.[49]

In the early 1990s, when Jim Zobrest played—sparingly, to be sure—the Salpointe boys' varsity basketball team attained its best record in a generation.

In his junior year, the Lancers compiled a gaudy 23–5 winning record and won the city's championship. In Jim's senior year, all five starters returned, consigning Jim to the bench once more. The team's win-loss record that year was 26–6. Again, the Lancers won the city's championship. A major reason for the team's success was the clutch performance of Sean Flannery—a star forward by any measure. During his high school career, Sean scored 2,332 points, then the fourth highest in Arizona history. He declined Lute Olson's offer to join the hometown Arizona Wildcats, which would go to the NCAA's Final Four without him, excelling instead at the University of San Diego. In what was a bitter irony, Jim's chief rival on the Salpointe basketball team thus rejected the elite school where Jim had hoped one day to play basketball.[50]

THE COST OF MAINSTREAMING

The cost of mainstreaming Jim Zobrest at Salpointe Catholic High School had been high. Jim had tried mightily to fit into the hearing world of his classmates, teachers, and coaches, but for the most part he remained in a world of his own. While Jim enrolled at Salpointe, his closest childhood friends scattered to other schools, and Jim did not develop similar friendships in high school. Deafness was, for most of Jim's classmates, a barrier they chose not to cross, whether by learning to sign, adjusting to his speech pattern, or telephoning him with special equipment. Salpointe had attracted Jim with its all-star athletic program, but he played sparingly on its championship-caliber basketball team, which disappointed him greatly. Sandi and Larry Zobrest came to see that their costly experiment in mainstreaming Jim had not produced the kind of social integration on which they had gambled their homelife and financial well-being. Jim's interpreter, Jim Santeford, came to realize he routinely ignored his own physical needs for adequate sleep and exercise, especially during the long basketball season that occurred between October and March. The result was Santeford suffered from mental and physical fatigue that by his own admission undoubtedly led to mistakes in interpretation and a lack of awareness he was making mistakes. Santeford developed a repetitive motion injury in his wrists called carpal tunnel syndrome—an ailment common to the signed interpretation profession—and left that line of work several years after signing for Jim Zobrest. In his own way, Jim Santeford might be considered another casualty of the mainstreaming experiment. Santeford ruefully realized he could have prolonged his career by alternating with another interpreter every twenty minutes. As appropriate as this idea was, a rotation of interpreters would have doubled the cost of this service, which had already pushed the Zobrests to the financial breaking point. Under any circumstance, Santeford proved hardly a machine.[51]

In looking back at his performance as an interpreter for Jim Zobrest, Santeford used the word *adequate*. Certainly, he had given his "all" while interpreting, as he would later say, but he had in his estimation "failed" to "educate the community of Salpointe High School" on the way in which communication with the deaf should work. Santeford maintained that his performance as an interpreter at Salpointe and as an advocate for deaf communication would have been better had he not worked by himself. It would have been preferable, in his estimation, if he had been part of a team with other interpreters who could have discussed particular challenges they faced in school and in sports. In addition, Santeford came to believe an administrator from Salpointe should have been assigned to work with him. As it was, Santeford had to forge his own relationships with every teacher, coach, and staff member at Salpointe. From Santeford's vantage point, the results were uneven.[52]

The results of the Zobrests' pioneering experiment in mainstreaming their deaf son had been dispiriting at times, but they thought, on balance, it had been worthwhile. When Sandi approached Salpointe Catholic High School about the admission of her son Jim, the principal said there was no prohibition on admitting deaf students, but he added that the school could not help him either. Given the opportunity to attend a prestigious school, Jim proved to his hearing teachers, classmates, and teammates that his deafness did not prevent him from succeeding in their world. Jim had compiled a solid record in the classroom with a B average, socializing with others in the best ways he could and doing well enough to earn a letter on the varsity basketball team. Jim's reading ability was especially noteworthy. He read at the same level as his hearing peers, when most deaf high school graduates typically scored at the fourth-grade reading level. If Jim had not played behind one of the greatest high school basketball scorers in Arizona history, he might well have done better in the sporting realm as well. Reflecting on the ups and downs of his high school experience a quarter century later, Jim allowed that he would reenroll at Salpointe, though he conceded his happiest day there was when he graduated. To complete that milestone day, Jim coached the assistant principal how to fingerspell his full name—James Lawrence Zobrest—as he proudly walked across the school's stage to receive his diploma. The question remained as to who would pay for Jim Zobrest's interpreter in a Catholic school. It was a question that had gone unanswered throughout Jim's high school career. In considering that question, the U.S. Supreme Court would grapple once again with the First Amendment's ambiguously stated guarantee of religious freedom.[53]

4 IN SEARCH OF RELIGIOUS LIBERTY

ORIGINS OF THE ZOBREST LAWSUIT

As long as Jim Zobrest attended Salpointe Catholic High School, the Zobrests had to pay for the sign language interpreter their deaf son required, which they believed was unjust and illegal. Jim received speech therapy at a public school after the day's classes ended at Salpointe, but deaf students could not wait until parochial school instruction was over to receive signed language interpretation in a public school building miles away. The Zobrests did not comprehend why the type of school Jim attended mattered, for he was "handicapped," in the parlance of that time, and required assistance that would remove otherwise insurmountable obstacles to being a successful student. Why, the Zobrests wondered, was it permissible for Jim to receive interpretation at public expense in his public elementary and junior high schools, but not in a sectarian high school? Didn't the First Amendment's Free Exercise Clause give them the right to follow their religious conscience and send their son to a religious school of their choosing? It had been the Zobrests' conclusion that state and federal laws regarding disability required that such assistance be provided at any school, including the religious school Jim attended. "What we're really fighting for is freedom of religion," Sandi Zobrest said. "We're being denied state services and funding because of his religious choice." The Zobrests' claim highlighted the tension within the First Amendment's guarantee of religious liberty. On the one hand, individuals like the Zobrests may practice the religion of their choice; on the other hand, the federal government is prohibited from assisting religion in general or preferring one religion over another, making religious accommodations for individuals problematic.[1]

Long in advance, the Zobrests had prepared for the day when Jim would enroll in a sectarian school in a district still without a public high school. Soon after Jim entered eighth grade at Orange Grove Junior High School in the fall of 1987, Sandi Zobrest met with the principal, Terry Downey, and informed her that Jim would attend Salpointe because of their religious convictions. Getting right to the point, Sandi asked Downey directly, "If Jim goes to Salpointe, will [the Catalina Foothills School District] provide an interpreter?" According to Sandi's recollection, Downey assured her, "Yes, I think so." Quite relieved, Sandi then took steps to register Jim at Salpointe. In Terry Downey's recollection, she explained to Sandi that the district could not say definitively whether the law would permit the school district to hire and pay an employee to work in a parochial school. The Zobrests were in for a rude awakening as the legal terrain shifted from provision for the disabled to constitutional concerns over church and state. The struggle over who would pay for Jim's interpreter went on for six years—five years in court—by which time Jim had graduated.[2]

Having never previously dealt with an issue that might rise to the level of constitutional permissibility, Terry Downey vowed to find out quickly whether the school district could provide the requested interpreter at Salpointe. She evidently discussed the matter with Superintendent Robert Hetzel, who brought it up to the school board, since the Zobrests' request was a "deviation" from what "most of us felt was the law at the time." The board supported Hetzel's plan to solicit legal advice on the matter, which became Downey's assignment. At no point, apparently, did the district formally consider the cost of providing appropriate services to disabled students, because the expense of Jim's interpreter was comparatively inconsequential and was, in any case, already a line in the district's budget. As the school district's attorney remarked, sign language interpretation amounting to thousands of dollars annually was not a "bank-buster," especially when compared to students with other kinds of physical disabilities such as paralysis. Downey later insisted no one in the Catalina Foothills School District had any interest in preventing Jim from attending Salpointe.[3]

On legal questions involving the district, Terry Downey typically conferred with the school's attorney but refrained from doing so this time. Thinking there might well be a constitutional issue involved in Sandi Zobrest's request, Downey called the Office of the Pima County Attorney, which was charged by state law to represent public school districts. JoAnn Sheperd, the deputy county attorney, fielded the query. Was it legal, Downey asked, for a public school district to provide a sign language interpreter for a deaf boy in a Catholic school? Sheperd, whose work regarding education usually involved contracts, personnel, and student discipline, reacted with surprise: "Oh, can they do that? Can they really pay for an interpreter to go to a parochial school?" When Downey asked whether an opinion from the Pima County Attorney's Office had the "force of law," Sheperd replied that the only legal effect such an opinion would have concerned shielding public officials, including school administrators such as Downey, from any personal liability for actions performed "in good faith reliance" on such opinions. Because the state attorney general had to review all county attorney opinions related to school matters, Downey would have to wait, as would the Zobrests.[4]

Impatient with this delay, the Zobrests made a formal request in October 1987 that the school district provide Jim with an interpreter at Salpointe. In the interim, Sandi Zobrest made a serendipitous telephone call across the country to an old friend on an unrelated matter that would greatly improve Jim's odds of getting the disability help he needed. She had called Ginny Ball Duncan, Jim's first speech therapist at the Barber Center in Erie, Pennsylvania, to congratulate Ball Duncan on getting married and, during the course of the conversation, expressed her ongoing frustration about what she saw as a bureaucratic runaround and a violation of federal law for disabled children. Sandi complained about the "flack" the district was giving her, and Ginny suggested, "maybe my dad can help you." Sandi had no idea Ginny's dad, William Bentley Ball, was one of the country's leading attorneys in the area of church-state jurisprudence and a stout defender of Catholic education. "Why would I want to talk to your dad?" Sandi asked. Ginny replied tersely, "That's what he does."[5]

As a favor to his daughter and always eager to tackle church-state questions that might protect what he characterized as religious liberty from "secularists," the indefatigable Ball readily agreed to assist the cash-strapped Zobrests on a pro bono basis. At first, he thought the Zobrests' complaint could be addressed simply by explaining the law to the school district. When it became plain the Catalina Foothills School District did not intend to pay for Jim's sign interpreter, Ball saw that the Zobrests' complaint fit neatly with his long-stated objective to lower the wall dividing church and state, especially with regard to tax-funded services for parochial school students. As a deaf young man, Jim Zobrest would be a sympathetic litigant with an undeniable disability requiring the services of an interpreter that his "impecunious parents" could not afford. This Arizona case, Ball firmly believed, would present a "very appealing case" to the U.S. Supreme Court—should it get that far—and give the justices another opportunity to "reinterpret" the Establishment Clause by accepting the doctrines of parental rights and the child benefit theory.[6]

WILLIAM BENTLEY BALL

The seventy-one-year-old William Ball was well disposed to take the Zobrests' case when it fell unexpectedly into his lap. The issue of disability was one in which Ball had considerable awareness and interest. He visited his college-age daughter Ginny when she spent her summers at an Easter Seals camp helping people with cerebral palsy, spina bifida, polio, and Down syndrome. Ginny was Jim Zobrest's first speech therapist, and she later earned a master's degree from Gallaudet University, the world's first institution of higher learning for the deaf and hearing impaired. Moreover, Ginny's husband and Ball's son-in-law—Sandy Duncan—was deaf and was president of the state association for the deaf in Pennsylvania. Ball and his wife Caroline had taken sign language instruction in order to learn how to communicate with him on a basic level, and Ball became competent in fingerspelling. In addition, Ball was a steadfast Catholic who, his daughter remarked, "truly believed he was a servant of Our Lord on earth." Ball knew the biblical accounts of Jesus of Nazareth miraculously healing the blind, the deaf, and the lame, and he took seriously his Savior's call for his disciples to help the hungry and the homeless as a way of serving him. On his way to or from daily Mass, Ball came across troubled or luckless people—some of whom evidently had serious psychological disorders—and, with his wife Caroline's consent, gave them money, took them out for a hot meal, invited them into his home, or found jobs or better housing for them. For Ball, individual acts of charity were required of faithful Christians. He saw no legitimate role for the ever-growing state to usurp what was for him a matter for individuals and private organizations.[7]

William Ball, "a short . . . pertinacious fellow with a bulging forehead," was also a skilled legal strategist with a remarkable memory, a ready wit, and a strong work ethic. He was an especially talented attorney in presenting church-state cases to the U.S. Supreme Court on behalf of groups he dubbed "nobodies in this world's affairs." Justice Harry Blackmun once remarked that Ball was "one of the finest oralists to ever appear before this Court." Throughout his high-profile career, Ball called for the High Court to treat "religious civil rights cases . . . with all the liberality accorded racial civil rights cases." His most widely recognized victory came in the *Yoder* case, when he successfully represented the Wisconsin Amish, a Protestant sect from Germany widely known for its plain living and horse-and-buggy mode of travel. On religious grounds, the Amish had objected to a state law compelling their children to go to school past the eighth grade. In addition, Ball sometimes provided free legal services to African Americans who had

William Bentley Ball, c. 1985. (Courtesy of Ball, Murren and Connell, LLC, Camp Hill, Pennsylvania)

been denied their civil rights, and he participated in the landmark case that struck down state laws banning interracial marriage.[8]

As one of his major themes, Ball persistently warned about the excesses of an ever-growing and intrusive government. He suggested at one point "the crazies, the materialists, the utilitarians" had moved America ever closer to becoming a "Bismarckian police state" where issues of right and wrong are decided not by "biblical principles" but by a democratic vote. To Ball, Catholic schools, with their emphasis on personal morality and social justice, offered an effective way of combating the nihilistic values that were increasingly dominant in a largely secular culture. The problem, as Ball saw it, was that Catholic education was in danger of collapsing due to rising costs, and so he railed time and again against the unfairness of Catholic parents having to pay taxes for public education while being denied tax benefits to support parochial education for their children. To prevent this calamity from occurring, Ball repeatedly sounded the alarm by writing essays in Catholic magazines, giving speeches, drafting and lobbying for state legislation, mobilizing the Catholic hierarchy, testifying before Congress, and battling "educational monopolists" in federal court. He also wrote or edited several books outlining the issues as he saw them, notably *In Search of a National Morality* and *Mere Creatures of the State?*[9]

For his legal work, William Ball received many honors and was once denominated as "God's Litigator." The Vatican made Ball a Knight of the Order of St. Gregory the Great for his numerous and consequential services to the Roman Catholic Church. At one point, there was speculation that President Ronald Reagan, whose political fortunes were closely connected to the Religious Right, might nominate Ball for the U.S. Supreme Court, an appointment that ultimately went to another conservative Catholic—Antonin Scalia. Fr. Richard John Neuhaus, a prominent Catholic priest and editor, described Ball as possessing "the courage and wisdom of a champion who will not give up [because] he is the kind of person who, by the grace of God, makes history." When Ball died at age eighty-two in 1999, he was lauded as a "prophetic voice," "a giant among men," and a "religious freedom fighter" who had defended the lives of unborn children and sought to provide accommodations, exemptions, and/or tax funds to help religious minorities obtain the kind of schooling they preferred for their children. A leading Catholic newspaper compared Ball to Thomas More, the sixteenth-century English lawyer who was executed for refusing to recognize Henry VIII as the head of the newly formed Church of England, which repudiated papal authority in civil and religious matters.[10]

Born in 1916, William Ball was a native of Rochester, New York, the son of a balladeer who sometimes appeared in tent revivals with William Jennings Bryan, the agrarian champion. Ball's mother was the daughter of Irish immigrants, a devout Catholic, and a piano teacher. The Ball family struggled financially and moved frequently, but a Catholic education was a family priority, with William attending his parish school and then the Cathedral Latin School in Cleveland, Ohio, before earning an undergraduate degree from Western Reserve University. To a large extent, Ball's staunchly conservative worldview was shaped by his traditional Catholic upbringing and the tumultuous times of the Great Depression. Ball's parents listened to—though they did not always agree with—the radio broadcasts of Fr. Charles Coughlin, the demagogic priest who embraced fascism, attacked Jewish financiers, and condemned President Franklin D. Roosevelt as "anti-God." Ball himself admired Martin Dies Jr., the anticommunist Texas congressman who chaired the House Un-American Activities Committee in the late 1930s and early 1940s. As a college student, Ball formed a Young Americanist League, which was avowedly Christian and which opposed a "government of dole," the existence of "isms" (communism, Naziism, and fascism) in the United States, and the growing fever for war in Europe from "cash-seeking whines." This league was especially eager to defend "Americanism" against the "subtle subversion of American government and ideals" by "Reds and Pinks" who were, as he was convinced, "determined to suffocate patriotism, wreck democracy, wipe out Christianity . . . [and] end America." Ball could not sit idly by while subversive forces aimed at "the destruction of God and government, family life and individual rights and liberties." It would be a credo by which Ball lived to the end of his days.[11]

After serving as a lieutenant commander in the U.S. Navy during World War II, Ball earned a law degree from the University of Notre Dame, America's citadel of Catholic higher education but not then known for preparing top-flight constitutional lawyers. He then worked in New York City for a few years as an in-house attorney for a leading chemical company and then for a pharmaceutical firm. Despite the prospect of financial security, Ball concluded the drudgery of corporate law was not his calling, and he joined the faculty at the new law school at Villanova University, a Catholic institution near Philadelphia, where he taught constitutional law. It was Ball's intention to serve the Catholic Church by becoming an expert in the First Amendment and by creating an institute of church and state at the university.[12]

In the 1960s, Ball left behind the worlds of business and academe to become executive director and general counsel of the newly established Pennsylvania Catholic Conference in the state capital of Harrisburg. He was the only full-time attorney for the Roman Catholic Church outside of Washington, and he worked unceasingly to ensure the religious liberty of the 4.5 million children who attended parochial schools. It was a position that allowed him to defend his Catholic faith and oppose social developments that alarmed him. To Ball's mind, the ascendant values of too many Americans in the late twentieth century revolved around the "imperial self," which could be seen in the hedonistic pursuit of material objects and the convenience of abortion, divorce, and euthanasia. In this "Kingdom of Man," the Bible's Ten Commandments were "no longer thought valid and necessary," which was the result of "the cocksure optimism of those whose fixed stare greets the blinding light of the glorious new dawn." Ball once poured out his despair about the direction of American society in a letter to Russell Kirk, one of the giants of the conservative movement and a founder of the *National Review*: "We are now faced with the development of a crisis . . . [which] is nothing less than the organized, highly financed drive to organize civilization without God." He blamed Hollywood, television, and the print media for this "monstrous evil" that threatened to enslave children.[13]

One solution to these growing secular trends was to have Catholic children learn Catholic values while attending Catholic schools. The problem was that the economic survival of these schools grew more imperiled with every passing year as Catholic families, on average, had fewer children and tuition rose sharply as salaried lay teachers replaced nuns and priests. Even so, Congress and the federal courts blocked "distributive justice" in the use of tax funds for sectarian schools, which would have reduced the expenses of the public school system. For Ball, this denial of financial assistance to Catholic schools stemmed from "a single gross presumption" that has been "the very foundation of the modern totalitarian state," namely, "that the state is the sole or superior educator." Ball regarded such thinking as another form of anti-Catholic bigotry, a bias that accompanied the Pilgrims and Puritans in planting Protestant colonies in New England. Some supporters of keeping church and state separate were indeed nativists, but others had different motives, including a fear of theocratic leaders requiring everyone to conform to unfamiliar or unpopular religious ideas.[14]

It had been Ball's hope that the U.S. Supreme Court would accept the concept of "higher" or natural law as found in the Declaration of Independence in order to permit religion to shape the values and behavior of American society. In the 1960s, Ball was outraged when the court forbade the use of public schools to promote religious exercises and permitted married women to use artificial birth control. Because he believed that American society was becoming unhinged, he felt compelled to seek new avenues to promote traditional morality. In this regard, Ball worked closely with the Most Rev. John Krol, the able but imperious and conservative archbishop (and later cardinal) for the archdiocese of Philadelphia, to oppose state and federal laws contrary to the Catholic Church's teaching and to convince the Pennsylvania legislature to adopt moral positions advocated by the church, especially regarding artificial birth control. Cardinal Krol was well on his way to becoming the "unofficial leader of America's 50 million Catholics," but he and Ball did not always see eye to eye on legal strategy, which sometimes led to bruised feelings on Ball's part.[15]

When the Catholic Church ignored Ball's considered advice to use the courts to defend its positions on church-state matters, Ball struck out on his own, forming a successful law firm with Joseph Skelly, one of his former students at Villanova. As far as Ball was concerned, the church's persistence in finding a "big name" to lobby for government aid to sectarian schools was "very foolish" because it would keep handing victories to separationists in the only venue that mattered—a court of law. Ball still performed legal work for the Pennsylvania Catholic Conference, but he could now also handle court cases of national significance and, perhaps, better implement his own strategy to restore religious liberty. Ball's independence of the church meant he would come to represent a wide variety of clients seeking religious freedom, including Evangelical Protestants and the Plain People, otherwise known as the Amish. One scholar characterized Ball as gaining national attention by the mid-1970s as a "Roman Catholic civil libertarian." Never lacking for clients, Ball did not engage in barratry—"ambulance chasing"—and did not take cases "willy nilly," as one of his law associates put it. Typically, church-state cases came to Ball as a result of his successful legal track record, his large circle of contacts, and his continuing high public profile due to his speaking engagements and magazine articles, which led others to think of him when there was a complaint involving religious discrimination. Over time, Ball's yeoman work in a small private law firm became ever more anachronistic, as religious liberty cases were increasingly taken on by large, public-interest law firms funded by substantial contributions. Ball could not hope to match these firms in terms of money spent or the number of attorneys who handled church-state cases, but he remained committed to this lifelong cause.[16]

Despite once confessing to a top Catholic Church official that he held "reactionary, hard-nosed, militant views," Ball's cultural views after he left the Pennsylvania Catholic Conference might be more accurately classified as "Catholic neoconservative" or the less familiar "theoconservative." This perspective developed in the United States in the wake of Pope John XXIII's Second Vatican Council in the early 1960s, a watershed event in which the Catholic Church reconsidered its position in the modern world. The Catholic neocons, who were influenced by Fr. Richard John Neuhaus, social philosopher Michael Novak, and theologian George Weigel, sought to identify and address several major threats to their religious beliefs. One of these threats arose from what they regarded as an insidious flowering of secularism in American life, a development they partly attributed to a constitutional system gone awry. From their vantage point, the U.S. Supreme Court had twisted the meaning of the First Amendment to require a "naked public square," meaning religious values had no place in public life. Deeply disturbed by the court's perceived amoral rulings, as well as society's culture war and the celebration of the "autonomous, unencumbered self," neocons believed that only the development of a "religiously informed public philosophy" could return the nation to its fundamental moorings. To develop a broader base of support for this thinking, Catholic neocons engaged in previously unthinkable ecumenical conversations with Evangelical Protestants who had feared and distrusted one another since the colonial period, with a particular emphasis on "life issues," a catch-all term referring to their unalterable opposition to abortion, sex education, euthanasia, and embryo experimentation. In this regard, Ball's endorsement of two declarations—the *Williamsburg Charter on the First Amendment* (1988) and *Evangelicals & Catholics Together: The Christian Mission in the Third Millennium* (1993)—which called for the reaffirmation of religion's primacy in American life and education, are notable.[17]

PREPARING THE LEGAL TEAMS

William Ball was admitted to practice in the courts of almost half the states, but not in Arizona, which meant he would have to work with a local attorney on the Zobrest suit. Sandi Zobrest had already contacted the Arizona Center for Law in the Public Interest in downtown Tucson, a nonprofit agency established in 1974 to promote "social, human, and environmental justice." Center staffer Rose Daly-Rooney, an advocate who typically handled two dozen cases involving special education at a given time, recalls that she was "blown away" by Sandi's unwavering commitment to her son and her knowledge of the issues. The matter of which services disabled children could receive in parochial schools was not one Daly-Rooney had handled frequently, if at all. She was aware that disabled students qualified for services such as speech therapy, as long as they occurred at a public school. During the course of the in-take conversation, Sandi offered to pay for Jim's interpreter in religion classes at Salpointe, as long as the Catalina Foothills School District paid for the interpreter in all other school settings. After the telephone call ended, Daly-Rooney researched what services Jim Zobrest was entitled to, and she grew "frustrated" at what she saw as the lack of "clear guidance" from the courts as to which services could be provided to special needs students, including the hearing impaired.[18]

Such matters had to be referred to the Center's attorney—Thomas Berning, who had come from a Catholic background, attended a Catholic school, earned his law degree at the University of Arizona, and specialized in disability law. When Sandi Zobrest spoke to Berning, he thought she had a "very good" case and could "fight this" denial of disability assistance. In order to take on the case, Berning had to convince the Center's board of directors of its worthiness, and its members were liberal lawyers who had a variety of interests, including voting rights, consumer affairs, utility rates, and immigration. Noting the church-state question was part-and-parcel of the case, some of the board members expressed surprise that the Center would take the side of the Zobrests rather than that of the school district. Berning's response was that the meaning of the First Amendment was debatable, and he reminded the board that the Center had a contract with the federal government to represent people under twenty-one years of age with disabilities, with a particular emphasis on special education. The board ultimately concurred and gave Berning permission to proceed with the Zobrests' complaint.[19]

William Ball then contacted Berning by telephone to hammer out their complementary responsibilities in handling legal questions on the federal level. As Berning recalled their conversation, Ball took the occasion to say in no uncertain terms that he "wasn't just some fool" when it came to the law. Ball, the "courtly," soft-spoken, conservative attorney from Pennsylvania, whose expertise was in the First Amendment, and Berning, the much-younger, bearded, public-interest progressive from Arizona, whose background was in special education law, would develop a fruitful relationship based on mutual respect for each other's skills. As the *Zobrest* suit moved forward, the issue of church and state relations took priority, in part because that is how the Catalina Foothills School District framed its unwillingness to pay for Jim's interpreter and in part because Ball, the senior partner for the petitioners, was highly experienced and far more interested in church-state questions than in disability law, which had few precedents to invoke on Jim's behalf.[20]

In the spring of 1988, Pima deputy county attorney JoAnn Sheperd released her conclusion about the Zobrests' request for a tax-funded interpreter. Sheperd reported that the Education for All Handicapped Children Act and its accompanying regulations did not expressly require a public school district to provide special education services at either a public or private school or to "concede to parental wishes" regarding the type and placement of such services. The rest of her advisory opinion hewed to the generally accepted meaning of the First Amendment, namely, that the Establishment Clause forbade the hiring of a government employee in a religious institution. Since the county attorney's office had been asked for a written opinion involving a school district, the state attorney general, Robert Corbin, was obliged to review it, a procedure that was more pro forma than anything else. After Corbin sided with the school district, School Superintendent Robert Hetzel conferred with the school district's attorney about the attorney general's decision. The school district's attorney replied to the superintendent that "the fact of the matter is the attorney general isn't the law," because "until a judge says 'yes' or 'no,' we don't really know what the law is." Years later, Sheperd conjectured that if the Catalina Foothills School District had approached her with a different request, one in which the district wanted to provide interpreter services at a parochial school for Jim Zobrest, the result might have been different. If Terry Downey had expressed a desire to provide the services at Salpointe that Jim had received in public school, there might never been a U.S. Supreme Court case titled *Zobrest v. Catalina Foothills School District*.[21]

Armed with the opinions of the county attorney's office and the state attorney general, Catalina Foothills school officials asked Sandi Zobrest to meet with them. They assumed these opinions would settle the matter by having the Zobrests choose a nearby public high school outside their district for Jim. After spending years of navigating—and surmounting—administrative barriers to help her deaf son, Sandi smelled a rat and asked Jamie Harris, whose son played Little League Baseball with Jim, to attend the meeting, too. "We were hell raisers," Sandi remembered, and she wanted to make sure her temper remained in check with a good friend in tow, so they would not miss anything important. Sandi told Harris, "I want you to come with me [as a witness] because I think we're going to have a problem here. You don't have to say anything. I just want you to listen." At the meeting, Superintendent Robert Hetzel and Assistant Superintendent Terry Downey informed Sandi that as much as they would like to keep providing Jim with an interpreter in high school, "we are not allowed to pay for anything in a Catholic school" because of the Establishment Clause. While Hetzel's main thought in this regard was "to protect the school district's best interest regarding what the state law is in Arizona," he also held out an olive branch. He told Sandi that the district would be happy to find a nearby public high school for Jim and arrange for the same support services that he had relied on in elementary and junior high schools.[22]

Unmollified, Sandi Zobrest became irate, saying, "I'm not happy with this," which was an understatement. She responded defiantly, "Well, [Jim's] going" there, regardless of any obstacle, including legal objections and financial costs. Hetzel was "quite taken aback" by Sandi's reaction, partly because he had never seen her express anger. Until this meeting, Hetzel regarded his and the district's relationship with Sandi as being on "very, very good terms" because the district had worked closely with her and provided Jim with an interpreter for three years running. Hetzel suggested the Zobrests consider sending Jim to Amphitheater High School, where his own children had thrived, but Sandi rebuffed the suggestion. Jim, she said categorically, "is not going there. He'll never go to that school," which had a reputation for drugs and violence. There was also the likelihood, Sandi feared, that Jim would be left to his own devices in a big, impersonal public high school. Sandi stormed out of the meeting, leaving behind her friend who heard the superintendent say with a sense of great relief, "I don't care if she's mad. I'm just happy she's not going to sue us." When Harris passed along this remark, Sandi confided to her friend in a voice of conviction, "He doesn't know me, does he?"[23]

This meeting set in motion a chain of events in the federal judiciary that began in federal district court in Tucson, moved to the U.S. Court of Appeals for the Ninth Circuit in San Francisco, and ultimately made it to the U.S. Supreme Court in Washington, D.C. Catalina Foothills School District officials hoped any threat of a lawsuit would be deterred by the weight of the county attorney's and state attorney general's opinions against permitting an interpreter in a parochial school. This hope was clearly misplaced, for a fortnight after the school district's notification, the Center for Law in the Public Interest filed suit to compel the school district to pay for Jim's interpreter at Salpointe. The Zobrests' attorney, Tom Berning, commented that the school district would be better off financially if it paid for Jim's interpreter at a parochial school than if it paid for his tuition at a high school outside the district. The Zobrests had no idea how complicated, lengthy, and expensive the process would be to see that their son received the assistance everyone agreed he needed to be a successful mainstreamed student. If the Zobrests triumphed in court, the result might be far-reaching because, as one legal scholar remarked, such a ruling would "leave the prevailing interpretation of the [F]irst [A]mendment's establishment clause in ashes." To mention one likely change of significance, tax-paid special education teachers and aides could provide a variety of services in parochial schools. In short, the public aid statutes and governmental practices once held to be an abridgement of the First Amendment might well pass judicial scrutiny in the future.[24]

Assistant Superintendent Terry Downey asked the Pima County Attorney's Office if it could provide legal representation at its expense. JoAnn Sheperd replied that even though such a request was permissible, this one could not be handled because "we just don't have the resources to do that here." Downey then turned to school attorney John Richardson, a shareholder in the prestigious and politically well-connected law firm of DeConcini McDonald Brammer Yetwin & Lacy, which had been established by Evo DeConcini, a former Arizona Supreme Court justice and the father of U.S. senator Dennis DeConcini. The firm, which then represented 75 percent of the school districts in the area, might have retained the services of John McDonald, who had been a school attorney and had served on the Catalina Foothills School Board, but this very experience would have made his involvement in the *Zobrest* suit awkward. As for the thirty-three-year-old Richardson, he had graduated first in his class at the University of Arizona's law school, where he had been a classmate and good friend of Tom Berning, who had helped the Zobrests sue the Catalina Foothills School District. After law school, Richardson joined the DeConcini firm, where he specialized in employment and education law, numbering among his many clients public school districts and community colleges. He typically handled school cases involving contracts, public records, open meetings, conflicts of interest, student discipline, privacy, and special education. There was also an occasional case involving constitutional concerns, such as the free speech rights of a schoolteacher. Three times he had gone to the U.S. Circuit Court of Appeals to block high school boys from playing on the girls' volleyball team.[25]

THE QUESTION OF RELIGIOUS ESTABLISHMENT

When the Zobrests' case entered the federal court system, the question of disability would take a back seat to the question of religious establishment. There was little jurisprudence regarding disability in education, and the Catalina Foothills School District had framed the issue in terms of church and state. The U.S. Supreme Court had long puzzled over the meaning of the Establishment Clause, which reads, "Congress shall make no law respecting an establishment of religion." The crucial question was whether the clause bans all government involvement with religion or permits certain kinds of interaction, cooperation, and accommodation between religious institutions and government. The most memorable and influential interpretation of this ambiguous clause came from Thomas Jefferson, author of the Virginia Statute for Religious Freedom and the Declaration of Independence. In an 1802 letter to the Baptists in Danbury, Connecticut, Jefferson interpreted the Establishment Clause by metaphorically describing the relationship as one involving separate and impermeable spheres: "I contemplate with sovereign reverence that act of the whole American people which declared that their Legislature should 'make no law respecting an establishment of religion, or prohibiting the free exercise thereof,' thus building a wall of separation between Church & State."[26]

In the twentieth century, the U.S. Supreme Court began systematically to address church and state questions involving education for the first time. In 1925, the U.S Supreme Court formulated what has been described as the "Magna Carta of private education," declaring states could not close non-public and primarily sectarian schools by requiring parents to send their children to public schools. Ball would refer repeatedly to this decision—*Pierce v. Society of Sisters of the Holy Names of Jesus and Mary*—as "a bedrock part of our constitutional law," because the court had declared "the child is not the mere creature of the state." Five years later, the Court used a "child benefit" test to permit students in Louisiana to receive textbooks paid for by the state.

This test would underlie much of Ball's arguments in seeking ever-increasing state aid for parochial schools. After World War II, the court in *Everson v. Board of Education* (1947) upheld a New Jersey statute using taxes to pay for the transportation of students attending Catholic schools, reasoning the law was neutral regarding religion, provided a public service for the common good, and only indirectly helped religious schools. In *Everson*, the court also formally embraced Jefferson's "wall" formula, even as it permitted this modest accommodation between church and state. In his opinion, Justice Hugo Black, once a Southern Baptist Sunday school teacher, insisted that the busing of Catholic children to Catholic schools had not cracked Jefferson's "wall," which "must be kept high and impregnable."[27]

With respect to religion and education, then, the court embraced two often conflicting principles—neutrality and separation—that would require continuous weighing by the justices in future cases. The results in church-state jurisprudence were inconsistent, as the court strove for the nebulous concept of neutrality, sometimes through separation, sometimes through accommodation, without abandoning the requisite rhetoric of separation. Attorney William Ball pronounced as "byzantine" the court's body of work concerning religion and accused the justices of concocting a "confusing mass of inventions" upon the Establishment and Free Exercise Clauses.[28]

As the landmark *Everson* case illustrates, government has sometimes accommodated religion, but other times it has not. For example, religious institutions receive tax exemptions, the Christian Sabbath and the birth of Jesus of Nazareth are legal holidays, and the federal government employs chaplains for American military personnel. In 1948, the year after the *Everson* decision, the court struck down religious instruction in public schools. In the early 1960s, when Ball worked for the Pennsylvania Catholic Conference, the court invalidated state laws providing for school-sponsored religious exercises in public schools. One of the state laws that was struck down came as a result of a case arising in a Philadelphia suburb. This Pennsylvania case—*Abington v. Schempp* (1963)—rescinded a state law requiring the reading of ten verses from the Bible without comment in every public school classroom. On one level, William Ball regarded *Schempp* as a disaster because it created "godless" schools. It meant, he explained, that "our children's inquiries regarding the meaning of life and the nature of good and evil are being answered in every public school of the land in programs that are loaded with life values divorced from God's Commandments and teachings." Collectively, all of these decisions reflected the two schools of thought on the High Court, as it wove a serpentine path between accommodation and separation on matters involving religion and education.[29]

Beginning in the late 1960s, the U.S. Supreme Court tackled a series of cases involving government aid to religious schools that went beyond the transportation of children to such schools. In what William Ball described as a "season of trial for Catholic education," the court struggled to decide the circumstances in which, and the extent to which, the government may help religious schools, with one scholar finding "at least six inconsistent theories" used by the justices. In the first of these cases, *Board of Education v. Allen* (1968), with Ball as co-counsel, the court upheld a New York practice requiring public school authorities to lend secular textbooks free of charge to secondary students in all schools, including religious ones. Justice Byron White wrote the opinion, conceding that the line between state sponsorship and state neutrality is not easily drawn. Borrowing from the *Everson* decision and applying the child benefit theory, White held as constitutional the textbook lending program, because the textbooks were loaned, not given, to students, rather than to religious schools. White asserted that sectarian schools had secular, as well as religious, functions, and the court could distinguish between the two. Justice Hugo Black, who had written the *Everson* opinion, excoriated the *Allen* ruling, characterizing the textbook loan as "a flagrant open violation" of the First Amendment amounting to a "great stride" toward "a state religion." Justice William O. Douglas also dissented, noting the books were chosen by teachers in religious schools where religious influence pervaded the learning environment. The result in *Allen* encouraged other states to assist parochial schools financially. In Rhode Island, for example, the state legislature added a 15 percent supplement to the salaries of parochial school teachers who taught secular subjects as they were taught in public schools.[30]

In the wake of the school prayer, Bible-reading, and textbook decisions, the two main factions regarding church and state plotted their next moves. For the separationists, there were meetings to present a united front when tackling future cases in this area. In the late 1960s, the American Jewish Congress joined with the American Civil Liberties Union (ACLU) and Americans United for Separation of Church and State (Americans United) to organize a "litigation consortium" that would ignore "borderline" church-state cases in favor of cases with "detailed and complete allegations concerning the religious nature" of institutions receiving state aid. Most importantly, for the separationists, the consortium should bring to the U.S. Supreme Court a case with a "substantially higher degree of aid than buses or textbooks." Time was important, for the consortium feared accommodationists of religion would carry the day by incremental means: "We should avoid making it easy for the Court to move by a series of small steps all the way down the road to full aid." This strategy meant separationists should pursue a case requiring "a large step or none" in the matter of parochial school aid, such as government funds going directly into religious schools.[31]

The other faction included William Ball and his fellow Catholics, who sought to reverse the separationists' interpretation of the Establishment Clause. Finding opportunity in a U.S. Supreme Court defeat, Ball thought the *Schempp* case presented a "fortunate coincidence" to secure parochial school aid and thereby finally break the state's monopoly on education for the nearly 25 percent of Pennsylvania students who attended sectarian schools. In that 1963 decision, the court maintained that the Establishment Clause precluded government financial support of religious activity and religion courses. Ball nonetheless inferred from the ruling that Catholic schools could serve as what one scholar described as "subcontractors of the state" in teaching secular subjects with tax money. To use the court's reasoning in his favor, Ball drafted the nation's first legislation directly reimbursing religious schools for some expenses, including teacher salaries and textbooks, as long as they were not related to "any subject matter expressing religious teaching, or the morals or forms of worship of any sect." With the strong backing of Cardinal Krol, the Pennsylvania legislature in 1968 enacted Ball's "purchase of services" bill—the Pennsylvania Nonpublic Elementary and Secondary Education Act. Soon thereafter, Alton Lemon, an African American secular humanist, social worker, and ACLU member in Philadelphia, sued David Kurtzman, the state's superintendent of public instruction, to overturn this law, which was expected to transfer up to $20 million in state horse and harness racing revenues to private schools, most of which were Catholic. Lemon believed that racial and ethnic minorities in public schools would be harmed by this parochiaid.[32]

Due to of the stakes involved for the Establishment Clause, the touchstone case of *Lemon v. Kurtzman* (1971) attracted two titans of church-state law. Leo Pfeffer, a Hungarian Jewish immigrant who was America's leading separationist attorney, represented several Pennsylvania taxpayers and civil liberties groups opposed to assisting religious organizations, a practice they believed abridged the Constitution's First Amendment. Serving the American Jewish Congress as counsel and working with the ACLU, Pfeffer had achieved major victories in the U.S. Supreme Court in the field of church and state, particularly involving school-sponsored religious activity. Pfeffer was highly critical of Roman Catholics as authoritarian and reactionary, because, as he put it, they "hope for an America in which, if not all will be Catholics, all will adhere to Catholic values: no divorce, no contraception, no abortion, no obscene books or pictures, no homosexuality, . . . government solicitous of and helpful to religion, and children and adults equally obedient to their parents and lawful authority."[33]

Pfeffer's legal opponent was William Ball, the devout Catholic who found Pfeffer irritating and regarded some of his legal work as "shallow." Ball and Pfeffer had debated each other on the topic of church-state issues at least a half-dozen times, and neither attorney-turned-cultural warrior would yield an inch on the controversial topic. In arguing *Lemon*, Ball understood full well he carried "the hopes, not merely of the [Catholic] Church, but of a great population of parents and Catholic people." It was his "obligation" to "a long, often bitter, often heroic past" against anti-Catholic sentiment "to advance the common cause" of "so many people [who] made such sacrifices for the parochial school." Cardinal Krol agreed with Ball on the importance of this case, telling Bishop Joseph Bernardin, the general secretary of the National Conference of Catholic Bishops, that *Lemon* represented a half century of effort on the part of the Catholic Church, and if the case were lost, "it will be a disaster" for parochiaid in states everywhere. Ball's legal theory in arguing *Lemon* was simple yet audacious: "Religiously affiliated and controlled agencies, which have a sacred, sectarian and religious function, also have a secular function, and that secular or public welfare function is publicly supportable." The *Lemon* case is crucial to understanding Ball's subsequent career in the field of church and state and explains why he took the *Zobrest* suit two decades later.[34]

Ball's fears over the *Lemon* case were realized, as the U.S. Supreme Court sided with Pfeffer and the separationists. Chief Justice Warren Burger admitted that the court found it difficult to determine what level of state aid to parochial schools was permissible: "Candor compels acknowledgement . . . that we can only dimly perceive the lines of demarcation in this extraordinarily sensitive area of constitutional law." Burger had become impatient with the increased time the court spent on religion cases, and so he and the majority built on the *Schempp* case to fashion a three-part test for laws involving religion, a test that was to be applicable to similar cases in this vein. To be permissible, under this "Lemon Test," a statute involving religion must meet the following requirements:

> It must have "a secular legislative purpose."
> It must not advance or inhibit religion in its "primary effect."
> It must "not foster an excessive government entanglement with religion."

In applying the new test, the court unanimously invalidated Pennsylvania's purchase of services law for violating the Establishment Clause, particularly because of the "comprehensive, discriminating, and continuing state surveillance" government officials would have to play in executing it in religious schools. Justice Byron White dissented, arguing that the states were merely supporting the secular functions of religious schools. He found "curious and mysterious" the claim that state aid had entangled the state and religious education because no evidence had been introduced to show that teachers were teaching or promoting religion.[35]

In what was the greatest defeat of his legal career, Ball conceded that separationists had won an "astounding" triumph. He predicted dire consequences in *Lemon*'s wake, including the legalization of the "evil" of abortion, which the U.S. Supreme Court permitted two years later. Ball had plenty of blame to pass around for the *Lemon* decision. He blamed residual anti-Catholicism, which allegedly still warped the thinking of the Protestant majority. He blamed the media for "holding open season on every failing and defect discoverable in the Church." The result, he claimed, was that "the Catholic Church is the good natured fat boy on the block whom all are free to push about," including the U.S. Supreme Court. He blamed Chief Justice Burger for revising the past in order to conclude the First Amendment contained the right to be free of religion. He blamed Justice William O. Douglas for unwittingly embracing the polemics of an evangelical Presbyterian who declared the real mission of Catholic schools was to "indoctrinate," not educate, their students in order to "make loyal Roman Catholics." In addition to Leo Pfeffer, Ball pointed an accusing finger at Harvard University's Paul Freund, the dean of American law professors, who maintained that state money for sectarian schools was unconstitutional because "religious controversy" seemed sure to follow, a notion Burger borrowed "lock, stock, and barrel" in his opinion. Ball maintained that the *Lemon* decision "barred the way to religious freedom of choice in education" and became "the great legal instrument for the enforced secularization of the national culture." Because the U.S. Supreme Court has usually relied on *Lemon* in cases involving government and religion in education, Ball would spend the rest of his life trying to curtail, if not reverse, it. When the *Zobrest* case came to him, Ball learned that the state of Arizona had referred to the *Lemon* decision to deny Jim Zobrest an interpreter at a Catholic school.[36]

The legal jousting between William Ball and Leo Pfeffer over government aid to nonpublic schools continued in the U.S. Supreme Court case of *Meek v. Pittenger* (1975). In 1972, the Pennsylvania legislature authorized the expenditure of millions of dollars for instructional materials and auxiliary services to children, including those with disabilities, who attended nonpublic schools. These services included psychological counseling, testing, speech and hearing therapy, and "related services for exceptional, remedial, or educationally disadvantaged students." Textbooks could be loaned to nonpublic school *students*, and instructional materials (periodicals, photographs, maps, charts, globes, recordings, cassettes, films, and slides) and instructional equipment (movie projectors, test tubes, and record players) could be loaned to nonpublic *schools*. Neither act required financial reimbursement by Pennsylvania's nonpublic schools.[37]

Since most of the state's nonpublic schools were religiously affiliated, a taxpayer named Sylvia Meek and groups Ball called "the same old gang"—the ACLU, Americans United, the Jewish Community Relations Council, and the National Association for the Advancement of Colored People—argued that the laws violated the Establishment Clause. As far as Ball was concerned, these groups still "grind away at the old, thinly concealed accusations" against the Catholic Church. In oral argument before the U.S. Supreme Court, Ball told the justices that speech and hearing services were "auxiliary, secular, and neutral," designed simply to help children with "learning disabilities" in the schools they happened to attend. As for the Lemon Test's possible application in *Meek*, Ball thought the laws in question had the secular purpose of educating citizens, and he dismissed any claims of entanglement between church and state as "fantasies." Pfeffer retorted that the Pennsylvania laws were "unconstitutional on their face." The court decided the constitutionality of government assistance depends on who receives the benefit. Textbooks in secular subjects that went to nonpublic students and not the schools they attended were permissible, which affirmed the *Allen* decision Ball had won earlier. Instructional materials and services received directly by nonpublic schools could be diverted to religious ends and were therefore unconstitutional, thereby affirming the *Lemon* decision Ball had lost.[38]

In the years between the *Meek* and *Zobrest* decisions, the U.S. Supreme Court decided several cases involving parochial school aid. Though the court continued to move erratically in this area, it is apparent the court was searching for ways to permit more tax aid to religious schools, which was exactly what William Ball had hoped for. In *Wolman v. Walter* (1977), the court decided that states could provide more aid than textbooks to private schools. While barring instructional materials, equipment, and field trips, the court cast aside its child benefit theory to approve a program in which public school employees provided speech, hearing, and psychological testing services for nonpublic school students at their schools. The court reasoned such limited diagnostic (testing) services, as opposed to ongoing therapeutic (counseling) services, had no "educational content," so there was no danger of proselytizing, a decision amounting to a legal pirouette away from the

Meek ruling. In the companion cases of *Aguilar v. Felton* and *School District of Grand Rapids v. Ball* (1985), the court struck down on-site delivery of special education programs in religious schools, marking the apex of the wall of separation between church and state. Drawing on its *Meek* and *Wolman* rulings, the court held such programs provided a "direct subsidy" to parochial schools and created a "symbolic union" between church and state that failed the Lemon Test. In *Witters v. Washington Department of Services for the Blind* (1986), however, the court used an "equal treatment" theory to permit Larry Witters, who suffered from a macular degenerative disease, to qualify for a state vocational scholarship for the visually impaired while he attended a Bible college. With state aid, Witters sought to change careers from washing laboratory dishes in Spokane to become a pastor, missionary, or youth director. In *Witters*, the court determined that the state law in question had a secular purpose in promoting vocational training, and the scholarship went to a disabled individual, who chose to pay tuition to a religious institution. For the first time, the court decided the Establishment Clause did not bar direct aid to a student in a religious institution, which offered an instructive and timely parallel for Ball and the *Zobrest* case.[39]

William Rehnquist, who would become chief justice of the U.S. Supreme Court, once offered a biting and ironic assessment of the court's "unworkable" and "unprincipled" rulings involving parochial school aid, some of which involved disability:

> [A] State may lend to parochial school children geography textbooks that contain maps of the United States, but the State may not lend maps of the United States for use in geography class. A State may lend textbooks on American colonial history, but it may not lend a film on George Washington, or a film projector to show it in history class. A State may lend classroom workbooks, but may not lend workbooks in which the parochial school children write, thus rendering them nonresuable. A State may pay for bus transportation to religious schools but may not pay for bus transportation from the parochial school to the public zoo or natural history museum for a field trip. A State may pay for diagnostic services conducted in the parochial school but therapeutic services must be given in a different building; speech and hearing "services" conducted by the State inside the sectarian school are forbidden, but the State may conduct speech and hearing diagnostic testing inside the sectarian school. Exceptional parochial school students may receive counseling, but it must take place outside of the parochial school, such as in a trailer parked down the street. A State may give cash to a parochial school to pay for the administration of State written tests and state ordered reporting services, but it may not provide funds for teacher-prepared tests on secular subjects. Religious instruction may

> not be given in public school, but the public school may release students during the day for religion classes elsewhere, and may enforce attendance at those classes with its truancy laws.[40]

For Rehnquest, then, there was no rhyme or reason for the court's jurisprudence involving the denial of parochiaid, and he had long vowed to do something about it. A Minnesota case gave him an opening to revive the child benefit theory that had lain dormant for a decade after the *Lemon* decision. If a way could be found by lawmakers to benefit educational institutions in a neutral, evenhanded manner in which religious recipients were not favored over nonreligious recipients, then there was no advancement of religion that might violate the Constitution. In the case of *Mueller v. Allen* (1983), a Minnesota statute granted tax deductions to taxpayers for most kinds of educational expenses, a financial gain available to parents of students attending all schools—public and private alike. The High Court sanctioned the statute as "evenhanded," even though public school parents had no need for the benefit and 96 percent of students in private schools attended religious schools. Further, the aid to religious schools was only indirect or incidental, the "result of decisions of individual parents," so there was "no "imprimatur of State approval" for religion in particular or in general. The significance of *Mueller* is that it was the first education case decided by the court to invoke neutrality as a way to block the *Lemon* "effects" test. In his opinion, Rehnquist took a jab at the Lemon Test by quoting another Supreme Court decision that described *Lemon* as "no more than [a] helpful signpost" in examining Establishment Clause cases. *Mueller* promised to be a useful precedent when the *Zobrest* case entered the federal courts.[41]

There the matter of nonpublic school aid stood, before William Ball took on the case of Jim Zobrest, a profoundly deaf student whose attendance at a Catholic school raised church-state questions as to whether the government would keep paying for the sign interpreter he needed and for which his cash-strapped parents could not pay. With Ball in charge of their case, it looked possible for the Zobrests to pass the Lemon Test as employed by the court in some of its recent cases.

5 SIGNING, SECTARIAN SCHOOLS, AND THE LAW

HIGH STAKES

The *Zobrest* lawsuit involved the human drama of a deaf young man who needed an interpreter's services to get an education that promised a "normal" life. Jim Zobrest was one of eighteen thousand profoundly deaf students in America, with eight thousand of them having an interpreter. What brought his case to the fore was his parents' claim that the government should pay for the interpreter in a sectarian school. Among other things, their suit presented an opportunity to untangle the U.S. Supreme Court's confusing jurisprudence involving church and state issues. University of Notre Dame law professor Douglas W. Kmiec characterized this jurisprudence as "profoundly amiss." Kmiec noted that "the Court has several formulas that it uses to analyze the First Amendment. These tests are extremely idiosyncratic and difficult to apply. It is important for the court to pick one standard, and it would be nice to have that standard go back to the original purpose of the First Amendment . . . to promote religious freedom by neither prohibiting beliefs nor prescribing them." The stakes in the *Zobrest* case, then, were high. If the Zobrests won, their eldest son—and the disabled children of other parents—would get the assistance they needed to succeed in whatever educational setting they chose, including sectarian schools. Moreover, the court might have to come to grips with its zig-zag jurisprudence involving religious establishment.[1]

FEDERAL DISTRICT COURT

All the while Jim Zobrest attended Salpointe Catholic High School, his parents looked to the courts to obtain financial relief concerning their son's interpreter. Though the intersection of disability and religious education was a singular feature of the Zobrests' lawsuit, fully 30 percent of all school litigation at the time involved disability in other contexts. The Zobrests did not ask the Catalina Foothills School District to pay for any school-related expenses, such as tuition and books. The Zobrests' twofold legal argument was, first, that the Education for All Handicapped Children Act (EAHCA) required the school district to pay for an interpreter for their deaf son and, second, that the Free Exercise Clause of the First Amendment guaranteed them the right to send Jim to a religious school. When Sandi Zobrest spoke to the media over a period of years about why her family should prevail in court, she alternated between emphasizing Jim's disability and her family's right to practice its chosen religion. At the time of the district court hearing, she argued that their case need not involve religion at all, because she believed the issue concerned disability alone. As she explained, "An interpreter is a living, breathing hearing aid" who "doesn't initiate any [religious] information; he just takes what is being said and transforms it into a form that Jim can understand."[2]

Because the Zobrests argued that federal law and the First Amendment were relevant to their complaint, they had to ask the federal courts for relief. In the federal court system, which typically considers cases involving federal statutes or the U.S. Constitution, there are three levels, starting with a district court before which a case will be tried or otherwise resolved by the court before trial. If the plaintiffs—those seeking the court's help—or the defendants—those who oppose the lawsuit—lose at this level, the losing party may appeal to the judges of the circuit court for their designated geographic region. In this circuit court of appeals, attorneys for both sides file briefs in which they state their views as to whether the district court's decision should be upheld (affirmed) or overturned (reversed). The losing party in this intermediate venue may request the U.S. Supreme Court to review the case—an extremely remote possibility, to be sure.

When the U.S. Supreme Court agrees to consider a case from a lower court, it issues a request (writ of certiorari) for that court's records; if the Supreme Court refuses to consider a case, it denies a petition for certiorari. This "court of last resort" typically hears cases when there are conflicting decisions in lower courts on a particular issue. As in the case of the circuit court, the parties directly involved—now called petitioners and respondents—file briefs stating their respective positions and must argue their claims in front of the justices, who usually render a decision several months later. Sometimes a case attracts organizations that are not part of the case but that want to make their views known to the court in order to affect the outcome. With the court's consent or the mutual agreement of the petitioners and respondents, these groups file an amicus (friend of the court) brief. The question the justices often must grapple with is which precedent or precedents should apply to the case they are then considering. As a general rule, the Supreme Court is reluctant to disregard precedent without justification, a practice intended to ensure stability in law and constitutional interpretation. The decision ultimately made by the Supreme Court cannot be appealed. It takes litigants years to move from the district court to the highest court in the land, a daunting and expensive process, with no guarantee of ultimate victory.

The first layer of the process involved the federal district court in Tucson, where the case was assigned to Richard Bilby, an unconventional judge and a life-long Republican who was appointed by President Jimmy Carter. The Zobrests' suit was brought by the Arizona Center for Law in the Public Interest, which asked Bilby to issue a preliminary injunction overruling the opinions of the county attorney and the state attorney general. At the hearing in August 1988, attorney Tom Berning argued that the school district had denied Jim Zobrest his constitutional right to practice his religion by refusing to provide a tax-paid interpreter at Salpointe. Berning then told the district court that it could not interfere with this right: "The Roman Catholic Church strongly recommends that students go to Catholic schools, so they won't be deprived of their religious beliefs. This court is in no position to substitute its opinion of religious faith under the First Amendment." Judge Bilby, an Episcopalian, retorted that as far as he knew a good Catholic did not have to attend a Catholic high school. "The church recommends it," he conceded, "but it is not a major tenet of the religion." When the school district's turn came, attorney John Richardson asserted that the Zobrests had the financial wherewithal to pay for their son's interpreter. Richardson then noted the U.S. Supreme Court had once held that public funds could not be used to provide on-site therapeutic services in religious schools. Observing how difficult such church-state questions could be, Richardson reminded the judge that the High Court had permitted the use of tax-paid textbooks for parochial students—but not world globes—because "you can't be sure how a religious teacher would interpret the globe."[3]

Judge Bilby declined to issue a preliminary injunction to force the school district to pay for Jim Zobrest's interpreter. Bilby maintained that "an interpreter for the deaf is neither therapeutic nor diagnostic" and therefore was not permitted under previous U.S. Supreme Court rulings. In an aside, Bilby commented that the Zobrests' suit would be a "perfect case to take to the Supreme Court to draw a line" on whether interpreter payments are constitutional. In the wake of this adverse ruling, Tom Berning approached the school district's attorney to see if the district would be willing to reimburse the Zobrests directly for the "costs of interpreter services," along the lines of the *Witters* case, which "would not involve direct interaction between church and state." In light of Bilby's preliminary decision, Berning's offer was understandably rebuffed.[4]

In July 1989, the *Zobrest* case reappeared in Judge Bilby's court for additional argument. This time the Zobrests retained William Bentley Ball, the renowned constitutional attorney from Pennsylvania, to present their case. Ball did not ask that the Zobrests be reimbursed for the cost of Jim's interpreter in his first year at Salpointe, but as Jim's sophomore year approached, Ball argued the Zobrests deserved a government-hired interpreter. Though he searched in vain for a "precise precedent," Ball believed the Zobrests were entitled to have a tax-paid interpreter because to deny their son this service would deny the family their right to worship as they pleased. Additionally, Ball argued that hiring an interpreter does not financially benefit a religious institution. "There is no subsidy to Salpointe," Ball observed, "just an exchange of services." Bilby was unconvinced. "Does the interpreter interpret classroom prayer?" the judge asked. Ball conceded that Jim's interpreter did so but maintained the interpreter did not advance any religious doctrine. At this point, John Richardson, the school district's counsel, pounced on Ball's admission. "You have a publicly paid employee standing in a classroom, repeating word for word Catholic doctrine," he pointed out in what he believed was the legal coup de grace to the *Zobrest* suit. As Ball began to respond, Judge Bilby cut him off. "Wait, stop," the judge said. "I can read it. I can read it. I know what it's . . . about." Ball was dumbfounded and reminded the court he had been promised fifteen minutes for oral argument. Bilby shrugged off Ball's objection, mentioning he had another commitment, and besides, he knew all about deafness because he had a deaf childhood friend. Bilby's offhand remark suggested the disability aspect of the Zobrest lawsuit would be relegated to the judicial backburner, if it were considered at all.[5]

When Judge Bilby issued his decision in the *Zobrest* case, he indicated that he had no doubt Jim Zobrest needed an interpreter to attend school, but in his mind, that was not the issue. The issue concerned where Jim Zobrest wanted to attend school and who would pay for the interpreter. The First Amendment, Bilby contended, along with the U.S. Supreme Court decisions in *Meek v. Pittenger* and *Wolman v. Walter*, barred government payment of an interpreter at a parochial school such as Salpointe. An interpreter, as Bilby made clear, would be required to interpret school prayers and lessons on Catholic doctrine, which would create an unconstitutional abridgement of the Establishment Clause. In Bilby's rendering, Jim's interpreter would have had the effect of "promoting James's religious development at government expense," in violation of the First Amendment. The interpreter, Bilby determined, would "act as a conduit for the religious inculcation of James." The way in which this hearing was conducted would present legal difficulties in the future because basic facts were not established, producing misunderstandings about disability and deafness and thereby producing bad law. As always, Sandi Zobrest was undeterred by this legal setback, telling a reporter "this is just the opening skirmish in the case." "We intend," she announced defiantly, "to take [the case] as far as we possibly can," which Judge Bilby had suggested be done. Jim, she continued, was "entitled" to the interpreter under the law, and she argued that the state denied her son "what is rightfully his because of his particular handicap."[6]

FINANCIAL STRUGGLES

When Jim first enrolled in Salpointe, the Zobrests absorbed the interpreter's expense by adding the annual bill of $8,500 to their company's budget. That plan was entirely feasible while the Zobrests were operating two profitable dry-cleaning chains in Tucson. When they bought a third dry-cleaning company in hopes of controlling more of the area's cleaning business, they got far more than they bargained for. The city's fire department informed the Zobrests that they had to remove large underground chemical storage tanks they had not known about and remediate the soil surrounding these tanks, a prohibitively expensive proposition. Then, a month after the federal district court ruled against the Zobrests' bid to have the government pay for their son's interpreter, they suffered a devastating financial blow. In August 1989, their main processing plant was destroyed by arson, leaving damage estimated conservatively at a million dollars. No one was ever arrested for the crime, which was one of several suspicious fires set in the area that year. With the insurance company delaying restitution, the Zobrests filed for bankruptcy. Now unable to pay for their son's interpreter, the Zobrests sold their cleaning business and began working, ironically, as debt collectors.[7]

If the Zobrests had sent Jim to any public high school in the area or to a nonreligious private school, the Catalina Foothills School District would have paid in full for the interpreter. The fact that the Zobrests did not choose this path demonstrates that their religious convictions were consequential to them and attests to their belief that Salpointe was the best school for their deaf son. They were also firmly convinced that they had a constitutional right to expect the school district to pay for the interpreter. They had no way of knowing they would one day—years into the future—be vindicated constitutionally and compensated financially. Undaunted by their precarious financial situation, Sandi Zobrest set about seeking donations to pay for the interpreter. Every week, she asked relatives and wrote to foundations, businesses, and almost anyone else she could think of, soliciting donations to pay for Jim Santeford's interpretation. "We need help to pay for this interpreter," she wrote. "We have a case pending. If we win, we pay you back; if we don't, we can't." It was a constant struggle to raise money for Jim's education. "I'd start getting low in my interpreter fund," Sandi admitted, "and hope I'd hear from another foundation and I'd send out a new batch of letters. Many nights I would be up until 11 o'clock typing letters and wishing I didn't have to do this. But it was worth it in the long run . . . to get Jim the parochial education at Salpointe."[8]

The situation had become so dire for the Zobrests by the spring of Jim's sophomore year that Fr. Leo McCarthy, Salpointe's principal, sometimes interceded on their behalf. He told a fellow Carmelite priest, "If funding is not found" for Jim's interpreter, "Jim will have to transfer to a public school." McCarthy added that Jim's parents "feel very strongly about the importance of a Catholic education for Jim and are willing to fight this battle in Court, all the way to the Supreme Court, if necessary." Donations arrived from the Carmelite Human Development Fund; the Knights of Columbus, the world's largest Catholic fraternal organization; a group of Tucson Catholic businessmen called the Conquistadores; the William R. and Virginia Hayden Foundation; and a local Ford dealership owner named Jim Click Jr., who had a disabled child and deliberately hired disabled workers for his businesses. When the Zobrests were down to their last ten dollars to pay for the interpreter, a check for a thousand dollars arrived. All told, the Zobrests received at least twenty-eight thousand dollars in contributions, more than three-fourths of the cost of Jim's interpreters over his four years at Salpointe.[9]

FEDERAL APPEALS COURT

Days after their defeat at the federal district court level, the Zobrests appealed to the U.S. Court of Appeals for the Ninth Circuit, which is headquartered in San Francisco. The Ninth Circuit had a reputation for being the most liberal appeals court in the United States, and the U.S. Supreme Court had overturned its rulings more than any other circuit court. Two other circuit courts had already decided that disabled children attending private sectarian schools were covered by the EAHCA. The *Zobrest* case could have been blocked from ever reaching the Supreme Court by another federal court case that arose at the same time in Stafford County, Virginia. There, Robert and

Kathleen Goodall sued their school district for refusing to pay for an interpreter for their deaf son in the Fredericksburg Christian School. The Fourth Circuit held that the EAHCA did not require a public school to provide a sign interpreter in a religious school.[10]

To a remarkable degree, the facts of the *Goodall* case mirrored those in *Zobrest*. In both cases, the male child was profoundly deaf, deaf interpretation for the child in public school was provided at no cost to the family, and the parents registered their son in a Christian school, which resulted in the public school district refusing to pay for the interpreter. In both cases, the petitioners cited the First Amendment and the EAHCA as the basis of their claims that the school board violated their religious rights and their rights as parents to direct their sons' education and upbringing. As these nearly identical cases traveled the same legal path through the federal courts at almost the same time, it was, oddly, the case considered first by the U.S. Supreme Court that fell by the wayside and was thus consigned to obscurity—the *Goodall* case.[11]

Though no one realized it at the time, a natural disaster in the San Francisco Bay area of California would tip the scales of justice in favor of the Zobrests. On October 17, 1989, a huge earthquake struck at the height of the afternoon rush hour and just before the first pitch of game three of Major League Baseball's World Series between the San Francisco Giants and the visiting Oakland Athletics. The shifting tectonic plates wreaked havoc, severing electrical lines, rupturing gas lines, interrupting telephone and television service, and generally leaving an urban landscape resembling a war zone, with dozens dead and thousands more injured or left homeless. Given the chaos of the earthquake, the Ninth Circuit concentrated on more urgent criminal cases than on First Amendment disputes. The delay meant the *Goodall* case, which had been argued after *Zobrest*, came up for consideration by the U.S. Supreme Court before *Zobrest* and was rejected. If *Zobrest* had been considered before *Goodall*, as it should have been, the Supreme Court would have dismissed *Zobrest* rather than *Goodall*. The reason the Supreme Court declined to hear *Goodall* was that Justice Thurgood Marshall, who favored a high and impregnable wall between church and state, was still on the bench. If Marshall had not retired from the court, the Zobrests' application to have the court consider their suit likely would have failed. When Marshall retired from the court in June 1991, he was replaced that fall by Clarence Thomas, who embraced a less restrictive position on the Establishment Clause. With Thomas on the court, the Zobrests' request for judicial review was granted in October 1992, and Thomas would later be the decisive fifth vote for the Zobrests when their case was finally decided.[12]

As the legal delays turned into years, the Zobrests grew increasingly restless, even angry. In mid-November 1991, the Zobrests wrote a remarkably frank letter to the Ninth District Court to prod the dilatory judges to decide their son's case very quickly. Their attorney, William Ball, had apprised them that despite repeated attempts he had been unable to learn when the *Zobrest* case would be decided, and he informed the Zobrests that unless the circuit court decided the case within the month they would have to wait another year for the U.S. Supreme Court to consider reviewing it, if they lost in the circuit court, as seemed likely. The Zobrests admitted their letter was probably ill-advised, and for that reason they had not cleared it with their attorney beforehand. But they were frustrated at the repeated delays they had encountered in the federal judicial process. The stakes, the Zobrests declared, were high indeed, not only for their son but also for "all deaf students that will need interpreter services in the future." The letter, which reflected the enormous financial and psychological cost the lawsuit had had on them, was sent to Judge Thomas Tang, not to the entire judicial panel, though the reason for doing so is unclear. Why, the Zobrests wanted to know, had the circuit court decided cases involving red squirrels before theirs? "This is not fair," they wrote. "We're talking about human beings here that are drowning in bureaucracy and can't do a thing about it."

> *PLEASE*, WE NEED A DECISION and we need it *NOW*. Your hesitation has already cost us a great deal of time and money, not to mention the anxiety and the embarrassment of having to borrow money from friends. We expect, no we DEMAND, that a decision be handed down in the next 10 days. You have had long enough. It's time to do the job that our tax dollars pay you to do.[13]

The December deadline came and went, and attorney William Ball penned his own letter to the appeals court in March. He was "appalled" by the dawdling of the judges and chastised them in blunt language: "My clients call me monthly *begging* for an answer. . . . This is not *General Motors v. United States* or a 100-party class action. Your delay, reminiscent of the Chancery Court in [Charles Dickens's novel] BLEAK HOUSE, is a most unfortunate example of 'wearying down the right.' The nation does not need more examples of people in positions of public trust who fail them. I am sure that the example of your glaring neglect has not been missed by my client, Jimmy Zobrest, a child when he came to your court, of college age today."[14]

Finally, the Ninth Circuit heard the Zobrests' appeal and affirmed Judge Bilby's decision. The majority opinion was signed by two liberal Carter appointees—Betty Binns Fletcher, a pioneering woman attorney and judge, and the irrepressible Stephen Reinhardt, whose frequent reversals by the nation's highest court led the justices to refer to him privately as a "renegade judge." The Ninth Circuit ruled that providing a state employee to communicate with the deaf would create "a symbolic union of government and religion," thereby failing the prevailing Establishment Clause test promulgated in *Lemon v. Kurtzman*, which, among other things, prohibits government action advancing religion. An interpreter paid by a public school district would have been, in the majority's view, an instrument for conveying and thus a sponsor of the parochial school's undeniable religious message. The court understood that in blocking payment for Jim's interpreter, it partly limited his parents' right to exercise their religion, but this denial was justified because the government had a compelling interest in ensuring that the First Amendment is not violated. In other words, the court of appeals ruled the Establishment Clause trumps the Free Exercise Clause.[15]

The circuit court's dissenter was Judge Thomas Tang, also a Carter appointee. Tang argued that Jim Zobrest's need for a sign language interpreter in a Catholic school did not violate the Lemon Test, because the program as a whole did not advance religion. His colleagues were wrong, Tang wrote, in looking at the specific use of a hearing aid in a religious school. Unlike the loan of instructional materials in *Meek v. Pittenger* and the use of public school teachers to instruct nonpublic school students in *School District of Grand Rapids v. Ball*, the financial compensation to Jim's interpreter did not end up in the hands of a sectarian school. Tang also disagreed that Jim's interpreter established a symbolic union between church and state, because the parochial school teachers, not the interpreter, were the source of religious doctrine. In Tang's mind, the First Amendment did not absolutely prohibit state employees from working in a parochial school classroom, because the constitutionality of parochial school aid does not depend on the recipient of the aid but rather the nature and quality of the aid provided. He observed that the parents, not the state, requested the interpreter, and only one student received this assistance. The logical conclusion the public should draw from Jim Zobrest's interpreter was that the government sought to "equalize the educational opportunities of all its students and to help handicapped students overcome barriers to their full academic development."[16]

As for sign language interpretation for profoundly deaf students, Tang reasoned that this method of communication in a parochial school did not pose a legal problem, because interpreters are the human equivalent of eyeglasses for students with vision problems or hearing aids for students with moderate hearing problems and are "not a potential fount of religious doctrine" as teachers could be. In his dissent, Tang also concluded that the Constitution permits limited supervision between government officials and parochial schools, because of the nature of sign language interpretation and because state officials would not need to become involved in religious matters. Tang pointed out the Zobrests and the school district had agreed that the interpreter's code of ethics obliges the interpreter "to translate communications completely, without altering, editing, or revising in any manner the content of the message." When the *Zobrest* case reached the U.S. Supreme Court, Tang's dissent would provide significant guidance to the majority.[17]

ON THE WAY TO THE U.S. SUPREME COURT

School board attorney John Richardson thought this second victory in the federal courts would finally discourage the Zobrests from pressing forward. His hunch was wrong. Within days of the Ninth Circuit's decision, William Ball began preparing a petition for a writ of certiorari, arguing the U.S. Supreme Court should hear the *Zobrest* case, which was a longshot at best as roughly 3 percent of such petitions are generally granted. As he worked on the petition, Ball turned his thoughts to God for strength and encouragement and kept up his daily ritual of attending Mass in St. Patrick's Cathedral in his hometown of Harrisburg, Pennsylvania.[18]

When word arrived that the Supreme Court would hear *Zobrest*, Ball was delighted to have another opportunity to challenge the court's church-state philosophy in support of separationism as it had developed for nearly a half century. Within days of this notification, he called University of Chicago law professor Michael McConnell, an authority on religious liberty and the Constitution, who had by then argued many cases before the Supreme Court, including *School District of Grand Rapids v. Ball* (1985). That case, which McConnell lost, applied the Lemon Test to invalidate secular classes for sectarian school students at public expense. McConnell, too, saw opportunity in the *Zobrest* case and recommended that Ball secure the assistance of U.S. Solicitor General Kenneth Starr and U.S. Attorney General William Barr in revising federal regulations against parochial school aid and to obtain a legal statement from the federal government favoring the petitioners.[19]

Church-state separationists, such as Americans United, saw considerable danger in the *Zobrest* case. According to Rob Boston, who edited Americans United's magazine, *Church & State*, there was the possibility the U.S. Supreme Court might discard the Lemon Test. In recent Establishment Clause cases, the court had adopted modifications of *Lemon* or bypassed it altogether to reach a majority decision, and five justices had doubts about that ruling, which had almost routinely invalidated incidental benefits to religious institutions. Separationists also discerned a legal strategy by the "parochiaid lobby" to represent student plaintiffs in sectarian schools who were disabled or otherwise disadvantaged, in the hope that courts would permit tax subsidies for sectarian schools. Once the court discovered this "newfound 'right'" in these "hard cases," Boston maintained, it would be "a relatively easy matter" to extend that right to all students, ultimately leading to outright state support for sectarian schools, which had been a prime goal of the Catholic Church since the early nineteenth century. Moreover, the *Zobrest* case presented yet another attempt to use the Free Exercise Clause as a justification for state support of sectarian schools. What made this attempt different, Boston argued, was that Jim Zobrest was a sympathetic disabled figure whose lawyers argued he was being discriminated against because of his religion. William Ball would have none of this implied notion that the Catholic Church had somehow conspired to manufacture a "carefully set up test" with a "deaf boy" from a "poor family" to tear down the wall separating church and state.[20]

With such high stakes involved, the *Zobrest* case attracted considerable interest from the federal government, church groups, public school officials, and civil liberties organizations hoping to persuade the U.S. Supreme Court of their arguments related to disability and the Establishment Clause. These groups submitted amicus briefs that dealt mainly with two questions: First, was it legal for a government to provide ongoing special educational assistance in a religious school to students with disabilities? Second, was a sign language interpreter an educator capable of promoting ideas, such as religion, or merely a neutral translating machine who happened to be a human being?

The U.S. Department of Justice (DOJ) supported the Zobrests' position, arguing that the Individuals with Disabilities Education Act (IDEA, formerly known as the EAHCA) had a secular purpose and did not "advance" religion. Any benefit to a religious school such as Salpointe was "indirect," because the interpreter, who was "merely a technical facilitator of communications," was "not himself teaching the child anything." Rather, the law was intended, as it stated, to "assure that *all* children with disabilities" receive necessary assistance, including those attending private schools. The DOJ brief pointed out that neither the IDEA nor the Establishment Clause restricted such assistance to nonreligious private schools.[21]

In a combined amicus brief, the Catholic League for Religious and Civil Rights, the Church of Jesus Christ of Latter-Day Saints (the Mormons), the Missouri Synod Lutherans, the National Association of Evangelicals, the National Council of Churches of Christ, and the Southern Baptist Convention went further than the DOJ, arguing that the school district's policy on religion plainly discriminated against religion. These groups urged the Supreme Court to regard the religion clauses of the First Amendment as "harmonious and mutually reinforcing provisions" to protect freedom of religion and use the *Zobrest* case to guarantee parental choice in education. The United States Catholic Conference likewise accused the school district of having "unjustly discriminated" against the Zobrests. The Arizona and national school board associations vigorously disputed the claim of discrimination and urged the court to apply the Lemon Test against the Zobrests. As far as the school boards associations were concerned, there was a considerable difference between a "static" hearing aid, which is "merely . . . a mechanical sound amplifier," and a "dynamic" interpreter, who was said to be part of an educational team, but they insisted that both forms of assistance were prohibited in a religious school when paid for by the government.[22]

The *Zobrest* case created a wedge between organizations ordinarily dedicated to strict separation of church and state. In a combined amicus brief, the American Civil Liberties Union, Americans United for Separation of Church and State, the American Jewish Committee, and the Anti-Defamation League reminded the U.S. Supreme Court it had "repeatedly and consistently" ruled that a state may not assist the teaching of religious beliefs in any manner. When diagnostic or therapeutic services were provided to parochial school students, the court permitted such services on the conditions they take place away from parochial school grounds and are not connected to the school's religious mission. Because a sign language interpreter would assist Jim Zobrest in studying Catholic theology at taxpayer expense, the interpreter would be a state employee, creating an "imprimatur of state approval." Moreover, this brief maintained, an interpreter is a living "representative of the state for all to see," not a mechanical device that cannot teach religious doctrine or anything else. There were innumerable opportunities for an interpreter who accompanies a deaf student all day to promote religion, whether intentionally or not. Accordingly, public school officials would have to monitor the interpreter closely and continuously, thus abridging the entanglement prong of the Lemon Test. Americans United legal counsel Steven Green thought that "people need to get past the fact of James Zobrest's disability and see the larger issue involved," which he argued was "not discrimination against religion, but government participation in religious education." Other civil liberties groups, including the American Jewish Congress and the Baptist Joint Committee on Public Affairs, argued in their amicus brief that there was no constitutional harm in a government providing a sign interpreter. They asserted that the fact that Jim's school was religious was "pure happenstance," based on the "personal choice" of the Zobrests. These ordinarily separationist groups supported the Zobrests because Jim suffered from a good principle "carried too far."[23]

On the surface, it seemed strange that the Zobrests received little support from the Deaf community, either in the form of financial assistance or in the form of a supporting brief to the U.S. Supreme Court. For many in the Deaf community, Jim Zobrest's mainstreaming experiment in his schooling was one they reflexively opposed as representing his abandonment of the minority culture into which he was born in order to adopt the ways of the dominant hearing world that would always regard him as disabled and inferior. Put another way, the Zobrests had made Jim a deaf turncoat. Only one national disability organization—the Alexander Graham Bell Association for the Deaf (AGBAD)—submitted a brief in support of the Zobrests' appeal to the Supreme Court. AGBAD's chief objective was to "ensure that deaf children become fully participating members" of the hearing society, in large part through the practice of mainstreaming. A key part of AGBAD's brief involved tutoring the court on the kinds of assistance deaf people need to understand the spoken word. Depending on the severity of a deaf person's hearing loss, assistive devices and services then included hearing aids, FM systems, induction loops, infrared systems, and oral (or sign language) interpreters. AGBAD defined an interpreter as "a human being who performs the simple, mechanical function of conveying the spoken word to a deaf person." Put another way, a sign language interpreter is "analogous" to a typist who types the spoken word. For AGBAD, there was no church-state violation when "the typist is human."[24]

MAKING A GAME PLAN

For the *Zobrest* case, William Ball undertook his usual meticulous preparation before appearing before the U.S. Supreme Court, this time with the help of his Arizona colleague, Tom Berning. Ball compiled a list of eleven recent Supreme Court cases on the Establishment Clause he wanted to review, a few of which were obscure and with only one involving disability. The cases Ball summarized and analyzed ranged from nativity scenes in public spaces to tax deductions for parochial school expenses to religious discrimination in employment. Ball also identified which justice authored each of these court opinions, the precedents cited in support of each opinion, the justices who joined or concurred in the rulings, and, in some instances, the justices who dissented. Ball took particular pains to mention when the court or even a single justice had called for the accommodation of religion, especially Sandra

Day O'Connor. In some of these cases, Ball added notes on how the court's decision in favor of strict separation of church and state did not govern the Zobrests' petition. One of Ball's major fears was that the Supreme Court would pass on the constitutional issue that formed the heart of the *Zobrest* case, in his opinion, and return the case to the lower federal courts in order to determine what the law required concerning students with disabilities in parochial schools. As the date for oral argument approached, an increasingly anxious Ball took refuge for a few days at his beloved lakeside home in the mountains of northeastern Pennsylvania, trying to regain his confidence as he battled "the worst the enemy can give."[25]

In advance of his first appearance before the U.S. Supreme Court, John Richardson also undertook elaborate preparations to defend the Catalina Foothills School District. Not only was he a novice at America's court of last resort, but, he joked, "every religious organization in the Western hemisphere [was] against me" and had filed briefs supporting the Zobrests and their conception of religious liberty. Richardson's chief aide in this regard was Brett Dunkelman, a Phoenix attorney who had attended law school with Richardson's wife and clerked for William Rehnquist before he became chief justice. In addition, the Arizona School Boards Association and the National School Boards Association called Richardson "all the time" with advice. The key justices, in Richardson's view, were Sandra Day O'Connor and Anthony Kennedy, because they were swing voters on many issues before the court, including church-state matters and because they had proposed their own modifications of the Lemon Test. Richardson crafted his arguments with this insight in mind and conducted mock trials at his alma mater, the University of Arizona.[26]

"We knew," Richardson said quite logically, "we had to press O'Connor's test for O'Connor and Kennedy's test with Kennedy." Sandra Day O'Connor, an Arizonan who had been appointed by Ronald Reagan as the first woman to the High Court, had devised an "endorsement" test to determine whether a given statute and the "unique circumstances" of its implementation abridged the First Amendment. Whereas the Lemon Test would strike down laws excessively entangling religion and government, O'Connor's endorsement test was set forth to determine whether the government favored or disapproved of religion over nonreligion or one sect over another. Would a "reasonable observer," the pragmatic O'Connor asked in a case involving a crèche on public property, believe a particular government action endorsed religion? If the answer was affirmative, this "contextual, fact-driven" test concluded the action was illegal. O'Connor's accommodationist approach permitted government officials to take religion into account when making public policy. She did not, for example, object to tutors from public schools assisting students in parochial schools.[27]

The mindset of the strait-laced Anthony Kennedy on the Establishment Clause was particularly unclear. He had been appointed by Reagan to the Rehnquist Court to be the deciding vote to reverse the Warren and Burger courts on a host of issues. An observant Catholic and former altar boy, Kennedy had once accused the court's liberal majority of "callous indifference" toward religion, but he had also written a separationist decision disallowing a cleric's prayer at a public school's graduation ceremony. By striking down this prayer, Kennedy pointedly refused to join the court's most conservative justices in redrawing the line between church and state. He had given other indications that he might abandon the accommodationist bloc, notably when he wrote that "substantial revision of our Establishment Clause doctrine may be in order." It was clear Kennedy disliked O'Connor's endorsement test, which he regarded as "flawed" and "unworkable," and offered his own variation on the meaning of the Establishment Clause. Kennedy argued that the government "may not coerce anyone to support or participate in any religion or its exercise."[28]

Attorney Richardson realized his "only chance" of winning was for the Supreme Court to respect its precedents regarding parochiaid, particularly three decisions forbidding the use of a public school tape recorder in a religious school. His mission, then, was to "shove those cases in their face." What made Richardson's task all the more difficult was that the Rehnquist Court had never settled on a constitutional theory to resolve the Establishment Clause cases that came before it. Douglas Laycock, a constitutional scholar of the University of Virginia Law School, observed that the court was ambivalent about such cases: "They don't feel bound by the Lemon Test but use it when convenient. The problem is that they can't agree on what to replace it with." Although Richardson spent considerable time in preparation, Brett Dunkelman told him bluntly, "You're going to lose, 5–4," because a passionate oral argument "hardly ever" changes a justice's mind. The more Richardson and Dunkelman talked about the case, the more they believed a strategic error had been made in not arguing that the federal statute only required the school district to pay for an interpreter in a public school. Now, it was too late to make this claim. The day before oral argument, Richardson went to the High Court for the first time in order to watch how the lawyers and justices conducted themselves in legal battle. He was struck by how small the chamber was—close enough, he thought, to spit on the justices accidentally.[29]

ORAL ARGUMENT

On Wednesday, February 24, 1993, a frigid and blustery day, the Zobrests finally got the opportunity to have their case argued before the justices of the U.S. Supreme Court. Five years had passed since they had filed their suit, Larry noted, and there had been "a lot of anguish, turmoil and a lot of ups and downs" during that time. With more than a bit of resentment over the delays in a legal process that appeared detached from the needs of the common man, Larry asked, "Let's face it, who does the court system benefit today? . . . Who are they serving when the child is already in college before we can get a decision? What's the point? What takes so long?" As far as Larry was concerned, the lower court federal judges wrongly focused on a church-state perspective to dismiss their suit. "We aren't out to push religion," he insisted. "We wanted my son to have the same rights and privileges that any other child has." After all, he observed, "it wasn't his choice to be born deaf." Moreover, Larry continued, none of the monies they had paid directly to the sign language interpreter ever went into the coffers of a Catholic church or school. As he saw it, the interpreter was "just a conduit to turn what was spoken into what Jim could hear" because "he's handicapped." His son Jim similarly rejected the notion that the interpreter was somehow promoting religion: "The role for the interpreter is to translate what the teacher tells the class and what I tell the teacher. That's all. They do not participate, and they do not teach anything." Sandi Zobrest thought the court would probably rule in their favor, simply because the Zobrests' case had been accepted for consideration. Still, she acknowledged, "nothing's ever a slam-dunk, so we have to hope and pray."[30]

The stakes were high, too, for William Ball, the Zobrests' seventy-seven-year-old attorney. He had devoted his long and illustrious legal career to religious liberty, meaning an end to what he saw as discrimination against religion in the public square. On the day of oral argument, Ball had awakened at 6:30 a.m. to go over his notes, which were written in large letters to "prompt [his] eyes and mind." If he could convince a majority of the Rehnquist Court to jettison the Lemon Test in authorizing tax funding of Jim Zobrest's interpreter, Jefferson's wall between church and state might be lowered enough to permit school vouchers, thereby encouraging educational choice. These thoughts must have been on Ball's mind when he, his wife, Caroline, their daughter, Ginny, and Ginny's husband, Sandy Duncan, who was deaf, came to the court early to eat breakfast.[31]

Ball was unusually on edge that morning, on a day that would mark his last argument before the U.S. Supreme Court. He had struggled to resist what he called "vain images of 'Bill's Last Hurrah,'" realizing full well that his duty was to lead the justices to focus on Jim Zobrest. Ball's daughter had "never seen [her father] so nervous," as he spoke in a slightly higher range while pointing out the justices, their clerks, and other personages of note who were also in the dining hall. Ball admitted he had been consumed by the case, which had been in his "system like a dye, coloring even [his] sleep."[32]

With limited reserved seats available, Larry Zobrest agreed to stay home while Sandi and their sons, Jim and Sam, attended this once-in-a-lifetime occasion. When the three Zobrests arrived, they were ushered to their seats in the front row, where they were simultaneously excited and nervous about the proceeding, as well as awestruck by the solemnity of it all. The court's somber chamber was "abuzz" that morning, school board attorney John Richardson remembered, because there were "strong feelings" about religion. There were two church-state cases to be heard by the court that day, the first one being *Lamb's Chapel v. Center Moriches Union Free School District*, which concerned a Long Island church's use of a public school's facilities after classes ended to show religious-themed films. The other case was *Zobrest*, which the court's marshal told Ball was "the most high profile case of this term so far." Ginny Ball Duncan, the daughter of the Zobrests' attorney and proficient in signed language, swiveled in her chair next to the aisle in order to start interpreting the proceedings for deaf people around her. One of the deaf members of the audience was Jay Innes, who taught at Gallaudet University and chaired the education committee of the National Association of the Deaf (NAD). He had come to the proceedings, even though NAD had not filed a brief in support of the Zobrests' case. The security guards demanded to know what Ginny was doing. She whispered, "I'm sorry. There are deaf people here for the next case. Out of courtesy, I'm allowing them to understand what's going on right now." The guards then relented. Ginny later thought that she may have done a "terrible job" because she did not know anything about the first case and because she had never translated legal terms such as *pursuant*.[33]

As the Zobrests waited for their own proceedings to begin, Sandi Zobrest noticed the sign language interpreter had arrived fifteen minutes into the *Lamb's Chapel* case but was standing to the side. There was no requirement that the court provide an interpreter, even in a case where the petitioner was deaf, so William Ball had made the arrangements himself, with the understanding the court would pay the fee. Sandi approached a Supreme Court police officer to have the interpreter move toward Jim Zobrest, Sandy Duncan, Jay Innes, and anyone else who might have been proficient in signed language, and she was promptly told to "Sit down, sit down!" Sandi replied forcefully, "But you don't understand. We have an interpreter. She needs to be up there." Ginny Ball Duncan also told Sandi to sit down, because "we're going to get thrown out of here." Sandi said, "This isn't right. This is why we're here." Eventually, the guard did permit the interpreter to move a little closer to the Zobrests.[34]

Although the Zobrests had lost the first two rounds in the lower federal courts, many legal observers believed they would ultimately prevail. Their attorney, William Ball, was one of the most experienced and respected litigators in front of the court, and his specialty was church-state jurisprudence, which would be the heart of the case. An unmistakable sign of Ball's popularity came when the four attorneys involved in the *Zobrest* case gathered in the clerk's office, and the clerk said, "Ladies and gentlemen, we have a special treat for you today. . . . Mr. Ball is here. Mr. Ball, could you stand up?" John Richardson of the Catalina Foothills School District thought to himself, "Holy mackerel. That's the last thing I need." The clerk continued, "It's such an honor to have you here again, Mr. Ball." Nor did a profile of the justices themselves bode well for Richardson. In looking at the justices, three of them—Antonin Scalia, Anthony Kennedy, and Clarence Thomas—had been educated in Catholic schools and seemed inclined to side with the Zobrests. Both Scalia and Thomas had graduated from a Jesuit high school and university, and Thomas had once planned to become a priest. Other justices, including William Rehnquist and Byron White, had criticized Jefferson's view of the First Amendment as erecting an imposing and impregnable wall between government and religion, and Rehnquist had sided with Ball in every church-state case he had heard Ball argue before the court. Moreover, in the last case involving the Establishment Clause before *Zobrest*, the court had sidestepped the Lemon Test while still upholding church-state separation on a different legal theory. Some observers thought *Lemon* itself hung in the balance when the court was to hear *Zobrest*.[35]

It was thus not altogether surprising that John Richardson came to Washington expecting to lose. He would have to rely in his defense on the Lemon Test—the Supreme Court's current definition of the Establishment Clause—but realized full well a majority of the court did not like *Lemon* and wanted "to put that pencil through its heart."[36]

At the stroke of 10 a.m., a gavel was struck, the robed justices filed in and took their seats, and the marshal chanted, "Oyez! Oyez! Oyez!" to command the attention of the assembled and commence the drama. Because the court was scheduled to hear the *Lamb's Chapel* case first, Ball had to wait an hour until his turn came. In his allotted fifteen minutes for oral argument, Ball introduced his client to the justices, noting Jim Zobrest was a "profoundly deaf boy" who had needed a certified sign language interpreter inside the college preparatory school of his choosing. Ball repeated himself to make indelible his contention that Jim's parents were hard working but financially pressed by the situation. Ball noted the college preparatory school that the Zobrests chose for their elder son was Roman Catholic and the atmosphere and academic curriculum in that school were "pervasively religious." Ball's characterization apparently was intended to cast the main issue in the case as primarily one of religious freedom and secondarily as one of disability. As Ball recognized, the Catalina Foothills School District made its decision to deny Jim the services of an interpreter solely on the basis of the Establishment Clause, rather than on what applicable disability laws and regulations permitted.[37]

Given the longstanding practice of the Supreme Court to avoid deciding cases on constitutional grounds, if possible, several justices raised the matter of whether there was a way to resolve this dispute by looking at the statutory and regulatory record. Sandra Day O'Connor wondered whether federal law and regulations required a public school district to provide a sign interpreter in a private school. In what was an overstatement, Ball responded that the IDEA indeed required services for children with disabilities in "all private schools." Additionally, Ball noted, Section 30 of the Code of Federal Regulations included "parochial" schools as eligible for such services. A parochial student, Ball insisted, "must be furnished [with] services of the same scope and quality as those provided for public school children." In actuality, the language of the IDEA was more limited and ambiguous than what Ball asserted, because the law allowed disabled students to receive appropriate aid in a private school if, and only if, a public school district could not provide such aid. The IDEA said nothing about a disabled student receiving such aid in a parochial school. Chief Justice Rehnquist then inquired as to whether the Catalina Foothills School District had ever used the IDEA or the relevant federal regulations to justify its refusal to provide an interpreter for Jim Zobrest at Salpointe. Ball replied, "None whatever."[38]

Ball then told the court the case should turn on whether a state-paid interpreter assisted religion within the meaning of the Lemon Test. In short, did this arrangement have a primary effect of advancing religion, which is what the school district claimed? Ball thought there was no such effect. In the first place, Salpointe received no money by accommodating an interpreter for one deaf boy. In the second place, Ball asserted, the school district "totally misconceives what certification of a sign language interpreter amounts to," which is "simply to translate American sign language into spoken English, spoken English into American Sign Language, and that's it." In fact, Jim Zobrest used a coding system—Signed Exact English—but Ball's point would have been the same in either case. On the other hand, the point hardly helped educate the justices on the communication options available to the deaf.[39]

Justice David Souter, a New England Republican who once contemplated entering the Episcopal priesthood, acknowledged that an interpreter does not originate a religious message. He suggested, nonetheless, that an interpreter is a "necessary functionary" to convey this message at a Catholic school such as Salpointe. Ball readily conceded that an interpreter would convey religious messages at a sectarian school but does so only as a hearing aid would allow a deaf student to understand what is said. As a mere "window of communication," in Ball's words, a sign interpreter would not therefore establish "a symbolic union of church and state," which was what the Ninth Circuit Court had ruled. Ball then injected some unexpected and uncharacteristic levity into his presentation. Ball realized "attempting humor before the Supreme Court is ill-advised," but he agreed with Erasmus, the Dutch Renaissance scholar, that "using it to expose folly is sometimes valuable." "I can," Ball remarked to the court, "only stretch my imagination so far, but it goes to the breaking point when I'm thinking of Jim's peers, these impressionable youngsters, saying something like, 'Guys, you see that fellow who's making those signs? Well, it's like *awesome!* Right here in chem lab we're seeing a violation of the Establishment Clause of the First Amendment." The courtroom erupted into laughter, a rare disruption in the invariably solemn proceedings.[40]

To make a strategic point, Ball asserted that the Zobrests had chosen a Catholic school for Jim to achieve their mainstreaming goals. They wanted "to get this boy equipped for the business of life" by having the same education he would receive in a public school in order "to become independent, to become self-sustaining, and to survive in a world not always hospitable to deaf people." Salpointe would teach him the "same math," "the same modern foreign languages," and the "same computer literacy" that a public school would offer. Surprisingly, Ball declined to ask the Court to scrap the Lemon Test he detested, insisting that "nothing in Lemon" barred a tax-paid sign interpreter in a religious school.[41]

The remainder of the petitioners' case was presented by Deputy Solicitor General William Bryson, a Republican holdover who had not yet been replaced by the new Clinton administration. Bryson maintained that providing a sign interpreter for a deaf student is "this child's ears" and would not convey "any implicit support on the part of the state for anything being said in providing the child with the means to hear what is said." Bryson compared Jim Zobrest's interpreter at Salpointe to a state-paid nurse who wheels a paralyzed child from class to class, so the child could attend a religious school. In neither instance, Bryson argued, would there be an endorsement of the religious message. Justice Souter questioned Bryson's comparison, seeing the performances of the nurse and the interpreter as "not inextricably bound up with communication of the message itself." The deputy solicitor general did not press the court to overrule its church-state precedents as that office had done during the administrations of Ronald Reagan and George H. W. Bush.[42]

It was then attorney John Richardson's turn to defend the Catalina Foothills School District. In his opening statement, Richardson stated categorically that neither the First Amendment nor the federal law IDEA permitted a public school district to pay and place an employee in a parochial school to "actively participate in a student's religious education." To paint the issue more starkly and to "personalize" the sign interpreter's obligation to convey religious dogma, Richardson distilled the essence of the Zobrests' lawsuit to the demand that the government should be forced to pay for an interpreter in a religious school who would repeat a theology teacher's declaration that "there's life after death." Ball thought Richardson had spoken "well" but privately criticized his handling of the case.[43]

Almost immediately, Richardson was "bombarded" with questions. Under questioning from Justice John Paul Stevens, a Ford appointee who voted for church-state separation in establishment *and* free exercise cases, Richardson admitted that the school district would have paid for Jim Zobrest's sign interpreter had he attended a nonreligious private school, but not a sectarian school such as Salpointe. Other justices asked what kinds of services a public school district could provide to a disabled student in a parochial school. Speech therapy was one such service, Richardson allowed, because that assistance was "unrelated" to the religious message of a parochial school. Sandra Day O'Connor asked whether the First Amendment permitted a school district to provide a hearing aid, as opposed to an interpreter, to a deaf child in a parochial school. Richardson saw a stark difference between a neutral mechanical device and a human being who would be "part of the educational team working in close cooperation with the school teacher to impart the educational lessons of the teacher," particularly in a parochial school whose curriculum includes "spiritual as well as secular" lessons. Returning to his theme that an interpreter would assist the religious message of a sectarian school, Richardson summarized what he was certain would happen: a public employee would be obliged "to convey to James Zobrest that Jesus Christ was the son of God or that he died to save his sins," the implication being that this uniquely Christian message would plainly abridge the First Amendment. Throughout, Richardson deliberately locked eyes on Justices O'Connor and Kennedy, hoping somehow to convince them to see the issue as one of illegal religious establishment.[44]

Next to question Richardson was Justice Antonin Scalia, a devout and outspoken "traditional" Catholic, who preferred the Latin Mass and was the father of nine children, one of whom became a priest. A self-described "originalist" who relied on the common understanding of the Constitution when it was adopted, Scalia repeatedly denied that his Catholicism determined his thinking about the law, particularly concerning abortion and school prayer. Some legal observers nonetheless noted that Scalia's judicial decisions in these areas synchronized closely with the views of the Catholic Church. Fiercely opposed to judicial activism, Scalia trusted the majority's will as expressed in the legislative branch to resolve disputes, especially when religious groups were involved. If state governments offered vouchers to parents sending their children to Catholic schools at public expense, Scalia applauded such school choice programs. During his tenure on the court, Scalia had repeatedly attacked the Lemon Test as a "jurisprudential disaster" for violating longstanding traditions and concocting psychological tests to assess the supposed damage that incidental exposure to religion might cause.[45]

Scalia asked whether John Richardson could accept a public employee as a bus driver for students attending parochial schools, where they would "learn about God." This question appeared somewhat disingenuous because the High Court had already approved of this arrangement decades earlier in the *Everson* decision. Richardson replied that this provision for parochial students was constitutional because the bus driver did not deliver a theological message. For the same reason, Richardson observed, the Catalina Foothills School District had readily provided Jim Zobrest with years of speech therapy at a public school. "We have no problem," Richardson summarized," with providing related services that don't make the public employee become integrally involved in the religious indoctrination that occurs in a parochial school classroom." Scalia then shifted gears, asking Richardson whether the state has an "obligation . . . not to impose upon a family with a deaf child a disincentive to go to a religious school." Is the state acting in a neutral fashion, Scalia wondered, if it tells the child, "'Go to any school you want. You will have an interpreter. But if you go to a religious school, no interpreter.'" Richardson said that the Establishment Clause forbade public employees from participating in religious activities. Citizens have a right to know, Richardson declared, that their taxes are not being misused to indoctrinate a student religiously. "The school board asks nothing more," Richardson said with a rhetorical flourish, "and the First Amendment commands no less."[46]

Byron White, an All-American college football player, a Rhodes scholar, and a Kennedy appointee to the court, had a well-earned reputation as a "relentless and difficult" interrogator of attorneys he faced, but he had been almost silent when Ball and Bryson presented their arguments on behalf of the Zobrests. A recent study of White's jurisprudence identified an "inconsistency" in his thinking when it came to church and state, while other scholars argued that White simply "refrained from inflexible, doctrinaire stands" in order to judge each case on its merits. In *Zobrest*, it appears that White's initial concern was procedural in nature. White grilled Richardson for not using federal law, rather than the First Amendment, to oppose the use of a government-paid interpreter in a sectarian school. Richardson replied that federal regulations prohibited the use of federal funds for religious instruction, and he forecast a "long, expensive trial" would result from using a statutory defense. When White asked whether a government-paid robot acting as an interpreter in a religious school would be permissible, Richardson compared it to another mechanical device—a tape recorder—which had been prohibited by the court in the *Meek* decision.[47]

Two justices appointed by Republican presidents did not participate in oral argument—Harry Blackmun and Clarence Thomas—and their views were polar opposite on church-state matters. Blackmun, who was appointed to the court by Richard Nixon, had joined the majority in crafting the Lemon Test in 1971 and relied on it consistently for two decades. In church-state cases before *Zobrest*, Blackmun asserted that the purpose of the Establishment Clause was "to create a complete and permanent separation of the spheres of religious activity and civil authority by comprehensively forbidding every form of public aid or support of religion." Since Blackmun had written that religion could "engender divisiveness" and thus be harmful to public discourse, Anthony Kennedy once accused Blackmun of outright "hostility toward religion," a charge that Blackmun characterized as "offensive" and "absurd."[48]

There was some doubt about Clarence Thomas's church-state leanings. Thomas had been baptized as a Baptist, converted to Catholicism under his grandfather's influence, and regularly attended Catholic Mass and his wife's charismatic Episcopalian church, where possession by the Holy Spirit and speaking in tongues were not unknown. At a symposium on Reagan's proposed school prayer amendment, Thomas criticized the Supreme Court for its ban on prayers authorized by school officials. "My mother," he said, "says that when they took God out of the schools, the schools went to hell. She may be right." Thomas, who had been nominated to the court by George H. W. Bush, nonetheless stated at his confirmation hearings that he had "no personal disagreement" with the Lemon Test and thought that Jefferson's "wall was an 'appropriate metaphor.'" After Thomas joined the court, however, he returned to his accommodationist mindset, once remarking that he had to follow "God's law" while on the bench.[49]

After Richardson concluded his presentation, William Ball had one minute for rebuttal. He took advantage of the fact that Richardson had just referred to the amicus brief filed by the Arizona School Boards Association, which included a report of the National Task Force on Educational Interpreters.

The report emphasized that a sign language interpreter's "priority" in the classroom was not in instruction, but interpretation, plain and simple.[50]

REACTION TO ORAL ARGUMENT

When William Ball and the Zobrests left the courtroom, Ball felt "great relief" after years of hard work for a worthy cause. Ball's daughter, Ginny Ball Duncan, remembers that her father was "never confident" about how well a case was received by the justices. At the conclusion of any case, Ball Duncan remembered, Ball habitually said something like, "I did my best. That's all I could do," as he replayed in his mind what he had said and how he had said it. There were hugs and kudos, reflecting a mixture of satisfaction and relief from the petitioners. Jim Zobrest remembered, "We all felt very good" about the proceedings. Still, Ball tried to temper the natural feeling of confidence emerging from that setting. "Anything can happen," he reminded the Zobrests. After dealing briefly with newspaper and television reporters, Ball, his family, and the Zobrests all headed to a luncheon organized by the Christian Legal Society and the Freedom Council for the people involved in the *Lamb's Chapel* case, including attorney Jay Sekulow of television evangelist Pat Robertson's American Center for Law and Justice. Sandi and Jim felt out of place at the luncheon, not because they were unwelcome but because it was so elegant. The Zobrests had watched every penny they spent in Washington, staying at a modest motel far from the Supreme Court building and bringing a crockpot in which to make chili. Afterward, the Balls dutifully went to Mass on Ash Wednesday at Washington's Shrine of the Sacred Heart.[51]

SUPREME COURT DELIBERATIONS

On the day the justices were to discuss the *Zobrest* case in conference, Harry Blackmun received a revealing memorandum from Radhika Rao, one of his law clerks. She advised Blackmun that there was "a move afoot" to sidestep the case's constitutional questions. In talking to other law clerks, she had learned that Sandra Day O'Connor, David Souter, and John Paul Stevens were inclined to send the case back to the Ninth Circuit Court to consider relevant state and federal laws, including the IDEA. Rao thought this approach was "prudent," reminding Blackmun that the U.S. Supreme Court had traditionally declined to address constitutional questions in a given case if the case could be handled without doing so. Moreover, Rao maintained, the parties in *Zobrest* "appear almost to have manufactured the Establishment Clause issue by refusing to litigate the very real and important statutory and state constitutional questions in the lower courts." Rao cautioned Blackmun that some justices might deliberately ignore such questions to use *Zobrest* as means of jettisoning the controversial Lemon Test and thereby upend the court's "longstanding" jurisprudence regarding the Establishment Clause. Such a development, Rao was convinced, would be "dangerous." Rao urged Blackmun to reverse and remand the case to the Ninth Circuit for reconsideration. If the Supreme Court nonetheless decided to address the federal constitutional question, Rao urged Blackmun to affirm the Ninth Circuit's denial of the Zobrests' claim for a government-paid sign interpreter for their son Jim.[52]

As it turned out, the key figure in the *Zobrest* case was not Sandra Day O'Connor or Anthony Kennedy, who said little in oral argument, but rather Chief Justice William Rehnquist, a Goldwater Republican and Reagan appointee from Arizona. Rehnquist believed the court's misreading of the Establishment Clause had produced a series of "unprincipled" decisions since World War II that displayed "a callous indifference to religious groups" and favored "those who believe in no religion over those who do believe"—exactly William Ball's position. Rehnquist, a devout Lutheran, had previously accused the court of paying lip service to the idea of neutrality involving religion in public life, while casting "its weight on the side of those who believe our society as a whole should be a purely secular one." Rehnquist's

Jim Zobrest interview in front of the Supreme Court, February 24, 1993, the day his case was heard. Sandi Zobrest acts as Jim's interpreter, and his brother Sam, center in trench coat, looks on. (Courtesy of Sandi Zobrest)

position on church and state was to accommodate religion's interests, as long as one religion was not favored over another. As a nonpreferentialist, he rejected the court's no-aid principle in favor of "evenhanded neutrality" and "private choice." To restore the First Amendment's original meaning, as set forth in the First Congress, Rehnquist aimed at knocking down Jefferson's "misleading" and "useless" metaphorical wall that, he insisted, was based on "bad history." The *Zobrest* case presented another opportunity to dismantle that obstacle and restore religious liberty as Rehnquist understood it.[53]

THE *ZOBREST* DECISION

The suspense over the Supreme Court's delay was agonizing to the Zobrests, their attorneys, and William Ball's daughter Ginny. The Zobrests had been calling Ball for news on their case, but he had "nothing to tell them." Finally, on Friday, June 18, 1993, Ball anticipated a decision from the court, so he paid particular attention to his appearance in the event reporters would interview him for his reaction. At 8:00 a.m., as was his custom, Ball went to St. Patrick's Cathedral in Harrisburg and told "Our Lord that I wanted to take it well if I lose and not be too loaded with vanity if I win." He wrote in his diary that he prayed "most especially" for the Zobrests. When he returned to his office, his staff was on edge. He asked his secretary to call the Supreme Court at 9:45 a.m. to find out if it had overturned the Ninth Circuit's ruling against the Zobrests. "Too early," came the reply. Wait a half hour. At 10:15 a.m., the secretary called again, raising her forefinger in the air as the announcement was about to be made. "Reversed?" she asked. "Reversed!" she said triumphantly. Ball shouted with joy and sank to his knees in thanksgiving. Everyone hugged each other. "A glorious moment!" Ball remembered, returning to the cathedral in gratitude to thank God.[54]

Since Rehnquist was in the majority, it was his prerogative as to who would write the *Zobrest* opinion, and he chose himself. One court observer described Rehnquist as a "master tactician," and with another Establishment Clause case to be adjudicated, Rehnquist did not want to entrust *Zobrest* to a colleague. Rehnquist spoke for a divided Supreme Court in reversing the rulings of the district and circuit courts to find in favor of the Zobrests. The court's ruling, which mirrored Ninth Circuit Court judge Thomas Tang's dissenting opinion, held that the First Amendment's Establishment Clause did not bar the Catalina Foothills School District from providing and paying for a sign interpreter to help Jim Zobrest learn. After decades of debate over the constitutionality of parochial school aid, the court for the first time allowed an employee paid for by public funds to be part of a religious school's instructional program. A veteran *New York Times* reporter on the U.S. Supreme Court wrote that *Zobrest* "lay at the intersection of two inherently inconsistent lines of precedent in the area of parochial aid," but this area of the law remained murky. Another observer noted that the court, which had been searching for some time for a means to further assist the disabled, had used *Zobrest* to reinforce the rights of disabled children.[55]

As the court considered the constitutionality of state aid granted to sectarian schools under the IDEA, Rehnquist relied chiefly on the accommodationist precedents of *Mueller* and *Witters*. He pointed out that the court had "consistently held that government programs that neutrally provide benefits to a broad class of citizens defined without reference to religion are not readily subject to the Establishment Clause challenge just because sectarian institutions may also receive an attenuated financial benefit." The provision of a sign language interpreter, observed Rehnquist, was not an act of establishment of religion but "part of a general government program that distributes benefits neutrally to any child qualifying as handicapped." If an individual who is handicapped, in this case Jim Zobrest, chooses to attend a parochial school, Rehnquist wrote, "we hold that the Establishment Clause does not prevent the school district from furnishing him with a sign language interpreter there in order to facilitate his education." The use of a publicly funded interpreter in a sectarian school was the result of an individual choice by the deaf child's parents. In providing this essential service, Rehnquist asserted, there was not a financial incentive for an individual to attend a religious institution. In this sense, Rehnquist's opinion, which was agreed to by Justices Anthony Kennedy, Antonin Scalia, Clarence Thomas, and Byron White, was a narrow one. The decision noted "no funds traceable to the government ever find their way into sectarian schools' coffers" under the IDEA, the federal law that provided services for disabled students.[56]

The majority's opinion hinged in part on its contention that a sign language interpreter would in no way advance the school's religious agenda. "Nothing in this record suggests that a sign language interpreter would do more than accurately interpret whatever material is presented to the class as a whole," Rehnquist wrote. An interpreter, as opposed to a teacher, "would neither add to nor subtract from that environment," and this kind of educational assistance was permissible. "The Establishment Clause," Rehnquist declared, "lays down no absolute bar to the placing of a public employee in a sectarian school." Rehnquist took considerable pains to distinguish *Zobrest* from two precedents emphasized by John Richardson on behalf of the Catalina Foothills School District. In *Meek v. Pittinger* and *School District of Grand Rapids v. Ball*, the court decided that the state government provided "massive aid" to religious schools when it gave them instructional materials, diagnostic and therapeutic services, and public school teachers for remedial classes, thereby reducing expenses for parochial schools. In the *Zobrest* case, the parochial school in question did not benefit directly because the interpreter was not teaching a course, but merely assisting the parochial school's sole disabled student. In addition, because religious schools did not customarily provide interpreter services, a tax-paid interpreter would not reduce the costs to them.[57]

The court declined to address "unrelated" issues in *Zobrest* because the parties pursued only the federal constitutional issue at the district and appellate levels. Rehnquist recognized the validity of the "prudential rule of avoiding constitutional questions," but he noted that on appeal, the court was presented with the "entire case," including "nonconstitutional questions actually decided by the lower court as well as nonconstitutional grounds presented to, but not passed on by the lower court." In the *Zobrest* litigation, the court found it significant that only First Amendment questions—rather than nonconstitutional grounds—were "pressed" before the Ninth Circuit and that, even before the district court, "the parties chose to litigate the case on the federal constitutional issues alone." The court concluded, "Given this posture of the case, we think the prudential rule of avoiding constitutional questions has no application. The fact that there may be buried in the record a nonconstitutional ground for decision is not by itself enough to invoke this rule." The court then proceeded directly to the First Amendment issue. Most notably, Rehnquist did not cite the Lemon Test in his opinion for the majority. Some observers speculated that Rehnquist did not have the votes to abolish the test. For many Roman Catholics, Evangelical Protestants, and conservative legal commentators, the opportunity for explicitly redirecting Establishment Clause jurisprudence away from the Lemon Test they despised had been lost.[58]

Rehnquist declared that the service of a sign language interpreter in this instance was "part of a general government program that distributes benefits neutrally to any child qualifying as disabled under the IDEA," without regard to whether the school attended was sectarian or nonsectarian, public or private. Rehnquist added that by giving parents the freedom to choose a school for their disabled children, the IDEA ensured a state-funded interpreter would be in a parochial school only because of parental decision-making. Rehnquist thus determined that because "the IDEA creates no financial incentive for parents to choose a sectarian school, an interpreter's presence there cannot be attributed to state decisionmaking." Rehnquist thought the religious school's economic benefit, if any, was indirect, and such benefit would have occurred only if the school made a profit on each student, if the student would have attended the school without the interpreter, and if the student's seat would have remained unfilled. He maintained that government aid to the student and his parents in the form of paying for his interpreter did not constitute a direct subsidy of the religious school, because the student—not the school—was the primary beneficiary of the IDEA.[59]

Another critical aspect of the case involved Rehnquist's understanding of what a sign language interpreter does. For him, a sign language interpreter's job is fundamentally different than that of a teacher or guidance counselor, because an interpreter does not add or subtract from the pervasively sectarian environment in which the student's parents had chosen to place him. Interpreters, Rehnquist argued, "transmit everything that is said in exactly the same way it was intended," making interpreters the human equivalent of a hearing aid—a visual hearing aid, in other words. Interpreter Jim Santeford would have agreed with the court in theory, but his experience during his years working with Jim Zobrest at Salpointe certainly seemed to suggest otherwise. As far as Rehnquist and the majority were concerned, a tax-paid interpreter signing to a student in a sectarian school did not violate the Establishment Clause, and so they reversed the Ninth Circuit Court's decision.[60]

The four dissenting justices were Harry Blackmun, Sandra Day O'Connor, David Souter, and John Paul Stevens. Writing for the minority, Blackmun rebuked the *Zobrest* majority for "unnecessarily address[ing] an important constitutional issue, [and] disregarding longstanding principles of constitutional adjudication." The dissent argued that the Court could have simply returned the case to the lower courts for a consideration of alternative grounds to resolve the dispute. The lower courts could have then construed the IDEA so as not to require an interpreter for a parochial school student, which was what happened in the *Goodall* case, as long as the school district provided an interpreter in a public school the child could attend. According to the dissent, the parties did not present briefs or make arguments concerning the "weighty" nonconstitutional issues because they wanted a ruling on the Establishment Clause question. Blackmun, in speaking for the dissenters, asserted that the avoidance doctrine is the most "deeply rooted" doctrine of constitutional adjudication, chiefly because it amounts to a "fundamental rule of judicial restraint."[61]

Turning to Rehnquist's opinion itself, Blackmun intoned forcefully, "Until now, the Court never has authorized a public employee to participate directly in religious indoctrination. Yet that is the consequence of today's decision." To permit Jim Zobrest to have a government-paid interpreter in a Catholic school would mean the government promoted a particular religious message, suggesting a clear violation of the First Amendment. The *Zobrest* decision, Blackmun argued, sanctioned "ongoing, daily, and intimate governmental participation in the teaching and propagation of religious doctrine." In a religious environment of the kind promoted by Salpointe Catholic High School, which was "so pervaded by discussions of the divine, the sign language interpreter's every gesture would be infused with religious significance." Souter joined Blackmun in this line of thinking on the constitutional merits of the case, but O'Connor and Stevens did not.[62]

IMMEDIATE REACTION TO THE *ZOBREST* DECISION

By the time the U.S. Supreme Court finally ruled, the Zobrests had begged for money to pay for their son Jim's interpreter, had endured bankruptcy, and had seen their son graduate from high school. Their attorney, William Ball, called the Zobrests at the collection agency where they worked with the good news. "You won!" he exclaimed. For Sandi Zobrest, her reaction ran the gamut of emotions. At first, she cried. "I got so emotional. You wait and you wait and you wait and then it comes. It's like the pressure's off." Sandi thought the whole affair had been well worth all of the trouble they had experienced. "I'm elated," she said, for the decision was more than a personal victory: "It's going to be easier now for handicapped students to have freedom of choice of schools and get the services they're entitled to." Sandi had never realized the significance of their case—"never knew it was as big a deal" as it was—until they began to get telephone calls from other parents with disabled children, thanking them for their pioneering legal victory. Thrilled as she was, Sandi still had the presence of mind to realize newspaper reporters would be looking to interview Jim, who was at home asleep. She called her sister-in-law to rouse him. "Get up, get up," Jim was told. "You won the case. Get dressed" to meet the press where his parents worked. By now a community college student, Jim also hoped the decision would help others with disabilities: "I think the case is a stepping stone for a lot of people that are in similar situations as we are. In the future, they'll be able to use our case as an example." Larry Zobrest, on the other hand, was a "little bitter" over the whole legal battle, because the school district had "squandered" $80,000 in attorney fees to keep Jim from having an interpreter at Salpointe. When the euphoria over winning their case receded somewhat, Sandi remembered—and fulfilled—her promise to repay those who had supported them financially.[63]

Although Barry Lynn, the executive director of Americans United, worried that the *Zobrest* decision had "the possibility of radically rewriting church-state law," conservative newspaper columnist James J. Kilpatrick saw a great possible benefit in the Rehnquist ruling. Kilpatrick looked forward to a day when the High Court would use the *Zobrest* decision to transform American education and end religious discrimination by accepting a system of vouchers to parents who would send their children to private schools, including sectarian ones. He ended his column by writing, "Thank you, Jim Zobrest, and thanks to William Bentley Ball, the brilliant First Amendment lawyer . . . who fought for a deaf boy through five years of court proceedings . . . and won." As for Ball, he observed that it had taken all that time "to get the monkey of *Lemon* off the back of justice—justice to a deaf boy."[64]

6 THE AFTERMATH

The consequences of the Zobrest case played out in judicial doctrine, in the practices of public school systems in their relationship to disabled students, in Tucson-area local politics, and, finally, in the lives of the Zobrests, who a quarter century after their brief moment in the middle of the nation's constitutional history continue to sort out the varied meanings of their experience of pursuing justice. In analyzing those consequences, it is possible to trace not only the evolution of church-state constitutional doctrine but also the changing understanding of disability in general, and hearing impairment in particular, in American society, culture, and law. Mainstreaming is and will remain controversial among the Deaf and their allies. However mainstreaming is regarded by those with the greatest stake in deaf education, the aftermath of the Zobrest lawsuit, both for the public order and for the Zobrests, indicates that there has been change in the direction of greater acceptance and inclusion of people with hearing impairments. That change has limits that continue to be obstacles for people who are hearing impaired. Jim Zobrest's life after the court decision is testimony to that.

THE FUTURE OF THE RELIGION CLAUSES OF THE FIRST AMENDMENT

Thomas Berning recalls that from a jurisprudential point of view, what his colleague William Bentley Ball sought in pursuing the Zobrests' lawsuit over the course of five years and at personal financial loss was not "a big, knockout blow" against the strict separationist doctrine that had prevailed in the Supreme Court. After decades of studying the U.S. Supreme Court and pleading before it, Ball knew its reluctance to extinguish years of rulings and suddenly head in a radically different direction. Ball hoped only, Berning recalls, for an "incremental step" toward a more accommodationist court.[1] After all his struggles toward that end, such a step would be significant enough progress. Nor was there probably any reason for Ball to anticipate that much would change for people with disabilities as the result of a positive decision, and to that extent, from the perspective of those concerned with the rights of people with disabilities, the proverbial tail was likely to wag the dog in the Zobrest lawsuit. Disability might well be the servant of the church-state agenda. After witnessing opinions against his clients' case from the Pima County Attorney's Office and the Arizona attorney general and being defeated in both the federal district and appellate courts, Ball had every reason to be cautious about prevailing at all, let alone obtaining a modestly favorable decision in the Zobrests' favor. The court had agreed to hear the case—a favorable sign, to be sure—but what sort of division among the nine justices would ultimately come out of its deliberations and what it might mean for the future was, to say the least, uncertain. "Incremental" steps seemed, realistically, as if it were the best Ball could expect.

On the other hand, Ball's longtime adversaries, the strict church-state separationists who led Americans United for Separation of Church and State (Americans United) and had filed a strong amicus brief on behalf of the Catalina Foothills School District, were not in doubt about the likelihood that the court's decision might be a blow to their position. They knew that on the strength of character and personal aspirations, Jim was a very sympathetic litigant. The fact that the court had agreed to hear the Zobrests' claim, which Americans United felt was a transparent assault on existing precedents that had been derived over two decades from the Lemon Test, and that there was a changing ideological composition of the court toward the Right with the arrival of conservative justice Clarence Thomas, portended, they feared, a radical reorientation of church-state doctrine. The court had declined to review the *Goodall v. Stafford County* case in 1991, a case presenting the same issues as *Zobrest* that had been decided against the Goodalls in the Fourth District Court of Appeals. Now the court was eager somehow to go back over the same territory on behalf of the Zobrests.[2] "The case stands the possibility of radically rewriting church-state law," American United's director, Rev. Barry Lynn, told the press just after the decision was announced. "I can't see why the court would take the case otherwise."[3]

Both parties proved correct. The case was of incremental value to Ball's longtime effort to shake loose public resources for parochial schools. This quest weighed especially heavily on his mind in the last decade and a half before his death in 1999 as he came to fear the combination of growing state power in society, especially in education, the rapid secularization of culture and society, and the abiding monopoly power of public education.[4] But it did not itself radically shift court doctrine as much as contribute to the work of gradually deconstructing it. In reaching to support the Zobrests' case, the five-member majority did not invoke the tight strictures of the Lemon Test at all. Absent from the majority opinion were the Catch-22 phrases of the past—*symbolic union* and *excessive entanglement*—that had bedeviled his and others' pleadings in the past. The *Zobrest* court's decision was rhetorically accommodationist. But it ruled rather strictly to the novel circumstances of the case—a deaf student and a sign interpreter who was really nothing more, the majority sought to believe without any inquiry into the matter, than a translating machine—even as it paid no attention to the contradictory, unpredictable, and ad hoc judgments often derived from the Lemon Test in the past. The decision cast doubt on the future of the Lemon Test, but it did not state that it was now dead or offer an explicit statement to the effect that a new test or doctrine was in the process of creation.[5]

The jurisprudential consequences of the *Zobrest* decision gradually emerged as the decision on its own and in league with other court rulings assisted in influencing the opinions of Supreme Court majorities in three prominent lawsuits—*Agostini v. Felton* (1997); *Mitchell v. Helms* (2000); and *Zelman v. Simmons-Harris* (2002)—heard by the Supreme Court between 1997 and 2002. Each decision assisted in relaxing the strict separation of church and state, but each decision was a narrow 5 to 4 ruling that suggested the court remained divided on the larger direction of Establishment Clause doctrine.[6]

There were two major doctrinal points made in *Zobrest* that assisted courts in confronting related points of law in these lawsuits. First, religious institutions, such as parochial schools, could not constitutionally be prohibited from participating in government-funded social welfare programs that neutrally distributed public resources to a broad class of citizens, such as people with disabilities or minority children whose families were poor, without explicit reference to religion. Such programs could not be seen as violations of the Establishment Clause simply because those religious institutions derived attenuated and indirect benefits from them. Thus, the public resources under the Education for All Handicapped Children Act/Individuals with Disabilities Education Act (EAHCA/IDEA) that, the court ruled, should have gone to Jim at Salpointe could not be construed as advancing religion, because the only benefit to Salpointe, not to mention the Roman Catholic Church, from the apportioning of those resources was the fact that Jim was enrolled there and paid tuition, a cost to his parents, not to the public. Under any circumstance, second, the attenuated benefit to Salpointe was not a consequence of a state mandate but of the private choice of individual citizens in their capacity, in this instance, as parents.[7] The latter argument, which was especially troublesome for advocates of secular public education, such as Americans United, which feared voucher programs would be the undoing of public school funding, had entered into other decisions before *Zobrest.* These decisions and *Zobrest* were cited in *Zelman v. Simmons-Harris*, a case in which the majority approved a Cleveland, Ohio, voucher plan, which was, in fact, conceived as a means to enable the parents of low-income minority students to send their children to tuition-based parochial schools at a time when there was a significant loss of confidence in the Cleveland public schools.[8]

Both of the points in the *Zobrest* decision served to protect providing a sign language interpreter at public expense from constitutional challenge, and in doing so created a singular precedent that was an incremental milestone from a jurisprudential point of view: a public employee or an employee paid for with public funds, such as the interpreter Jim Santeford, might work routinely in a parochial institution. This point had been under contention for decades in adjudicating state laws that attempted to provide for the sharing of resources, such as might assist in paying for afterschool enrichment and compensatory education programs, between public and parochial schools. Furthermore, under certain restricted circumstances, that employee could even be involved in religious matters.[9] Other court decisions had begun to speak generally of there being no constitutional bar necessarily in accommodating religion or religious institutions in governmental contexts, if religious indoctrination or devotional practice were not explicitly encouraged.[10] *Zobrest* in this respect went further but, again, on the incorrect assumption, contradicted in the experience of Jim Zobrest and Jim Santeford, that a sign interpreter is less an active, multidimensioned human being than a passive translating machine.

In this connection, *Zobrest* was of assistance to the accommodationist majority in reaching its conclusions in the first of the three lawsuits. *Agostini v. Felton*, in effect, repealed a decision made a dozen years before in *Aguilar v. Felton*, in which the court had ruled unconstitutional a costly and well-intended New York City program providing public resources, in the form of public school teachers, for compensatory education for poor minority students, among whom were numerous children with learning disabilities, in afterschool programs within parochial schools. If Jim's interpreter, who might actually be in a position to interpret Catholic doctrine in religion class, was no threat to the Establishment Clause, one might legitimately now ask how a public school math or reading teacher offering remedial services, without any intellectual proximity to religious content, could be such a threat.[11]

The second of the three cases, in chronological order, was *Mitchell v. Helms*. It involved, not public employees, but the status of instructional materials under a Louisiana law. Justice Thomas's majority opinion created a metaphysical leap that moved *Zobrest* from animate to inanimate public resources. If a sign interpreter were simply translating, in a machinelike manner, religious messages rather than creating them, how could a math textbook or a textbook on grammar be any more at risk of indoctrinating students? If the same public resources created no problem under the Establishment Clause at secular public schools, how could they do so at parochial schools? The court's answer in the past had been that perhaps those in charge of using them could not resist the temptation to direct secular resources in religious directions. But like the strictures against putting tax-supported employees in parochial institutions, those against trusting them and trusting parochial school employees with public material resources were collapsing. Also collapsing was the argument that measures put into effect to make sure that remedial arithmetic or reading instruction would involve an insidious, excessive entanglement of church and state. Justice Thomas's decision said, in effect, that this level of surveillance, costly and plodding, was a waste of time.[12]

In these and other decisions, the *Zobrest* decision has played a role in directing a reorientation of church-state jurisprudence in educational matters that has gained momentum in the twenty-first century. It has spoken directly to disability less frequently. Most cases citing *Zobrest* have not been about services to disabled students at the K–12 level. Of the 9 cases heard by the Supreme Court in which *Zobrest* has been cited, in fact, only the very significant *Agostini v. Felton*, and then only in part, and not as a principle point of the lawsuit, involved services for disabled students at the K–12 level. A survey of all 65 cases, to be found in Appendix 2, heard in the Supreme Court and at the federal district-court and appellate-court levels in lawsuits between 1993 and 2017 in which *Zobrest* was cited suggests the uses of the decision in church-state and other matters. Fourteen of the 65 lawsuits (21 percent) were about educational services for disabled students at K–12 levels. Eight involved cases like the Zobrests' involving parochial schools and public resources for students with disabilities, and 6 involved disability and education outside church-state issues. The latter were lawsuits involving conflicts over Individualized Education Program (IEP) negotiations or secular private school enrollments for children with multiple disabilities who, public school officials had argued, could not be accommodated in public schools.

Of the remainder of the cases, 24 (37 percent) concerned the ongoing work at a general level of defining the boundaries of church and state within K–12 public education, and 15 other cases (23 percent) concerned church-state boundaries outside education. The balance of 12 cases (18 percent) concerned federal-state jurisdictional issues, judicial process issues, and funding equity and race within public school systems.[13]

Where the Zobrest decision may lead the Supreme Court in the future is a matter for speculation beyond the scope of this work. It may suffice to say that for all of the resistance to change in constitutional jurisprudence, the twisting paths of constitutional interpretation are unpredictable. As precedent, court decisions have been known to surface and recede, only to resurface, sometimes decades later. To that extent, *Zobrest v. Catalina Foothills School District* may well await new applications, whether in church-state or education or disability law.

THE PRACTICES OF PUBLIC SCHOOL DISTRICTS

What have been the practical effects of the decision for students with disabilities, the latter-day Jim Zobrests, who seek to take public resources into nonpublic schools? When we consider the consequences of the decision for individual disabled students and for the practices of public school districts under the EAHCA/IDEA, the picture tends to grow more complicated than we might expect. The law remains complex, as does its local application. The Zobrests' victory in 1993 did not necessarily usher in a new era everywhere throughout the nation for students like Jim Zobrest; yet in some places it certainly did. Thoughtful observers anticipated that on balance, the outcomes would be tentative. Paul Siegel, a hearing (and fluent American Sign Language signer) professor of communications and media law, who was then on the faculty at Gallaudet University, gave expression to this tentativeness in an early, postdecision assessment of the decision. Referencing the *Zobrest* majority's incorrect view of the work of sign language interpreters, Siegal titled his essay, "What They Didn't Know May Have Helped Us."[14]

Anticipating the decision in the Zobrests' lawsuit, or reacting to it just after it was announced, most commentators focused on the hope for a general resolution of the problem of church-state boundaries in availability of public resources for parochial schools. Thus, when the influential Jesuit scholar, public intellectual, and Georgetown University law professor Fr. Robert Drinan commented on the decision, he spoke of "a glimmer of hope for aid to Catholic schools" but noted that he did not think it necessarily held out as much for disabled students.[15] It was not uncommon in these commentaries to focus on Jim's deafness as an interesting detail of the case but then go directly to the familiar and longstanding First Amendment issues. Of course, that was the way the lawsuit had been argued and the ground on which it had been adjudicated since its origins, so public commentaries were logically directed by court arguments and decisions. Moreover, even without much knowledge of the Constitution, individuals could be assumed to find church-state controversies significant. Public opinion had been aroused for years, in the context of an increasing politicization of faith, with issues such as abortion and contraception, school prayer, the public display of religious symbols, and the teaching of Darwinian evolution and creationism. Church-state issues fused ideology and emotion in believers and secularists alike, so it was logical to assume that court decisions on such issues made compelling reading.

Even *Silent News*, self-described as "the world's most popular newspaper of the deaf," hit the same note in reprinting a widely circulated article by Aaron Epstein on the impending decision in the lawsuit that presented Jim's disability more in human interest terms than as the context for a precedent-setting ruling on assistance to students with disabilities. Such articles might focus, for example, on the work of sign language interpreters, not in terms of their varied roles in the classroom and in the school at large or the problems of interpreting speech into signed language in such challenging intellectual contexts as theology-based religion classes, but rather on the problem for the Constitution of a publicly funded sign interpreter translating Catholic doctrine. In such reporting, an opportunity was lost, just as it was lost in the way the court majority expressed its opinion, to raise the question of what resources and degrees of public support disabled students actually needed if mainstreaming were to be made a viable program.[16]

However, parents of disabled students in Jim's situation and those educators who faced the necessity of negotiating resources for students in private and parochial schools focused instead on the hope for a strong precedent that would clarify what was possible under law for assisting students with disabilities. Catholic educators seemed cautious in speaking about these hopes during the process of adjudication of the Zobrest lawsuit as if in fear of creating an anti-Catholic reaction. After the decision by the Supreme Court was announced, they expressed their opinions publicly. The superintendent of the Catholic schools of Erie, Pennsylvania, Sister Mary Arnold Tann, for example, told the Diocese of Erie's *Lake Shore Visitor*, which featured the Zobrests' story because of its local connections, that there were no deaf children in diocesan schools because "the cost of providing interpreters for them would be prohibitive." "In regards to the Zobrest case," she continued regarding disabled students, "I would like to see funding available to educate a child at the school of the parent's choice."[17] Catholic educators in Phoenix agreed. Mary Beth Mueller, the superintendent of the Diocese of Phoenix school system, which then had more than ten thousand students, explained that the diocese regularly turned away disabled students for whom it could not fund assistive services. The principal of Brophy Catholic High School in Phoenix, Fr. Robert Mathewson, made the same observation about his school but stated that he looked forward to the possibility that a decision for the Zobrests would open Catholic schools to more disabled students than could currently be accommodated.[18]

These were the same themes mentioned by individual parents contacting the Zobrests for advice in the wake of the decision. Sandi noted in a letter to William Bentley Ball four years after the court's decision that she still received "calls from parents all over the country who need information about how to get started in their fight against [public] school districts."[19] These were parents such as Mary Jo Green of Dallas, Texas, who wrote the Zobrests soon after the court announced its decision to explain how the lawsuit might aid Christopher, her hearing impaired four-year-old. He had been receiving publicly funded resources at a Catholic preschool. This assistance was removed at some time after public school district authorities discovered that the Zobrests had lost their appeal in the Ninth Circuit Court of Appeals. Green now anticipated it might be restored. She also marked the way in which the lawsuit worked as an inspiration for such parents. Encountering resistance from their local public school administrators, who invoked what appeared to parents to be vague legal precedents and complex legal processes, it was not surprising that parents were intimidated and that there was a temptation to give up the effort to attain assistance. Although she hoped for cooperation from those local administrators, she cited the Zobrests' "fortitude and courage" and added, "We certainly plan to fight hard for it."[20]

The court's decision, however, was not as definitive a guide for the future as these parents and Catholic educators hoped. As Justice Harry Blackmun noted with exasperation in his minority opinion, the majority was eager to reach its conclusion on the church-state issues without ever examining what the EAHCA/IDEA actually mandated in cases such as the Zobrest lawsuit. What the law, in fact, allowed was discretion on the part of school districts in the use of public funds for disabled students in parochial or secular private schools: school districts were not obliged to provide such resources but could if they were inclined to be of assistance to students like Jim.[21]

The law has gone through several changes since then. Revised in 1997, because of recognition by Congress of confusion as to what it actually said about assistance to students with disabilities in nonpublic schools, the law now narrowed the opportunity afforded students like Jim. It removed any sense of obligation, while not making it unlawful to provide resources in nonpublic schools for disabled students, and it provided parents of these students with the right to appeal only to a hearing officer. Today, the latest iteration of the EAHCA/IDEA (2011) appears somewhat more generous, at least formally. It mandates that a proportion of school budgets, determined by a fixed formula set by the U.S. Department of Education, must be given over to providing such assistance. What precisely the sum determined by that formula is used for, however, ultimately remains a matter to be determined by local public school administrators. They may choose, for example, to use all of the money for purposes such as private school teacher training in subjects that will educate these teachers to assist disabled students. If monies are made available for assistance to individual students, they are not automatically expended when a need is declared, but are subject to negotiation between local public school boards and parents, so that parents like the Greens may indeed have to struggle to receive what they believe their children require but to which they do not necessarily possess a legal entitlement.[22]

The federal courts themselves have reinforced this lack of clarity in the legal obligation to attend to the needs of disabled students enrolled in nonpublic schools since the *Zobrest* decision. In 1995 the Goodalls, the Virginia couple with the hearing impaired son whom they had wished to place in an Evangelical school with publicly provided assistive resources, took heart from the *Zobrest* decision and reinstituted their lawsuit against the local public school district. Their hopes for a different outcome, however, were denied by the Fourth Circuit Court of Appeals, and the U.S. Supreme Court again declined to review the case. Unlike the Zobrests, the Goodalls had the misfortune of having their case heard in courts in which the EAHCA/IDEA was adjudicated, and under that law, provision of such services was lawful but not mandatory. In fact, that the decision in *Zobrest* did not address the nature of the EAHCA/IDEA allowed the appellate court to take the same position that had worked against the Goodalls in their first lawsuit. Thus, although the situation of the Zobrests and the Goodalls was the same, the outcomes were diametrically opposed because of the different terms on which the issues were adjudicated. Also, the appeals court ruling, based on prior federal cases that it is not a burden on individuals when the state makes the practice of their religion more expensive for them—because their situation was the result of personal choice, not coercion imposed by the state—was a further blow to the Goodall case.[23]

That judicial thinking continues to stand, legitimizing refusals of local school districts to provide assistive resources in nonpublic schools. In 2016, when an Orthodox Jewish couple, Akiva and Shani Leiman, sued a Maryland school district for its refusal to provide such resources to their learning disabled daughter at a religious academy, the federal courts at both the district and appellate levels ruled against them on the grounds presented by local public school district administrators: the resources were available to them at public schools in the district. The Leimans had conceded that point but based their case on the ground of religious liberty, which the district school board was, in this instance, not obliged to respect.[24]

Yet such refusals did not necessarily represent the practice of all school boards, and observers needed to look no further than Catalina Foothills to see a counterexample. On the tenth anniversary of the *Zobrest* decision, the *Arizona Daily Star* approached Terry Downey, now the district's associate school superintendent, and other Catalina Foothills School District administrators to ask whether the line between public and parochial was still as bright in practice as it had been a decade before. The answer was that "a whole lot of gray" now characterized the practices of the district. Nancy Sargeant Abbate, the district's director of special education services, explained that as a consequence of the *Zobrest* decision, the district in the past school year had, in addition to visual impairment services, "offered orientation and mobility services, speech and occupational therapy and tutoring to about 25 parochial school students." Terry Downey had contended throughout the course of the lawsuit and in later interviews that out of a sense of responsibility to all students in the district, the school system would have been pleased to accommodate Jim wherever he went to high school. It would have done so, said Downey, had it not been for the decisions of the county attorney and the Arizona attorney general, which established that if it had done so, it would have been engaged in unlawful behavior that may have imperiled its access to federal education grants. She reiterated this sense of obligation on the tenth anniversary of the lawsuit the district lost. Pointing to the present cooperation of the district, parents, and the parochial schools, she said, "It's one more responsibility. They're our community's children and we're working together to make sure their needs are being met."[25]

But not all public school systems have judged the situation in the same light. The general logic of the 1982 *Rowley* Supreme Court decision—that disabled children are entitled to an education comparable to their nondisabled peers, but fiscal realism in fulfilling that mandate was a legitimate exercise of school board prudence—continues to guide school boards, which realistically must work within their budgets in deciding to what extent they will make money available for disabled students in religiously based schools. Moreover, the rapid proliferation of voucher programs in the states, by which public money is made available to individual children to attend schools of their parents' choice, including private religious schools, has added another element of complexity to the funding situation. A U.S. Government Accounting Office report released in September 2016 found that many private voucher school students with disabilities, though entitled to assistive services under the EAHCA/IDEA, were not getting them. In some instances, the voucher school administrators were found to be uninformed or confused about their responsibilities under the law, evidence perhaps that the rapid expansion of these programs in recent decades has outstripped the knowledge of the individuals in charge of them of their responsibilities under the law. In other instances, however, private voucher schools have unilaterally opted out of providing such services, arguing that the process of getting the monies available and of meeting a student's needs simply involved too many administrative difficulties.[26] Thus, it remains the case that access to public resources for disabled students in, or aspiring to be in, religious or secular private schools remains more or less at the discretion of local public school boards or in some instances of the schools they attend.

LOCAL OPINION AND POLITICS IN THE TUCSON AREA

In addition to the claim that the Catalina Foothills school system would have been willing to accommodate the Zobrests had it not been for the two opinions that it had received from local and state legal officials, Terry Downey stated at the time the lawsuit was in the courts that accommodating the Zobrests might well have created an angry, polarizing backlash among the local public about the diversion of public resources to a private religious school. She believed, in effect, that many parents, especially non-Catholics, would say to themselves, "Why should my tax money be diverted to help send someone attend a religious school?"[27] There was little sign of such public controversy over the issues, however, during the long course of the lawsuit from 1988 to 1993. Though it was acknowledged that the lawsuit had possibly significant constitutional implications, it was treated in the press and on television locally as a human interest story and hence emphasized, for example, either how Jim communicated or his basketball skills. After the decision, while there was a brief controversy over the financial settlement resulting from the decision, what was most notable about it, from a disability perspective, was what did *not* happen. Aside from individual private carping of the sort of which Larry Zobrest says he was aware at the time, there was never any *public* criticism of the implications of the court's decision for future practices, nor any stated public opposition to the Zobrests being compensated, or their attorneys being compensated, for their time and expenses.[28]

Opinions in the community that a student with a disability should not receive state assistance getting an education in a nonpublic school were wholly absent from local public discussion, as was evident in the absence of reactions to editorials in the two daily newspapers on opposite sides in evaluating the court decision. The *Arizona Daily Star* editorialized in support of the court's decision, stating that the lower courts had gotten the matter wrong from the beginning in neglecting to see the disability connections in the lawsuit. In supporting the rights of those with disabilities, said the newspaper, it was true that Jim had gotten access to public resources that had not been available before, but that was to the good. "Sometimes," the editorial concluded, "making things equal means giving some people something extra."[29] In the discussion of the court's decision, this was not only the sole public statement about the integration of people with disabilities that opened the question of what mainstreaming might actually require (an investment of public resources) and why it was necessary (for the sake of equality), but one that also bucked the national political trend away from providing government assistance to individuals. No angry letters to the editor protesting such strongly pro–social welfare views followed this statement. In light of the dislike of many late twentieth-century Americans for taxation and legal entitlements, and the widespread belief that government agencies and institutions regularly wasted and misused revenue derived from taxes, this is noteworthy in itself.

Similarly, a *Tucson Citizen* editorial, just after the Supreme Court hearing of the case in February, called for a decision against the Zobrests on the basis of church-state separation and for the use of public money exclusively to support public schools, but it also failed to prompt a more general community discussion on its *Letters to the Editor* page. No one responded to the editorial either to call for denying Jim resources or to approve of his getting them.[30]

In the absence of a politicized, vocal local response to the case, we may well see traces of emerging positive attitudes about the integration of people with disabilities into society, even though that integration often requires public resources to make mainstreaming a reality. In fact, by paying attention to what was *not* being said, such as the lack of a hostile response to these editorials, we may detect an emerging consciousness in the majority of nondisabled people of the need to make room in the public sphere for people with disabilities. That no one offered the public comment in the wake of the court's decision that Jim's deafness was his and his family's problem to confront, or that it was wrong to ask the public to pick up the bill for assisting him, may be the most telling evidence of all of local reaction.

What *was* said about the case, in one especially relevant cohort of the local population, was telling. Among students at Salpointe, there was outspoken support when they were asked to state their opinions by a reporter for the *Crusader*, the student newspaper. When the question was put to them in March 1993, as interested observers awaiting the court's decision, the six students who were asked strongly agreed that Jim, who had graduated the year before, should win his case on the basis of religious liberty and disability equality claims.[31] None of the six gave evidence of caring about, nor did they even acknowledge, theoretical or ideological apprehensions about the symbolic union of church and state in such funding arrangements that had bedeviled claims such as those the Zobrests had presented in the past in the courts. That fear of the appearance of a symbolic union had been invoked in court decisions in the past, especially in speaking about the impression that would be made on K–12 students. The justices had long considered the appearance of a symbolic union as a bad civics lesson for young people. Like most of the area's parents perhaps, the students were unaware of just what the state of church-state constitutional law was at the time, and perhaps, just as William Bentley Ball said in his unexpectedly humorous remarks during oral pleading at the Supreme Court, they thought more or less that it was "awesome" that Jim get the assistance he required. The matter resolved itself for them on practical equity grounds. Knowing Jim as they did—smart, earnest, friendly, and athletic—they could not see how abstract principles should get in the way of practical assistance to one hardworking deaf classmate. As sophomore Johnny Schultz said, Jim had the right to choose whatever school he wanted to go to and "shouldn't be at any disadvantage just because he is deaf. . . . He should have the same rights that we do."[32]

Even in this small sample of opinion, there is a suggestion of what mainstreaming accomplished for cohorts of nondisabled students who were now being exposed to peers with disabilities for the first time since the gradual implementation of the EAHCA. We have seen the difficulties Jim faced as a pioneer in mainstreaming, in return for which he got the type of education in the hearing world that his parents wanted for him and that he had come to want for himself. That came with a variety of difficulties, not the least of which was social marginalization in the community of the school. But the emerging new world of disability educational rights and inclusion had a significant basis not only in court decisions and laws, but also in the hearts and minds of people, especially young people. They were being exposed, as previous generations had not been, to disability through sharing space daily in school with peers with disabilities, whom to one extent or another they came to find much like themselves and worthy of dignity and respect. The limits of the situation were apparent, of course, for Jim remained at the fringe of the school community. Interpersonal relations were freighted with awkwardness and aversion, mostly because in Jim's case communication was difficult. But that his presence may have made a difference in creating a lasting feeling of support for opportunities for people with disabilities is certainly worthy of consideration.

The sole source of a local controversy that did result from the court's decision had nothing to do with the Constitution or directly with assistance to Jim Zobrest. It arose instead from the fact that the court's decision neglected to address the matter at the heart of the lawsuit: the compensation to which the Zobrests might be entitled for the approximately $34,000 they had paid to the sign language interpreters who had assisted Jim during his four years at Salpointe. (Compensation for the cost of tuition at Salpointe was not and had never been in contention; it was universally acknowledged to be impossible under the law; Jim could not go to a Catholic high school at public expense.) The newsletter of the national Catholic League, while celebrating the court's recent decision, pointed to the very real possibility that the Zobrests might "not have seen the last of courts and judges just yet."[33] Furthermore, though it was not a matter that the Supreme Court would have addressed explicitly under any circumstance, there were also the legal fees of both parties that needed to be confronted. The board had spent about $90,000 employing John Richardson and his associates and also, as the usual obligation of the losing party to a lawsuit, owed more than double that sum to Ball and Berning, who had waived their fees and worked on a pro bono basis during the course of the lawsuit but now had claims, should they choose to make them, on the losing side for compensation.[34] These questions did not excite constitutional discussion nor criticism or defense of the Zobrests but were argued on grounds familiar to late twentieth- and early twenty-first-century political and ideological discourse: populist anti-elitism and distrust of public bureaucracies and the experts who headed them. Though for very different reasons, there was an undercurrent of discontent about the public schools that united the Zobrests, who had rejected those schools in 1988, with the local politicians who were questioning how the Zobrests were to be compensated for the costs of Jim's sign interpreter. No one directly involved with the case or observing it from the general community questioned whether they should be paid or argued for continued litigation of this question.

Both sets of counsels agreed that further litigation on these questions would be expensive and time-consuming and agreed to a figure that represented the compensation of Ball and Berning. The school district paid the Zobrests for the costs of four years of sign interpretation at Salpointe directly out of its budget, and this enabled Sandi, in turn, to compensate the individuals, institutions, and organizations that had given them money during 1988–92 to cover that expense. This left the school district with the problem of coming up with the money to compensate Berning and Ball, who adjusted their compensation at a lower figure than their estimate of $210,000 for their time over the course of five years. (The board's counsel, John Richardson, had already been compensated.) The sum ultimately agreed to in toto for Berning and Ball was $98,500.[35]

Already concerned about declining state support to school districts throughout Arizona that appeared likely to impose a $50,000 cut ($15 per student in the district) in the next year's budget, the school board sought help from the county Board of Supervisors. Under Arizona law, in order to avoid depriving students of educational resources, it was permissible for a school district fearing fiscal problems in consequence of a lawsuit to ask the county Board of Supervisors to levy a one-time tax on homeowners to raise the necessary sum. In this case, the size of the levy would burden the average homeowner possessing a house valued at around $150,000 approximately $6.50. The board approved the financial terms for the settlement of the lawsuit but, backed by the *Tucson Citizen*, the three-member Republican majority on the board initially took exception to the school board's request for the tax levy on the ground that a wealthy district like Catalina Foothills should not have to depend on taxpayers to solve special problems of this type.[36]

What's noteworthy for our purposes is that the question of the Zobrests' right to compensation for the costs of sign language interpretation over four years and the needs of a disabled student did not come into question, even among those fiscal conservatives wary of extensions of rights by court decree that ended up creating expensive mandates and entitlements. The *Tucson Citizen* editorialized that the school district was in the middle of "a mess of its own creation." "It seems strange that Catalina had enough money to fight Zobrest for five years, but not enough to cover the debt it now owes him." The school district's budget was $15.8 million, the newspaper noted, so $100,000 should be no problem. Marshalling heavy sarcasm, the paper challenged the professional employees of the district: "Why not skip a few of those academic blab fests that teachers and administrators love to attend? Or take a one-time cut from the school administrators' salaries? Or eliminate a day's worth of vacation time from the generous perks given to teachers?"[37] Ed Moore, the Republican chair of the board known for his outspoken criticisms of government waste, agreed: "More money from government is not the answer." If the school board, with its large budget, could not find the money, Moore said, "I'll find it for them. If they don't want me to do it, we'll send over a couple of five-year-olds."[38]

The school board and district administrators advanced a successful defense of their position, pointing out, as did Terry Downey in an interview, what the obligation to pay these legal costs combined with a decline in state allocations would mean—the loss of three teachers—in terms of cutbacks to core educational needs. To the argument that it should not have gotten itself into the position it was in, board member Charlotte Ackerman explained that the board had no choice, because the points at law were important, and, under any circumstance, by exercising their right to sue and then to appeal, the Zobrests had extended the school board's financial obligation, the closest anyone came to laying the fault for the situation on the plaintiffs in the lawsuit.[39] Taking the position that it was better to err on the side of supporting the district's students, Republican supervisor Mike Boyd switched his vote, and the tax levy was approved after he joined the two Democrats on the board when the matter was reheard. The political contentions over Catalina Foothills School District's obligations then faded from public view.[40]

That little of this struggle had to do with the basic question of services outside the public schools for students with disabilities is testified to by the fact that, in the next decade, the district took up the obligation to support them, wherever they were locally enrolled.

JIM ZOBREST AND HIS FAMILY IN THE AFTERMATH

In 2015, Sandi Zobrest returned as a tourist with her friend Mary Prus to the Supreme Court for the first time since the court's hearing in the Zobrest lawsuit twenty-two years earlier. It was an occasion less for nostalgia than for stocktaking about what an ordinary American family had accomplished in seeking justice. She was reminded of that accomplishment by employees of the court. She casually mentioned that she had been there once before as a litigant, and they told her how reluctant the court was to review lower court decisions and how much rarer it was to encounter someone who had played that role, let alone won the case.[41] Of course, the lawsuit and the family's day in court have never been far from the Zobrests' collective consciousness. Though William Bentley Ball is no longer alive to congratulate them after Supreme Court decisions in which their lawsuit is cited as a precedent or is the subject of a law review essay, from time to time eminent popular writers on the court and the First Amendment have reminded them: the journalist Aaron Epstein has written about the lawsuit, and later the constitutional law scholars Peter Irons and Robert S. Alley have anthologized the pleadings and the decision in volumes of notable First Amendment cases. Epstein went to Tucson to interview the Zobrests as sources for telling their own story and highlighted, in doing so, their place in history.[42] Closer to home, the case forms a unit of instruction in Marco Enriquez's civil rights and civil liberties class at Salpointe.[43] Sandi has accumulated a significant personal archive on the lawsuit that she keeps at her home and continues to sort through from time to time.

The story of the lawsuit has not remained the same for the Zobrests over time. The arrangement and the relevance of the facts—from Sandi's emotional confrontation in the spring of 1988 with Terry Downey and Robert Hetzel, in which she was told that Jim would not get the assistance from the Catalina Foothills School District at Salpointe, to the phone call she received from William Bentley Ball in June 1993 informing her of the U.S. Supreme Court's positive decision—have not changed. The highpoints of that five-year journey through the courts, such as Judge Bilby's perfunctory judgment in the case in federal district court, or Sandi's and Ball's individual letters to the Ninth Circuit Court of Appeals judges urging them to hear the case once and for all, are well-remembered and well-rehearsed symbolic vignettes of her narrative of those five years of struggling for justice. So, too, are the details of the personal sacrifices and financial difficulties that accompanied raising the money to pay for Jim's educational resources, such as the contacts with the generous people and foundations, locally and throughout the nation, that contributed to help the Zobrests.

What has changed instead is the ultimate meaning, the core goal, of that journey through the courts, which has taken on a different emphasis over time. For the Supreme Court and for William Bentley Ball, the lawsuit the Zobrests initiated was about the meaning of the Establishment Clause of the First Amendment to the Constitution. Moreover, while religious liberty itself was not litigated, the Zobrests' Catholicism and choice of a Catholic education for Jim certainly formed an implicit legal foundation for the lawsuit and, in an even larger sense, for their moral legitimacy as litigants. While their explanation of their motivation tended to be inconsistent, they generally accepted this logic at the time and often explained themselves in those terms. "First of all," Sandi told the *Arizona Daily Star* in 1992, explaining the decision to send Jim to Salpointe and fight for the resources to keep him there, "we are Catholics, and we wanted him . . . to attend a Catholic school."[44] Of course, this line of explanation also served both the direction of the argument that William Bentley Ball wished to advance and Ball's long-term strategy on behalf of public resources for Catholic parochial schools. But one doubts it had to be urged upon the Zobrests. It certainly suited Ball's efforts among Catholic individuals and institutions to raise funds to finance the litigation to stress that the Zobrests were "faithful Catholics" who "testify well to their religious faith."[45] The language he used in his efforts was influential in the Zobrests' own fund-raising appeals. From the beginning of their search for a high school for Jim to their decision to seek justice through the courts, the virtues of *Catholic* schooling were integral to their decisions. Besides, if one were around Ball, one almost naturally felt more Catholic because of his overwhelming enthusiasm for the religion and its institutions, his love for its rituals and belief in the promise they held for Catholics, and his singlemindedness in pursuing rights for Catholics.

To that extent, from a disability perspective, disability became at least publicly the servant of another agenda in the Zobrest lawsuit. For the Zobrests over time, however, their view of their aspirations and what they had accomplished changed in its emphasis, and disability and mainstreaming came to be more central to an understanding of what they had sought and accomplished.

In part, this reevaluation may have been indirectly shaped by their reevaluation of their Catholicism. Whatever feelings to seek religion he may have had as an adolescent, Jim has never really taken to it. As a student at Salpointe, he chose not to attend Mass, and he has remained religiously indifferent as an adult. Sandi, on the other hand, greatly appreciates the value of religion and of a certain amount of devotionalism in her life. She feels that her adult life has been an unrelenting struggle, especially to assist Jim, and she takes comfort in faith amid that struggle. But she came to feel alienated from the religion into which she was born and indoctrinated as a girl in Catholic schools in Pittsburgh and at Mercyhurst College in Erie, and she eventually came to define herself as a "non-practicing Catholic."[46] She was pushed in that direction by the feeling that the suburban parish where she had attended Mass for some years was pervaded by a type of formality and social snobbishness she disliked. In contrast, she experienced democratic feeling and warm spirituality while looking for alternatives at the Grace to the Nations, a nondenominational Evangelical congregation, fusing Anglo and Hispanic communities and Catholic and Protestant practices, that met in a rented space in a shopping mall.[47] In this, she parallels the course of religious evolution of many older ethnic stock Catholics who have left the Catholic Church and, more generally, of many Americans among those baby boomers who came to be known as "seekers" and who in recent decades have embarked on a pursuit of the spiritual along many different paths. They seek a personal relationship with God that feels authentic and is sustaining. They have much less concern about where, in the sense of denomination and doctrine or physical setting, they may find it than have previous generations of Americans.[48]

But this disaffection from or, on Jim's part, ultimately indifference to Roman Catholicism is only part of the source of the changing emphasis the Zobrests have come to bring to their story. Sandi says today that in their struggle for justice, Jim represented the deaf, who are to be sure far from united around the mainstreaming goals the Zobrests adopted, but she does not reference his representation of Catholics. Moreover, if Sandi says today that when that struggle began, "I thought this was just about a deaf kid who liked to play basketball and wanted to go to a Catholic high school," in that order, she emphasizes, not religious liberty, but instead Jim as a "deaf kid" seeking to find his way in the world, with his own talents and ambitions, who needed encouragement and assistance if they were to be realized.[49] Deafness, as a disabling condition in the world—in other words, as a literal *handicap* in the various competitions constituting life in America that serves to limit opportunities and curb aspirations—was at the center of the Zobrest family's existence then and has remained so over the last three decades. Religion may wax and wane in the life of the Zobrest family, but deafness and disability are always there. Jim's future continues to be, at one level, a family project for the Zobrests, even as Jim has entered his mid-forties.

Jim's adult life has not been easy. Never at home in the Deaf community, the ASL signers who identify with Deaf history and culture, he does not sign its language fluently or identify with its history and its ideologies or the struggles over language and pedagogy that have defined it. He has not found it possible, however, to enter the world of the hearing. He received a cochlear implant as an adult but ended up unplugging it after nine months. He stored the expensive technology away, perhaps never to be used again. Like many people born with very little hearing, he found it difficult to process the diversity of sounds made available to him, imperfectly rendered by the implant technology under the best of circumstances. The hearing aids he had worn for years continued to prove more effective in assisting him to use what limited hearing he has. The ambitions of his adolescence—to play college basketball in a Division I institution and to have a career in movie production—were not realized. Jim dropped out of his community college, where he did not play basketball, and has never obtained a B.A.[50] He has had a series of unchallenging jobs, none of which seems to make use of his intelligence and none of which has amounted to an investment in creating a career. In this, he is not unlike most other hearing impaired people. In 2014, when the Zobrests began to make plans to relocate once more, 47 percent of people between twenty-one and sixty-four years of age with hearing impairments, including the profoundly deaf, were out of the labor force, and another 4.6 percent had been working but were then unemployed.[51] Jim has worked in his relatives' real estate business, had data entry jobs, and at one time had his own small dog-walking business. At times, his hearing impairment was explicitly a factor in limiting his employment options, as was the case when one employer did not want to take on the burden of having a sign language interpreter around to assist Jim. Sandi and Jim sought the assistance of the Arizona Department of Economic Security's Vocational Rehabilitation Services but experienced repeated delays getting an appointment, let alone real help. As they entered their late sixties, and Sandi says she hoped life would slow down, Sandi, Larry, Jim, and Sam, his wife, and their three children relocated to North Carolina in 2017 in the hope that Jim would get some assistance there in finding work. They will continue to live close by each other, as they did in Arizona. In the meantime, relatives in North Carolina will help them resettle. It is a recognized pattern in their lives, recapitulating their move four decades ago from Erie to Tucson, where they also joined relatives, when they resettled half the country away in search of better educational opportunities for Jim.[52] What stays the same is the struggle to overcome the limitations that are imposed, by design or indifference, by the hearing world.

The U.S. Supreme Court did not choose in 1993 to speak directly to those limitations, the larger context of the Zobrest lawsuit. To that extent, what benefits there have been in the decision for the hearing impaired and other students with disabilities have been incidental to the main thrust of the court's purpose, the long-standing issue of the height of the wall of separation between religion and government. Of course, the court is constrained to rule on the issues placed before it. Though there is a tradition in the court of not rushing to judgment about what the Constitution says in fear of causing doctrinal confusion, this case progressed unrelentingly toward that end. Both sets of attorneys were united, along with the Pima County district attorney and Arizona attorney general, Judge Bilby in the U.S. District Court of Southern Arizona, and a two-judge majority in the Ninth Circuit Court of Appeals, in presenting the issues in the case as church-state issues and not investigating its disability dimension. A perplexed Justice Blackmun asked in his dissent about what the EAHCA/IDEA actually said about claims such as those made by the Zobrests and challenged the majority to figure that out before ruling in the case. Yet, inadequate as the judicial reasoning process may seem, the decision and the related decisions it influenced, notably *Agostini v. Felton*, and the larger descriptions of Jim's mainstreamed high school experience the media brought to coverage of the lawsuit have done students with disabilities as well as poor and minority students a great deal of good, if unevenly. To that extent, the Zobrests were agents of significant social change, and their struggle for justice, as they have increasingly come to conceive of it—as above all else a contribution to the advancement of students with disabilities—is inseparable from the narrative of the ongoing struggle of people with disabilities and without disabilities for equality and opportunity alongside other Americans.

APPENDIX 1
FEDERAL COURT DECISIONS CITING THE *ZOBREST v. CATALINA FOOTHILLS SCHOOL DISTRICT* DECISION

United States Supreme Court

Board of Education of Kiryas Joel Village School District v. Grumet, 1145 S. Ct. 2481, 2498+. June 27, 1994.§
Rosenberger v. Rector and Visitors of the University of Virginia, 115 S. Ct. 2510, 2526+. June 29, 1995.*
Agostini v. Felton, 117 S. Ct. 1997, 2001+. June 23, 1997.†
City of Chicago v. International College, 118 S. Ct. 523, 527+. December 15, 1997.#
Columbia College v. Clarke, 119 S. Ct. 2357, 2358. June 14, 1999.†
Mitchell v. Helms, 120 S. Ct. 2350, 2531+. June 28, 2000†
Zelman v. Simmons-Harris, 122 S. Ct. 2460, 2465+. June 27, 2002.†
Locke v. Davey, 124 S. Ct. 1307, 1311. February 25, 2004.†
Van Orden v. Perry, 125 S. Ct. 2854, 2861. June 27, 2005.*

Federal District and Appellate Courts

Gonzales v. North Township of Lake County, Indiana, 4 F.3d 1412, 1419+, 7th Cir. (IN). September 10, 1993.*
Pifl v. Massachusetts Department of Education, 9F.3d 184, 189+, 1st Cir. (MA). November 16, 1993.‖

Source: *Westlaw Services*
Key:
* Church-state establishment clause issues or religious liberty issues (non-education)
† Church-state in education
§ Church-state and disability in education
‖ Disability and education, without church-state connection
\# Federal government jurisdictional or procedural question

Hedges v. Wauconda Community Unit School District No. 118, 9 F.3d 1295, 1297, 7th Cir. (IL). November 23, 1993.†

Hawley v. City of Cleveland, 24 F.3d 814, 822+, 5th Cir. (OH). May 18, 1994.*

Brown v. Woodland Joint United School District, 27 F 3d 1373, 1382, 9th Cir. (CA). June 15, 1994.†

Harris v. Joint School District, No. 241, 41 F.3d 447, 456+, 9th Cir. (ID). November 18, 1994.†

Walker v. San Francisco Unified School District, 46 F.3d 1449, 1458+, 9th Cir. (CA). January 30, 1995.† [As continued in 62 F.3d 300, 303+, 9th Cir. (CA). August 2, 1995.]

Goodall by Goodall v. Stafford County School Board, 60 F.3d 168, 170+, 4th Cir. (VA). July 27, 1995.§

Federal Election Commission v. Survival Educational Fund, Inc., 65 F.3d 285, 290. 2nd Cir. (NY). September 12, 1995.#

Hsu By and through Hsu v. Roslyn Union Free School District No.3, 85 F.3d 839, 864, 2nd Cir. (NY). September 12, 1995.†

Miller v. Benson, 68 F.3d 163, 164, 7th Cir. (WI). October 6, 1995.†

Hartmann v. Stone, 68 F.3d 973, 987, 6th Cir. (KY). November 2, 1995.*

People v. Materne, 72 F.3d 103,106, 9th Cir. (Guam). December 12, 1995.#

Hamilton v. Schriro, 74 F.3d 1545, 1559+, 8th Cir. (MO). (January 12, 1996)*

U.S. v. Cusumano, 83 F.3d 1247, 1251+. 10th Cir. (WY). May 8, 1996.#

Russman by Russman v. Sobol, 85 F.3d 1050, 1053+, 2nd Cir. (NY). June 12, 1996.§

Cefalu on behalf of Cefalu v. East Baton Rouge Parish School Board, 103 F.3d 393, 395+, 5th Cir. (LA). January 3, 1997.§

Stark v. Independent School District, No. 640, 123 F.3d 1968, 1076+, 8th Cir. (MN). August 21, 1997.†

Rojas v. Fitch, 127 F3d 184,189, 1st Cir. (RI). October 9, 1997.*

Thomas R.W. By and Through Pamela R. v. Massachusetts Dept. of Edu., 130 F3d 477 478+, 1st Cir. (MA). November 17, 1997.‖

Peck by Peck v. Lansing School District, 148 F.3d 619, 622+, 6th Cir. (MI). June 29, 1998.§

Russman v. Board of Education of City of Watervliet, 150 F.3d 219, 220+, 2nd Cir. (NY). May 15, 1998.‖

Helms v. Picard, 152 F.3d 347, 355+, 5th Cir. (LA). August 17, 1998.†

Peter v. Wedl, 155 F.3d 992, 997, 8th Cir. (MN). September 15, 1998.§ [As continued in *Peter v. Jax*, 187 F.3d 829, 831+, 8th Cir. (MN). August 13, 1999.]

Doe v. Sante Fe Independent School District, 168 F.3d 806, 831, 5th Cir. (TX), February 26. 1999.†

Doe ex rel. Doe v. Beaumont Independent School District, 173 F.3d 274, 288, 5th Cir. (TX). April 19, 1999.†

Adler v. Duval County School Board, 174 F.3d 1236, 1270, 11th Cir. (FL). May 11, 1999.† [As continued in *Adler v. Duval County School Board*, 206 F.3d 1070, 1089, 11th Cir. (FL). March 15, 2000.]

Strout v. Albanese, 178 F.3d 57, 61+, 1st Cir. (ME). May 27, 1999.†

Coles ex rel Coles v. Cleveland Board of Education, 183 F.3d 538, 539, 6th Cir. (OH). June 11, 1999.*

KDM ex rel WJM v. Reedsport School District, 196 F.3d 1046.1050+, 9th Cir. (OR). November 15, 1999.§

Johnson v. Economic Development Corporation of County of Oakland, 241 F.3d 501, 509+, 6th Cir. (MI). February 27, 2001.†

Doe v. Beaumont Independent School District, 240 F.3d 462, 481, 5th Cir. (TX). January 26, 2001.†

DeStefano v. Emergency Housing Group, Inc., 247 F.3d 397, 414+, 2nd Cir. (NY). April 20, 2001.*

Columbia Union College v. Oliver, 254 F.3d 496, 500+. 4th Cir. (MD). June 26, 2001.†

Independent School District No. 284 v. A.C., by and through her parent, C.C., 258 F.3d 769, 775. 8th Cir. (MN). August 3, 2001.†

Knight v. Connecticut Department of Health, 275 F.3d 156, 165+, 2nd Cir. (NY). April 20, 2001.*

Steele v. Industrial Development Board of Metropolitan Government Nashville, 301 F.3d 401, 406+, 6th Cir. (TN). August 14, 2002.†

Maine School Administrative District No. 35 v. Mr. R., 321 F.3d 9, 14, 1st Cir. (ME). February 24, 2003.‖

Nieves-Marquez v. Puerto Rico, 353 F.3d 108, 116. 1st Cir. (Puerto Rico). December 24, 2003.‖

American Jewish Congress v. Corporation for National and Community Service, 399 F.3d 351, 356. D.C. Cir., March 8, 2005.*

Republican Party of Minnesota v. White, 456 F.3d 912, 919. 8th Cir. (MN). June 20, 2006.#

U.S. v. Vilches-Navarrete, 523 F.3d 1, 23, 1st Cir. (Puerto Rico). April 10, 2008.#

Brotherhood of Locomotive Engineers and Trainmen General Committee of Adjustment, Central Region v. Union Pacific Railroad Corporation, 522 F.3d 746, 750, 7th Cir. (IL). April 9, 2008.#

Winn v. Arizona Christian School Tuition Organization, 562 F.3d 1002, 1016+, 9th Cir. (AZ). October 21, 2009.† [As continued in 586 F.3d 649, 652+, 9th Cir. (AZ). October 21, 2009.]

American Atheists, Inc. v. City of Detroit Downtown Development Authority, 567 F.3d 278, 289, 6th Cir. (MI). May 28, 2009.*

Herandez v. Astrue, 380 F. App'x 699, 702, 9th Cir. (AZ). May 28, 2010.#

U.S. v. Tennessee, 615 F.3d 646, 657+, 6th Cir. (TN). August 4, 2010.#

A.M. ex rel Marshall v. Monrovia Unified School District, 627 F.3d 773, 782, December 15, 2010.‖

Doe ex rel. Doe v. Elmbrook School District, 658 F.3d 710, 730+, 7th Cir. (WI). September 9, 2011.*

Grote v. Sebelius, 707 F.3d 850, 862, 7th Cir. (IN). January 30, 2013.*

Rubin v. City of Lancaster, 710 F.3d 1087, 1099, 9th Cir. (CA). March 26, 2013.*

Williams v. California, 764 F.3d 1014, 9th Cir. (CA) August 19, 2014.§

Smith v. Jefferson County Board of School Commissioners, 788 F.3d 580, 593, 6th Cir. (TN). June 11, 2015.†

Brumfield v. Louisiana State Board of Education, 806 F.3d 289, 300+, 5th Cir. (LA). November 10, 2015.§

PHH Corporation v. Consumer Financial Protection Bureau, 839 F.3d 1, 58+, D.C. Cir., October 11, 2016.#

M.K., et al. v. Joshua Starr, et al., 185 F Supp. 3d, 679, 4th Cir. (MD). May 5, 2016.§

APPENDIX 2
INTERVIEWS*

Terek Amin, March 18, 2017 (telephone)
Caroline Ball, May 29, 2015 (telephone)
Virginia Ball Duncan, May 22, 2015, August 16, 2016 (in-person, Camp Hill, Pennsylvania)
Thomas Berning, June 24, 2015 (in-person, Tucson, Arizona)
Mark Bruenkant, November 7, 2015 (telephone)
Camille Shadegg Catsaros, January 11, 2017 (telephone)
Kim Chumley, June 26, 2015 (in-person, Tucson, Arizona)
Richard Connell, May 22, 2015 (in-person, Camp Hill, Pennsylvania)
Rose Daly-Rooney, June 25, 2015 (in-person, Tucson, Arizona)
Terry Downey, June 23, 2015 (in-person, Catalina Foothills, Arizona)
Sandy Duncan, March 5, 2016 (questionnaire)†
Brett Dunkelman, September 25, 2015 (telephone)
Denise Jensen Erickson, March 14, 2016 (telephone)
Bruce Goldstein, February 11, 2016 (telephone)
Derek Hersha, March 21, 2017 (telephone)

---

* Transcripts (or in a few instances written notes) of these interviews or, when used as an alternative to oral interviews, written questionnaires are available in the office of Professor Bruce Dierenfield at Canisius College in Buffalo, New York. Oral interviews and questionnaires were supplemented in the case of almost all the informants with emails soliciting more information. The emails are in the possession of Bruce Dierenfield and David Gerber.

† The authors conducted an interview of approximately five hours with the Zobrests at their home. Sandi Zobrest signed for Jim Zobrest and translated his signing during the course of the interview. Jim Zobrest also answered some of our questions with oral speech.
Other communication with our two deaf informants, Jim Zobrest and Sandy Duncan, were done through a questionnaire or by email.

Robert Hetzel, February 8, 2016 (telephone)
Chris Koester, December 2, 2016 (telephone)
Patty and Richard McBride, April 4, 2016 (telephone)
Philip Murren, May 22, 2015, August 16, 2016 (in-person, Camp Hill, Pennsylvania)
Mary Prus, February 22, 2017 (telephone)
John C. Richardson, June 24, 2015 (in-person, Tucson, Arizona)
Salpointe faculty and administration (Sister Helen Timothy, Kay Sullivan, Jim Flannery), June 25, 2015 (in-person, Tucson, Arizona)
Jim Santeford, August 21, 2015, November 23, 2015, July 14, 2016 (questionnaires)
JoAnn Sheperd, November 30, 2015 (telephone)
Francis Viglietta, February 9, 2017 (telephone)
James Weinstein, February 14, 2016 (telephone)
Mary Rita Wechsler, July 15, 2016 (questionnaire)
Zobrest family interview, Sandi Zobrest, Larry Zobrest, Jim Zobrest, Sam Zobrest), June 23, 2015 (in-person, Catalina Foothills, Arizona)*
Sam Zobrest, January 30, 2017 (telephone)

NOTES

INTRODUCTION

1. Douglas Baynton, "Disability and the Justification of Inequality in American History," in *The New Disability History: American Perspectives*, ed. Paul K. Longmore and Lauri Umansky (New York: New York University Press, 2001), 52.

2. Catherine Kudlick, "Review Essay: Disability History: Why We Need Another 'Other,'" *American Historical Review* 108 (June 2003): 763–93.

3. *Zobrest v. Catalina Foothills School District*, 509 U.S. 1 (1993).

4. All references to the Zobrests' narrative, as they related it to the authors, are derived from two types of sources: a long oral history interview with Larry, Sandi, Jim, and Sam, done at the family home in Tucson, Arizona, on June 23, 2015; and email correspondence with Sandi, Jim, and Sam Zobrest periodically over approximately three years. Unless otherwise indicated, all references to the Zobrests that assume their perspectives and memories are to the oral history interview. This and the other oral history interviews were done under the guidance of the Institutional Review Board protocols of Canisius College, Buffalo, New York. Transcriptions and permissions forms are in the office of Professor Bruce Dierenfield at Canisius College.

5. Mitchell Yell, Antonis Katsiyannis, and M. Renee Bradley, "The Individuals with Disabilities Education Act: The Evolution of Special Education Law," *Handbook of Special Education*, ed. James M. Kauffman and Daniel P. Hallahan (New York: Routledge, 2011), 61.

6. Audra Jennings, *Out of the Horrors of War: Disability Politics in World War II America* (Philadelphia: University of Pennsylvania Press, 2016).

7. Lennard Davis, *Enabling Acts: The Hidden Story of How the Americans with Disabilities Act Gave the Nation's Largest US Minority Its Rights* (Boston: Beacon Press, 2015); Fred Pelka, *What We Have Done: An Oral History of the Disability Rights Movement* (Amherst: University of Massachusetts Press, 2012); Doris Zames

Fleischer and Frieda Zames, *The Disability Rights Movement: From Charity to Confrontation* (Philadelphia: Temple University Press, 2011); John B. Christiansen and Sharon N. Barnett, *Deaf President Now: The 1988 Revolution at Gallaudet University* (Washington, D.C.: Gallaudet University Press, 2003); Richard Scotch, *From Good Will to Civil Rights: Transforming Federal Disability Policy* (Philadelphia: Temple University Press, 1984); Margret A. Winzer, *From Isolation to Integration to Inclusion: A History of Special Education in the Twentieth Century* (Washington, D.C.: Gallaudet University Press, 2009), 118, 126–27.

8. "Education for All Handicapped Children Act," Pub.L. No. 94-142, 89 Stat. 773 (1975), codified as amended at 20 U.S.C.A. 1400–1485 (1990) and as the "Individuals with Disabilities Education Act," Pub.L. No. 121-476, 104 Stat. 1141 (1990), codified as 20 U.S.C.A. 1400 (a) (1990); Yell, Katsiyannis, and Bradley, "Individuals with Disabilities Education Act," 62.

9. "Enforcing the Right to an 'Appropriate' Education: The Education for All Handicapped Children Act of 1975," *Harvard Law Review* 92/5 (March 1979), 1103–27; 3 chapters in Kauffman and Hallahan, *Handbook of Special Education*: Mitchell Yell and Jean B. Crockett, "Free Appropriate Education," 77–90; Barbara D. Bateman, "Individual Education Programs for Children with Disabilities," 91–106; and Michel Rozalski, Jason Miller, and Angie Stewart, "Least Restrictive Environment," 107–19; Andrew M. I. Lee, J. D., "Individuals with Disabilities Education Act (IDEA): What You Need to Know," https://www.understood.org/en/school-learning/your-childs-rights/basics-about-childs-rights/individuals-with-disabilities-education-act-idea-what-you-need-to-know (accessed Aug. 8, 2018); Margaret Winzer, *The History of Special Education: From Isolation to Integration* (Washington, D.C.: Gallaudet University Press, 1993).

10. *Board of Education of the Hendrick Hudson Central School District v. Rowley*, 458 U.S. 176; Robert C. Smith, *A Case about Amy* (Philadelphia: Temple University Press, 1996); Dena Kleiman, "First Deaf Lawyer Goes before the Supreme Court," *New York Times*, March 24, 1982; Amy June Rowley, "*Rowley* Revisited: A Personal Narrative," *Journal of Law and Education* 37/3 (July 2008): 311–28.

11. Office of Educational Research and Improvement, *State Comparisons of Education Statistics: 1969–70 to 1996–97* (Washington, D.C.: United States Department of Education, 1998), 31, 33.

12. Joyce Martin, "Special Education and the Non-Public School Child: A Handicap is a Non-Sectarian Condition," *Law and Inequality: A Journal of Theory and Practice* 5/3 (Jan. 1988): 561–62.

13. Richard J. Murname and Sean F. Reardon, "Long Term Trends in Private School Enrollments by Family Income," AERA *Open* 4/1 (Jan.–March 2018): 3; Carol Ann McGregor, "Why the Decline of Catholic Schools Matters," Scholars Strategy Network, Mar. 2, 2013, https://scholars.org/contribution/why-decline-catholic-schools-matters (accessed Aug. 8, 2018).

14. Martin, "Special Education and the Non-Public School Child," 562–66; *School District of Grand Rapids v. Ball*, 473 U.S. 373 (1985); *Aguilar v. Felton*, 105 U.S. 3232 (1985).

15. We use the now-conventional capital *D* for the word *deaf* when discussing deafness as the source of a culture, group identity, and the center of a disability ideology. On mainstreaming, see, for example, Claire L. Ramsey, *Deaf Children in Public Schools: Placement, Context, and Consequences* (Washington, D.C.: Gallaudet University Press, 1997); Irene W. Leigh, *A Lens on Deaf Identities* (New York: Oxford University Press, 2009), 67–86; Linda Watson and Stephen Powers, eds., *Deaf and Hearing Impaired Pupils in the Mainstream*, rev. ed. (Abington, U.K.: Routledge, 2016).

16. This rethinking is summarized in and epitomized by Anthony S. Bryk, Valerie E. Lee, and Peter B. Holland, *Catholic Schools and the Common Good* (Cambridge: Harvard University Press, 1993) from research done throughout the decade of the 1980s in a variety of American communities.

17. The History of Salpointe Catholic High School, http://www.k12academics.co./national-directories/catholic-school/salpointe-catholic-high-school (accessed June 3, 2015); "Reverend Leo McCarthy" (obituary), *Arizona Daily Star*, Nov. 25, 2009. Jim Flannery, Sister Helen Timothy, and Kay Sullivan, interview, June 25, 2015; Denise Jensen Erickson, interview, March 14, 2016.

18. Terry Downey, interview, June 23, 2015; Robert Hetzel, interview, Feb. 8, 2016.

19. John C. Richardson, interview, June 24, 2015; John Richardson to David Gerber, emails, July 10, Oct. 23, 26, 2015.

20. The trend of Supreme Court decisions in the late twentieth century is conveniently summarized in Ronald Flowers, *That Godless Court? Supreme Court Decisions of Church-State Relations*, 2nd ed. (Louisville: Westminster John Knox Press, 2005).

21. *Cochran v. Louisiana State Board of Education*, 281 U.S. 370 (1930); *Board of Education v. Allen*, 392 U.S. 236 (1968); *Everson v. Board of Education*, 330 U.S. 1 (1947).

22. *Lemon v. Kurtzman*, 403 U.S. 602 (1971).

23. Both Sandi Zobrest and Robert Hetzel remember this meeting in similar ways; Zobrest family interview, June 23, 2015; Robert Hetzel, interview, Feb. 8, 2016.

24. Andrew Solomon, *Far from the Tree: Parents, Children, and the Search for Identity* (New York: Scribner, 2012).

25. Sandi Zobrest to David Gerber, emails, Sept. 15, 2015, Feb. 15, 2016.

26. David M. Engel, "The Oven Bird's Song: Insiders, Outsiders, and Personal Injuries in an American Community," *Law and Society Review* 18/4 (1984), 551–82, "Law, Culture, and Children with Disabilities: Educational Rights and the Construction of Difference," *Duke Law Journal* 25/1 (Feb. 1991): 166–205, and *The Myth of the Litigious Society: Why We Don't Sue* (Chicago: University of Chicago Press, 2016).

27. Engel, "Law, Culture, and Children with Disabilities," 195–201; Carol Gilligan, *In a Different Voice: Psychological Theory and Women's Development* (Cambridge: Harvard University Press, 1982).

28. Totaling hundreds of pages, there were twenty-eight friend-of-the court briefs supporting the Catalina Foothills School District's position on antireligious establishment and religious liberty grounds, while eighteen briefs supported the Zobrests' case.

29. Rob Boston to David Gerber, email, Oct. 8, 2015.

30. Rob Boston, "Hearing Problems: Why a Deaf Student's Supreme Court Case Has Church-State Separationists Worried," *Church & State* 46/2 (Feb. 1993): 4–8.

31. Wolfgang Saxon, "William Bentley Ball Is Dead at 82: Defended Religious Rights," *New York Times*, Jan. 18, 1999; Edward McGlynn Gaffney Jr., "William Bentley Ball (1916–1999)," *First Things* 92 (April 1999): 77–78; "Religious Freedom Attorney Dies at 82," *Harrisburg Patriot News*. Jan. 12, 1999; "In Memoriam: William Bentley Ball," National Lawyers Association, *NLA Review* 3/1 (Spring 1999): 2.

32. Thomas Berning, interview, June 24, 2015. Berning summarized his affection, respect, and debt of gratitude for Ball's mentorship in a post–Supreme Court hearing letter to Ball; Thomas Berning to William Ball, March 26, 1993, copy in possession of Larry and Sandi Zobrest.

33. Boston to Gerber, email, Oct. 8, 2015 (1).

34. Most notably in *Agostini v. Felton*, 521 U.S. 203 (1997), in which the Supreme Court overturned one of its own decisions in *Aguilar v. Felton*, 473 U.S. 402 (1985) to allow for the use of public resources in New York City parochial schools in remedial education programs especially serving poor and minority children; and in *Zelman v. Simmons-Harris*, 536 U.S. 639 (2002), in which the court approved an Ohio voucher program that included parochial schools. The informal influence of the Zobrests' effort and their success are evident in letters they received from parents who wanted to take public resources for a disabled child to parochial schools and were initially denied until school officials became aware of the court's decision in the Zobrests' case; Mary Jo Green to Mr. and Mrs. Zobrest and James, June 20, 1993, copy in the possession of the authors.

35. On the Supreme Court's readiness for an ideological pivot in the late 1980s and early 1990s, just prior to the *Zobrest* decision, see David Savage, *Turning Right: The Making of the Rehnquist Supreme Court* (New York: John Wiley and Sons, 1992), esp., 116–23, 321–26. That is also Rob Boston's evaluation of the state of court doctrine, while simultaneously giving credit to William Bentley Ball as an "effective advocate," Boston to Gerber, email, Oct. 8, 2015 (2).

36. Paul Siegel, "What They Didn't Know May Have Helped Us: How the Supreme Court Misinterpreted the Role of Sign Language Interpreters," *American Annals of the Deaf* 140/5 (Dec. 1995): 386–95.

CHAPTER 1. PARENTING, TRAINING, AND SCHOOLING: THE ZOBRESTS ENCOUNTER DEAFNESS

1. Andrew Solomon, *Far from the Tree: Parents, Children, and the Search for Identity* (New York: Scribner, 2012), especially 49–114, on families with a hearing impaired child.

2. Zobrest family interview, June 23, 2015.

3. Zobrest family interview, June 23, 2015; Kathleen Arnos and Arti Pandya, "Advances in the Genetics of Deafness," in *Oxford Handbook of Deaf Studies, Language and Education*, ed. Marc Marschark and Patricia Elizabeth Spencer, vol. 1, 2nd ed. (New York: Oxford University Press, 2011), 392–405.

4. Unsigned, "Jimmy Zobrest: Hearing Evaluation," Arizona School for the Deaf and the Blind, April 16, 1980 (Phil Ubernaga, audiologist), April 14, 1981 (Phil Ubernaga, audiologist), April 9, 1982 (Phil Ubernaga, audiologist), March 24, 1983 (Phil Ubernaga, audiologist), April 2, 1984 (Gail D. Rochlin, audiologist), Jan. 10, 1985 (Gale D. Rochlin, audiologist), Zobrest Student Records, Catalina Foothills School District, Catalina Foothills, Ariz. (hereafter CFSD); T. D. Wyatt, audiologist, Ear, Nose, and Throat Associates of Southern Arizona, P.C., "Audiological Examination: James Zobrest. July 21, 1986," Zobrest Student Records, CFSD; unsigned, "Progress Notes, 1986–1987," Zobrest Student Records, CFSD.

5. Sandi Zobrest to David Gerber, email, Nov. 17, 2016.

6. Solomon, *Far from the Tree*, 53.

7. Harlan Lane, *When the Mind Hears: A History of Deafness* (New York: Vintage, 1989).

8. Jim Zobrest to David Gerber, email, June 30, 2016; Arthur Rothstein, "Justices to Give Tucson Student a Court Interpreter," *Arizona Daily Star*, Feb. 22, 1993, 1A. The observation has been confirmed by one who perhaps knew better than anyone else Jim's situation in high school, Jim Santeford, his frequent sign language interpreter: Jim Santeford questionnaire, Oct. 31, 2015, and Jim Santeford to David Gerber, email, July 14, 2016.

9. Tom Humphries and Carol Padden, *Inside Deaf Culture* (Cambridge: Harvard University Press, 2005); Harlan Lane, Richard C. Pillard, and Ulf Hedberg, *The People of the Eye: Deaf Ethnicity and Ancestry* (New York: Oxford University Press, 2011); Paddy Ladd and Harlan Lane, "Deaf Ethnicity, Deafhood, and Their Relationship," *Sign Language Studies* 13/4 (Summer 2013): 565–79.

10. Zobrest family interview, June 23, 2015; Mary Prus interview, Feb. 22, 2017.

11. Sandi Zobrest to David Gerber, email, Nov. 17, 2016.

12. David M. Engel, "Law, Culture and Children with Disabilities: Educational Rights and the Construction of Difference," *Duke Law Journal* 1991, 1 (Feb. 1991): 198.

13. Irene W. Leigh, *A Lens in Deaf Identities* (New York: Oxford University Press, 2009), 71; Virginia Ball Duncan, interview, May 22, 2015.

14. Lennard J. Davis, *Enabling Acts: The Hidden Story of How the Americans with Disabilities Act Gave the Largest US Minority Its Rights* (Boston: Beacon Press, 2015).

15. Ball Duncan, interview, May 22, 2015.

16. Prus, interview, Feb. 22, 2017.

17. Thomas Berning, interview, June 24, 2015.

18. Sandi Zobrest to Gerber, email, Nov. 17, 2016.

19. Zobrest family interview, June 23, 2015.

20. Zobrest family interview, June 23, 2015.

21. John C. Richardson to Thomas J. Berning, July 27, 1989, letter in the possession of Sandi Zobrest.

22. Engel, "Law, Culture, and Children with Disabilities," 198.

23. Prus, interview, Feb. 22, 2017. Prus explained to a reporter a few days after the case was argued at the Supreme Court, "Sandi has had to fight every inch of the way

to get the services for Jim. She has elected to raise Jim in a hearing world." Mary Benson, "Mercyhurst Grad Takes Son's Case to the U.S. Supreme Court," *Lakeshore Visitor*, Feb. 26, 1993.

24. Prus, interview, Feb. 22, 2017; Sandi Zobrest to David Gerber, email, May 24, 2017.

25. Sandi Zobrest to Gerber, email, May 24, 2017.

26. Zobrest family interview, June 23, 2015.

27. Virginia Ball Duncan, interview, Aug. 16, 2016; "Erie, Pennsylvania," Wikipedia, https://en.wikipedia.org/wiki/Erie,_Pennsylvania; CBS News, "Erie Is Definitely a Sinking Ship, and You'd Be Crazy Not to Get Off," Feb. 27, 2017, www.cbsnews.com/news/america-manufacturing-erie-pennsylvania/ (accessed June 5, 2017).

28. Zobrest family interview, June 23, 2015.

29. Zobrest family interview, June 23, 2015; Prus, interview, Feb. 22, 2017; Sandi Zobrest to David Gerber, email, May 11, 2017.

30. Zobrest family interview, June 23, 2015; Prus, interview, Feb. 22, 2017.

31. Zobrest family interview, June 23, 2015; Sam Zobrest, interview, Jan. 30, 2017; Prus, interview, Feb. 22, 2017.

32. Zobrest family interview, June 23, 2015; Prus, interview, Feb. 22, 2017.

33. Ball Duncan, interviews, May 22, 2015, Aug. 16, 2016; Prus, interview, Feb. 22, 2017; Zobrest family interview, June 23, 2015.

34. History of the Barber National Institute, https://www.barberinstitute.org/history-of-dr-gertrude-barber (accessed Feb. 14, 2016); Anne Marie Welch, "Cause for Canonization for Sainthood of Dr. Gertrude Barber Opened by Diocese of Erie," Dec. 17, 2019, prweb.com/release/cause_for_canonization_for_sainthood_of_dr_gertrude_barber_opened_by_diocese_of_erie/prweb16794364.htm (accessed Feb. 6, 2020).

35. Douglas Baynton, *Forbidden Signs: American Culture and the Campaign against Sign Language* (Chicago: University of Chicago Press, 1998); R. A. R. Edwards, *Words Made Flesh: Nineteenth-Century Deaf Education and the Growth of Deaf Culture* (New York: New York University Press, 2012).

36. William C. Stokoe, *Sign Language Structure: An Outline of the Visual Communication Systems of the American Deaf*, Studies in Linguists: Occasional Papers no. 8 (Buffalo: University of Buffalo, Department of Anthropology and Linguistics, 1960); Margalit Fox, *Talking Hands: What Sign Language Reveals about the Mind* (New York: Simon and Schuster, 2007); Jane Maher, *Seeing Language in Sign: The Works of William Stokoe* (Washington, D.C.: Gallaudet University Press, 2010).

37. Gerilee Gustason, *Signing Exact English: Seeing instead of Hearing* (Los Alamitos, Calif.: Modern Signs Press, 1972); Sheila Lowenbraun, *Teaching the Hearing Impaired through Total Communication* (Columbus: Charles E. Merrill, 1980); Hilde S. Schlesinger, "Total Communication in Perspective," in *Deafness in Perspective*, ed. David M. Luterman (San Diego: College Hill Press, 1986), 87–116.

38. Claire L. Ramsey, *Deaf Children in Public Schools: Placement, Context, and Consequences* (Washington, D.C.: Gallaudet University Press, 1997).

39. Ramsey, *Deaf Children in Public Schools*, for a critique of mainstreaming and analysis of the benefits of a separate environment for young deaf students; Solomon, *Far from the Tree*, 54.

40. Mary Rita Weschler, questionnaire, July 2016; "CSJA Profile: A Journey towards Home; an Interview with Mary Rita Weschler, CSJA," www.csjboston.org/assets/associates/Mary-Rita-Weschler (accessed July 6, 2016).

41. Ball Duncan, interviews, May 22, 2015, Aug. 16, 2016; Aaron Epstein, "U.S. Supreme Court to Rule on Interpretation in Religious Schools," *Silent News* (March 1993).

42. Weschler, questionnaire, July 2016; Ball Duncan, interviews, May 22, 2015, Aug. 16, 2016; Virginia Ball Duncan to David Gerber, email, June 30, 2016.

43. Ball Duncan, interview, Aug. 16, 2016; Virginia Ball Duncan to David Gerber, email, June 29, 2016.

44. Ball Duncan, interviews, May 22, 2015, Aug. 16, 2016; Weschler, questionnaire, July 2016.

45. Sandi Zobrest to Gerber, email, May 11, 2017, June 22, 2017; Virginia Ball Duncan to David Gerber, email, May 28, 2017.

46. Zobrest family interview, June 23, 2015.

47. Ball Duncan, interview, Aug. 16, 2016; Zobrest family interview, June 23, 2015. The John Tracy Clinic was founded by Louise Treadwell Tracy, whose own profoundly deaf son led her to a lifelong interest in the education of children with hearing impairments. It is now known as the John Tracy Center. John Tracy Center, www.jtc.org (accessed Dec. 30, 2019).

48. "Motorists Get the Message: A Sign Points out the Danger When Children Are Playing along Route 99," *Erie Times-News*, undated clipping [1977] in the possession of Sandi Zobrest; Zobrest family interview, June 23, 2015; Benson, "Mercyhurst Grad Takes Deaf Son's Case."

49. Tony Pasquale and Bill McKinney, "Feds Probe Charges Erie Schools Discriminate against Deaf Children," *Erie Times-News*, undated [1978] clipping in the possession of Sandi Zobrest; Sandi Zobrest to David Gerber, email, Jan. 26, 27, 2016.

50. Zobrest family interview, June 23, 2015.

51. St. Mary's School for the Deaf, https://www.smsdk12.org (accessed June 4, 2017).

52. Sandi Zobrest to David Gerber, email, May 24, 2017.

53. Sandi Zobrest to David Gerber, emails, May 31, 2017, June 2, 2017; Jack Gannon, *Deaf Heritage: A Narrative History of Deaf America* (Silver Spring, Md.: National Association of the Deaf, 1981); John Vickery Van Cleve and Barry A. Crouch, *A Place of Their Own: Creating a Deaf Community in America* (Washington, D.C.: Gallaudet University Press, 1989), 88–89, 93–94, 136–38, 140–41, 157–60.

54. Gannon, *Deaf Heritage*, 47, 48, 54, 63, 277, 301; Arizona School for the Deaf and the Blind (hereafter ASDB), https://asdb.az.gov/about/about-asdb/ (accessed June 1, 2017).

55. Sandra Zobrest, "Parent Statement—Program Placement," ASDB, n.d. [probably 1980]; "Jimmy Zobrest: Results of Previous Evaluations, 1984 [results of standardized tests given at ASDB, 1980, summarized], Zobrest Student File, CFSD.

56. Department for the Hearing Impaired, "Individual Education Program—Participants, James Zobrest," Aug. 18, 1984. James Zobrest student file contains approximately 250 pages of grade reports, evaluative exercises, standardized test scores, and teachers' comments. It is especially complete for the 1984–85 school year, probably because these were the records that accompanied him when he transferred to the Catalina Foothills School District for the 1985–86 school year. They constitute a formidable record of oversight and diagnostic analysis. Among the standardized tests are the following: WISC-R Performance; Hiskey-Nebraska Test of Learning Aptitude; Gates MacGinite Reading Test; Brigance Inventory of Basic Skills; Woodcock Reading Mastery Test; and Stanford Achievement Test. Each of the individual disciplinary and hearing impairment related goals of the annual IEP produced extensive evaluation: reading; auditory training; speech; expressive language; written language; receptive language; and mathematics. There are summary reports on each of these evaluations by his homeroom teacher as well as evaluations of his classroom performance by his subject teachers.

57. Sandi Zobrest to David Gerber, email, June 3, 2017.

58. Sandi Zobrest to David Gerber, email, June 2, 2017.

59. Sandra Zobrest, "Parent Statement—Program Placement," ASDB, two undated, and the final one dated Feb. 5, 1985, for the shifting criteria for enrollment at ASDB; Zobrest Student File, CFSD. The final form does not check off "Parent preference for student at ASDB," indicating that by that time the Zobrests had made the decision to transfer Jim to the Catalina Foothills School District.

60. Sandi Zobrest to Gerber, email, June 2, 2017; "Bilingual-bicultural (Bi-bi): Learning American Sign Language," raisingdeafkids.org/communicating/choices/bibi.php (accessed Dec. 20, 2019); Shawn Neal Mahsie, *Educating Deaf Children Bilingually—with Insights and Applications from Sweden and Denmark* (Washington, D.C.: Gallaudet University Press, 1995).

61. Zobrest family interview, June 23, 2015.

62. Unsigned, "James Zobrest, Counseling," ASDB, n.d., Zobrest Student File, CFSD.

63. Zobrest family interview, June 23, 2015; Sandi Zobrest to David Gerber, email, May 11, 16, 2017, Dec. 18, 2019.

CHAPTER 2. INTO THE MAINSTREAM

1. Zobrest family interview, June 23, 2015; "Tucson, Arizona," Wikipedia, https://en.wikipedia.org/wiki/Tucson,_Arizona (accessed July 19, 2017).

2. Chris Koester interview, Dec. 2, 2016; Rose Daly Rooney interview, June 25, 2015; Judge Thomas Berning interview, June 24, 2015; John C. Richardson interview, June 24, 2015.

3. "Catalina Foothills, Arizona," Wikipedia, https://en.wikipedia.org/wiki/Catalina_Foothills,_Arizona (accessed July 19, 2017); Terry Downey interview, June 23, 2015; Robert Hetzel interview, Feb. 8, 2016.

4. "Tucson, Arizona;" "Catalina Foothills, Arizona."

5. Zobrest family interview, June 23, 2015.

6. Zobrest family interview, June 23, 2015; Sam Zobrest interview, Jan. 30, 2017; Terek Amin interview, March 18, 2017; Koester interview, Dec. 2, 2016.

7. Jean F. Andrews, Pamela C. Shaw, and Gabriel Lomas, "Deaf and Hard of Hearing Students," in *Handbook of Special Education*, ed. James M. Kauffman and Daniel P. Hallahan (New York: Routledge, 2011), 233–46; Unsigned, "Jimmy Zobrest—Results of Previous Testing," n.d. [standardized test scores: 1978, 1980, 1981, 1982], in "Psychoeducational Evaluation [James Zobrest], Dec. 4, 1984 and Jan. 15, 1985," Zobrest Student File, Catalina Foothills School District (CFSD).

8. As noted in his end-of-the-term grade report, cited in extended form in note 13.

9. Zobrest family interview, June 23, 2015.

10. Zobrest family interview, June 23, 2015.

11. Unsigned, "Educational History," n.d., Arizona School for the Deaf and the Blind (ASDB), Zobrest Student File, CFSD. The summary noted that Jim had made "good progress in meeting the goals and objectives as stated in his IEP" and further noted his "good understanding of language," but it added, "His biggest barrier is his classroom behaviors which interfere many times with his learning as well as the learning of others." While comments like these were not uncommon in Jim's early school record, they were mixed with comments about the improvement in his classroom behavior and his good school citizenship.

12. Zobrest family interview, June 23, 2015.

13. Jeanette Hansen, Upper Elementary Department for the Hearing Impaired, "Jim Zobrest—March 18–May 31, 1985, Fourth Quarter" (grade report, ASBD), Zobrest Student File, CFSD. Jim received the following grades in his academic subjects: E in Language, Reading, and Science/Social Studies; E- in Spelling; G in Mathematics; and S- in Communication Skills, where E was excellent, G was good, and S was satisfactory.

14. Unsigned, "Jimmy," n.d. (evaluation, ASDB), Zobrest Student File, CFSD.

15. Zobrest family interview, June 23, 2015; Mary Prus interview, Feb. 22, 2017; Virginia Ball Duncan interviews, May 22, 2015, Aug. 16, 2016; Sandi Zobrest to Bruce Dierenfield, email, July 27, 2017; Sandi Zobrest to David Gerber, email, April 11, 2018; Deborah McQuaid, "A Family's Fight Takes on National Significance: Ex-Erie Couple Goes to Supreme Court over Deaf Son's Rights," *Erie Morning News*, Feb. 18, 1993. Jim's identity negotiations have hardly been uncommon among younger deaf people; see Sarah Katz, "Is There a Right Way to Be Deaf?," *New York Times*, Nov. 7, 2019, https://www.nytimes.com/2019/11/07/opinion/health/is-there-a-right-way-to-be-deaf.html (accessed Nov. 9, 2019).

16. Sandi Zobrest to Gary Londer, Catalina Foothills School District, n.d. (c. 1985), Barbara Schofield, Special Education Coordinator (CFSD) to Colleen Wilcox, Director of Adaptive Education, Tucson Unified School District, April 29, 1985, MKH [?] to Barbara Schofield, memo, April 25, 1985, Zobrest Student File, CFSD.

17. Terry Downey interview, June 23, 2015; Terry Downey obituary, *Arizona Daily Star* (Tucson), Feb. 25, 2017, http://www.legacy.com/obituaries/tucson/obituary.aspx?n-terry-t-downey.

18. Robert Hetzel interview, Feb. 8, 2016; Downey interview, June 23, 2015; Zobrest family interview, June 23, 2015.

19. Downey interview, June 23, 2015.

20. Zobrest family interview, June 23, 2015.

21. Sandi Zobrest to David Gerber, email, June 12, 2017.

22. Unsigned, "Jimmy Zobrest" (nine-point program), May 24, 1985, Zobrest Student File, CFSD; Downey interview, June 23, 2015.

23. "Point 8—Behavior modification program," "Jimmy Zobrest" (nine-point program), May 24, 1985, Zobrest Student File, CFSD.

24. Downey interview, June 23, 2015; Catalina Foothills School District, Mary K. Hodgson, evaluator, "Speech, Language, Learning, Jim Zobrest, Sept. 21, 1988; this was the "Individual Education Plan" for Jim Zobrest and is in the possession of Sandi Zobrest; Sandi Zobrest to Gerber, email, June 12, 2017; unsigned, "Child-Study Team—Student Referral Checklist, Jim Zobrest," n.d. (c. Sept. 1985), Zobrest Student File, CFSD, which notes areas of evaluation covering physical health (including hearing), psychology and behavior, academic and intelligence testing, psychology and behavior, classroom teacher commentary, academic subject performance, and parent conference and IEP meeting. Also, Christie T. Young, Resource Room Teacher, "Conference Request—Jim Zobrest, semester review, Jan. 15, 1986," Zobrest Student File, CFSD, which notes that at the Feb. 3 meeting with the Zobrests reviewing Jim's first semester in the system, the following people may be in attendance: "principal, classroom teacher, resource teacher, psychologist, speech therapist, or any other person involved in evaluation."

25. Hodgson, "Speech, Language, Learning, Jim Zobrest, Sept. 21, 1988."

26. Sandi Zobrest to Gerber, email, June 12, 2017.

27. Robin Konrad, "James Zobrest, Fifth . . . Grade Progress Report," Zobrest Student File, CFSD. Jim received the following grades: A+ (Reading); A (Mathematics; Composition; Spanish); A- (Spelling); B+ (Resource Room); and B (Science; Social Studies; Grammar).

28. Sandi Zobrest to Bruce Dierenfield, email, July 27, 2017; Hodgson, "Speech, Language, Learning, Jim Zobrest, Sept. 21, 1988."

29. Downey interview, June 23, 2015; Zobrest family interview, June 23, 2015; Sandi Zobrest to Gerber, email, June 12, 2017.

30. Downey interview, June 23, 2015; Sandi Zobrest to Gerber, email, June 12, 2017; Sam Zobrest interview, Jan. 30, 2017.

31. Downey interview, June 23, 2015.

32. Zobrest family interview, June 23, 2015; Hodgson, "Speech, Language, Learning, Jim Zobrest, Sept. 21, 1988."

33. Zobrest family interview, June 23, 2015.

34. Gina Oliva, *Alone in the Mainstream: A Deaf Woman Remembers Public School* (Washington, D.C.: Gallaudet University Press, 2004), especially 74–99, in which Oliva quotes from a number of interviews she has done with mainstreamed hearing impaired individuals about their public school experiences. For reviews and sum-

maries of the experiential literature of mainstreaming and its evaluation, see Irene W. Leigh, *A Lens on Deaf Identities* (New York: Oxford University Press, 2009); and Janet Cerney, *Deaf Education in America: Voices of Children from Inclusion Settings* (Washington, D.C.: Gallaudet University Press, 2007). One of the landmarks of this literature was written by Bonnie Poitras Tucker, a hearing impaired attorney and professor of law who assisted in writing a friend-of-the-court brief to the Supreme Court for the Alexander Graham Bell Association on behalf of the Zobrests' lawsuit; see Bonnie Poitras Tucker, *The Feel of Silence* (Philadelphia: Temple University Press, 1995).

35. Hodgson, "Speech, Language, Learning, Jim Zobrest, Sept. 21, 1988."

36. Zobrest family interview, June 23, 2015; Sam Zobrest interview, Jan. 30, 2017; Terek Amin interview, March 18, 2017; Downey interview, June 23, 2015; Sandi Zobrest to Gerber, email, June 12, 2017.; Sandi Zobrest to Bruce Dierenfield, email, July 27, 2017.

37. The medal in basketball is noted in the grade report cited in note 13.

38. Zobrest family interview, June 23, 2015; Sam Zobrest interview, Jan. 30, 2017; Amin interview, March 18, 2017; Downey interview, June 23, 2015; Derek Hersha interview, March 21, 2017; Larry Copenhaven, "Suing Public District: Deaf Student Wants Interpreter Funded at Private School," *Tucson Citizen*, Aug. 4, 1988.

39. Amin interview, March 18, 2017.

40. Amin interview, March 18, 2017; Prus interview, Feb. 22, 2017; Jim Zobrest to David Gerber, email, May 19, 2017; Sam Zobrest interview, Jan. 30, 2017; Sandi Zobrest to Dierenfeld, email, July 27, 2017.

41. Amin interview, March 18, 2017; Zobrest family interview, June 23, 2015.

42. Downey interview, June 23, 2015; Richardson interview, June 24, 2015; Hetzel interview, Feb. 8, 2016; Camille Catsaros to Bruce Dierenfield, email, Jan. 11, 2017.

43. Zobrest family interview, June 23, 2015; "Amphitheater High School," Wikipedia, https://en.wikipedia.org/wiki/Amphitheater_High_School (accessed July 19, 2017), "Sabino High School," Wikipedia, https://.en.wikipedia.org/wiki/Sabino_High_School (accessed July 19, 2017).

44. Zobrest family interview, June 23, 2015; Sandi Zobrest to Dierenfield, email, July 27, 2017; Berning interview, June 24, 2015; Kristen Cook, "Justices to Weigh Appeal by Deaf Tucson Student," *Arizona Daily Star*, Oct. 6, 1992. What we have called the perception of a *moral crisis*, sociologists have called *moral panic*. For a significant analysis of the phenomena of moral panic, such as the authors believe took place in the 1980s in the United States over drug addiction and pornography, see Erich Goode and Nachman Ben-Yehuda, *Moral Panics: The Social Construction of Deviance* (Malden, Mass.: Wiley-Blackwell, 1994), 197–217, 218–44. A moral panic is the widely held perception, usually disproportionate to the evidence, that a real social problem that is ultimately rooted in individual behavior has reached a quantitative level that transforms it qualitatively into a societal crisis.

45. "Amphitheater High School"; "Sabino High School." Even with the peculiarities of Wikipedia authorship in mind, the statement made in the entries for both Amphitheater High School and Sabino High School about the centrality of sports

and achievement in sports to the self-understanding of both institutions would be remarkable.

46. Zobrest family interview, June 23, 2015; Downey interview, June 23, 2015; Hetzel interview, Feb. 8, 2016.

47. Salpointe faculty and administration interview (Sister Helen Timothy, Kay Sullivan, and Jim Flannery), June 25, 2015; Zobrest family interview, June 23, 2017; Mark Bruenkant interview, Nov. 7, 2016; Denise Jensen Erickson, March 14, 2016; "Salpointe Catholic High School," Wikipedia, https://en.wikipedia.org/wiki/Salpointe_Catholic_High_School (accessed Aug. 11, 2014); "History," Salpointe Catholic High School, https://www.salpointe.org/about/history (accessed Aug. 11, 2014).

48. Anthony S. Bryk, Valerie E. Lee, and Peter B. Holland, *Catholic Schools and the Common Good* (Cambridge: Harvard University Press, 1993), 10–11.

49. Jay P. Dolan, *The American Catholic Experience* (Garden City: Doubleday, 1985), 262–93.

50. Sandi Zobrest to Bruce Dierenfield, email, July 26, 2017; Kevin M. Schultz, *Tri-Faith America: How Catholics and Jews Held Postwar America to Its Protestant Promise* (New York: Oxford University Press, 2011); William R. Hutchinson, *Religious Pluralism in America: The Contentious History of a Founding Ideal* (New Haven: Yale University Press, 2003); John Courtney Murray, *We Hold These Truths: Catholic Reflections on the American Proposition* (New York: Sheed and Ward, 1960); Philip Gleason, "The Crisis of Americanization," in *Contemporary Catholicism in the United States*, ed. Philip Gleason (South Bend, Ind.: Notre Dame University Press, 1969), 3–31.

51. Andrew M. Greeley, *The American Catholic: A Social Portrait* (New York: Basic Books, 1977); Andrew M. Greeley, *American Catholics since the Council: An Unauthorized Report* (Chicago: Thomas More Press, 1985); James Hudnu-Beumler, *Looking for God in the Suburbs: The Religion of the American Dream and Its Critics, 1945–1965* (New Brunswick: Rutgers University Press, 1994); Gleason, "Crisis of Americanization," 3–31.

52. Andrew M. Greeley, William C. McReady and Kathleen McCourt, *Catholic Schools in a Declining Church* (Kansas City: Sheed and Ward, 1970); Andrew M. Greeley and Peter H. Rossi, *The Education of American Catholics* (Chicago: Aldine, 1966), 118–46; National Catholic Educational Association, *The Catholic High School: A National Portrait* (Washington, D.C.: National Catholic Educational Council, 1985).

53. Bryk, Lee, and Holland, *Catholic Schools and the Common Good*, 33–41; Andrew M. Greeley, *Catholic High Schools and Minority Students* (New Brunswick, N.J.: Transaction Books, 1982); National Catholic Education Association, *Catholic High School*.

54. Bryk, Lee, and Holland, *Catholic Schools and the Common Good*, 93–100, 132, 142, 165, 283; Peter L. Benson and Michael J. Guerra, *Sharing the Faith: The Beliefs and Values of Catholic High School Teachers* (Washington, D.C.: National Catholic Educational Association, 1985).

55. Zobrest family interview, June 23, 2015; Salpointe faculty and administration interview (Timothy, Sullivan, Flannery), June 25, 2015; Sam Zobrest interview, Jan. 20, 2017; Denise Jensen Erickson interview, March 14, 2016.

56. Arthur G. Powell, Eleanor Farrar, and David K. Cohen, *The Shopping Mall High School: Winners and Losers in the Educational Marketplace* (Boston: Houghton-

Mifflin, 1985); Philip A. Cusick, *The Egalitarian Ideal and the American High School* (New York: Longman, 1983); Theodore R. Sizer, *Horace's Compromise: The Dilemma of the American High School* (Boston: Houghton-Mifflin, 1984); Gerald Grant, *The World We Created at Hamilton High* (Cambridge: Harvard University Press, 1988); Michael W. Sedlack, Christopher W. Wheeler, Diane C. Pullin, and Philip A. Cusick, *Selling Students Short: Classroom Bargains and Academic Reform in the American High School* (New York: Teachers College Press, 1986).

57. Bryk, Lee, and Holland, *Catholic Schools and the Common Good*, 207–36.

58. Zobrest family interview, June 23, 2015; Sandi Zobrest to David Gerber, email, July 3, 2017.

59. Charlotte Harris to Bruce Dierenfield, email, July 7, 2017.

60. Bruenkant interview, Nov. 7, 2016; Erickson interview, March 14, 2016; Richard and Patty McBride interview, April 4, 2016.

61. Zobrest family interview, June 23, 2015.

62. Zobrest family interview, June 23, 2015; Sandi Zobrest to Gerber, email, July 3, 2017; Mike Urbanski to Kay Sullivan, email, April 25, 2018; Michele Brubaker to Bruce Dierenfield, email, May 3, 2018.

63. Jim Zobrest to David Gerber, email, June 30, 2016.

CHAPTER 3. MAINSTREAMING IN A CATHOLIC SCHOOL

1. Education for All Handicapped Children Act, Pub. L. 94-142, 1975; Kathryn M. Coates, "The Education for All Handicapped Children Act since 1975," *Marquette Law Review* 69/4 (1985): 51–81; Greg Aiken to Bruce Dierenfield, email, July 11, 2018.

2. "Tuition Information," *Salpointe Catholic High School: Parent-Student Handbook*, 1988–89, 21.

3. Salpointe Catholic High School, *Horizons* yearbooks, 1990, 218–21; 1991, 25–33, 36, 38.

4. Salpointe Catholic High School, *Horizons* yearbook, 1989, 13, 15, 22, 160.

5. Salpointe Catholic High School, *Horizons* yearbook, 1989, 7–8, 10–11, 18, 20, 27, 45–46, 48–50, 110, 122, 136, 139, 143; 1990, 210.

6. Gina A. Oliva, *Alone in the Mainstream: A Deaf Woman Remembers Public School* (Washington, D.C.: Gallaudet University Press, 2004), 75, 88–92; Laura Foley, "Learning through Hands," *The (Salpointe) Crusader*, Sept. 16, 1988, 4.

7. Candace Flores Carrillo, telephone message for Bruce Dierenfield, Feb. 12, 2016; Oliva, *Alone in the Mainstream*, xi, xvi, 87–88; Jim Zobrest to Bruce Dierenfield, email, July 25, 2017; Arthur H. Rotstein, "Justices to Give Deaf Tucson Student a Court Interpreter," *Arizona Daily Star*, Feb. 22, 1993; James Santeford, questionnaire, Oct. 31, 2015; Zobrest family interview, June 23, 2015.

8. Sam Zobrest, interview, Jan. 30, 2017; Jim Flannery, interview, June 25, 2015; Camille Shadegg Catsoros, interview, Jan. 11, 2017; Derek Hersha, interview, March 21, 2017; Chris Koester, interview, Dec. 2, 2016; Patty McBride, interview, April 4, 2016.

9. Janet Cerney, *Deaf Education in America: Voices of Children from Inclusion Settings* (Washington, D.C.: Gallaudet University Press, 2007), 27; Jeri Banks, *All of Us Together: The Story of Inclusion at the Kinzie School* (Washington, D.C.: Gallaudet

University Press, 1994), 193; Sandi Zobrest to Bruce Dierenfield, email, July 27, 2017; Oliva, *Alone in the Mainstream*, 81–83; Hersha, interview, March 21, 2017; Salpointe Catholic High School, *Horizons* yearbook, 1992, 56; Arthur H. Rotstein, "Justices to Give Deaf Tucson Student a Court Interpreter; Terek Amin, interview, March 18, 2017.

10. Denise Jensen Erickson, interview, March 14, 2016; Kris Kaul to Bruce Dierenfield, email, Feb. 22, 2016; McBride, interview, April 4, 2016.

11. "How the Deaf Developed a Phone of Their Own," *ITU News*, June 2011, 36–37; "TTY and TTY Relay Services," National Association of the Deaf, https://www.nad.org/resources/technology/telephone-and-relay-services/tty-and-tty-relay-services/; Jim Zobrest to Bruce Dierenfield, email, July 25, 2017; Koester, interview, Dec. 2, 2016; Ken Arcia to Bruce Dierenfield, email, June 21, 2017; Sandi Zobrest to Dierenfield, email, July 27, 2017.

12. Joel Feldman, "Yes—the Deaf (and Those with Hearing Loss) Are Allowed to Drive and Do So as Safely as Hearing Drivers," End Distracted Driving, Dec. 12, 2016, https://www.enddd.org/end-distracted-driving/enddd-presentations/yes-deaf-are-allowed-to-drive/; Sandi Zobrest to Dierenfield, email, July 27, 2017; Jim Zobrest to Dierenfield, email, July 25, 2017; Foley, "Learning through Hands," 4; Jack Gannon, *Deaf Heritage: A Narrative History of Deaf America* (Silver Spring, Md.: National Association of the Deaf, 1981), 384–87; "A Brief History of Captioned Television," National Captioning Institute, https://web.archive.org/web/20110719060406/http://www.ncicap.org/caphist.asp.

13. Michele Brubaker to Bruce Dierenfield, email, April 26, 2018; Zobrest family interview, June 23, 2015; Richard McBride, interview, April 4, 2016; Jim Zobrest to Dierenfield, email, July 25, 2017.

14. "Speech/Language/Hearing evaluation of Jim Zobrest," Sept. 21, 1988, James Zobrest student file, Catalina Foothills School District (CFSD).

15. "Speech/Language/Hearing evaluation of Jim Zobrest," Sept. 21, 1988.

16. Cerney, *Deaf Education in America*, 30–31.

17. "Tucsonan Wins High Court Case," *Tucson Citizen*, June 18, 1993; James Santeford, questionnaire, Oct. 31, 2015.

18. Karen Bontempo, Jemina Napier, Laurence Hayes, and Vicki Brasher, "Does Personality Matter: An International Study of Sign Language Interpreter Disposition," *Translation & Interpreting* 6/1 (2014): 24; Hubert Demers, "The Working Interpreter," in *Topics in Signed Language Interpreting: Theory and Practice*, ed. Terry Janzen (Philadelphia: John Benjamins, 2005), 201–5, 207, 210–11, 214, 217–20, 222–23; Melanie Metzger, *Sign Language Interpreting: Deconstructing the Myth of Neutrality* (Washington, D.C.: Gallaudet University Press, 1999), 2–3; Angela Stratiy, "Best Practices in Interpreting: A Deaf Community Perspective," in Janzen, *Topics in Signed Language Interpreting*, 235; Ann McIntosh, book review of Oliva, *Alone in the Mainstream*, Gallaudet University Press News, n.d., http://gupress.gallaudet.edu/reviews/AITMrevw2.html.

19. Cerney, *Deaf Education in America*, 29–30, 46.

20. Rev. Leo McCarthy, "A Greeting," *Salpointe Catholic High School Annual Report, 1986–1987*, i; "Philosophy and Objectives of Salpointe Catholic High School," *Salpointe Catholic High School: Parent-Student Handbook*, 1988–1989, 4; "Introduction," *Faculty/Staff Handbook: Policies and Procedures, 1988—1989*, Salpointe Catholic High School, 1; "Carmelite High Schools," *Faculty/Staff Handbook: Policies and Procedures, 1988–1989*, Salpointe Catholic High School, 6; "Philosophy," *Salpointe Catholic High School Annual Report, 1986–1987*, 2.

21. Kay Sullivan, interview, June 25, 2015; Salpointe Catholic High School, *Horizons* yearbook, 1989, 117, 132, 141, 187, 202, 207; "Reverend Leo McCarthy" (obituary), *Arizona Daily Star*, Nov. 25, 2009, http://www.legacy.com/obituaries/tucson/obituary.aspx?n=leo-mccarthy&pid=136420698; "Academic Program," *Salpointe Catholic High School: Parent-Student Handbook, 1988–1989*, 10–11; Stipulation of Facts, *Zobrest v. Catalina Foothills School District*, U.S. District Court for the District of Arizona, April 6, 1989; Jim Flannery, interview, June 25, 2015; Erickson, interview, March 14, 2016; Hersha, interview, March 21, 2017; Aaron Epstein, "Supreme Court Hears Case of Tucson Family Caught between . . . Church and State," *Phoenix Gazette*, Feb. 2, 1993.

22. Salpointe Catholic High School, *Horizons* yearbook, 1989, 21, 25, 29, 116–17, 119, 122, 154.

23. Epstein, "Supreme Court Hears Case of Tucson Family," A4; Salpointe Catholic High School, *Horizons* yearbook, 1990, 128; 1992, 122; Erickson, interview, March 14, 2016.

24. Salpointe Catholic High School, *Horizons* yearbook, 1989, 111, 120; 1992, 20.

25. Erickson, interview, March 14, 2016; *Salpointe Catholic High School: Parent-Student Handbook, 1988–1989*, 31; Zobrest family interview, June 23, 2015.

26. Hersha, interview, March 21, 2017; Zobrest family interview, June 23, 2015; Sandi Zobrest to Dierenfield, email, July 27, 2017; Jim Zobrest to Dierenfield, email, July 25, 2017.

27. Erickson, interview, March 14, 2016; Mark Brunenkant, interview, Nov. 7, 2016; Flannery, interview, June 25, 2015; Brubaker to Dierenfield, email, April 26, 2018.

28. High school transcript for James Zobrest, Salpointe Catholic High School, 1992; Richard McBride, interview, April 4, 2016; Sandi Zobrest to Dierenfield, email, July 27, 2017; Jim Zobrest to Dierenfield, email, July 25, 2017; Erickson, interview, March 14, 2016.

29. High school transcript for James Zobrest, Salpointe Catholic High School, 1992; Michele Brubaker to Bruce Dierenfield, email, May 3, 2018; Donald F. Moores and David S. Martin, eds., *Deaf Learners: Developments in Curriculum and Instruction* (Washington, D.C.: Gallaudet University Press, 2006), 33–36; Brunenkant, interview, Nov. 7, 2016; Richard McBride, interview, April 4, 2016; Zobrest family interview, June 23, 2015.

30. Richard McBride, interview, April 4, 2016; Erickson, interview, March 14, 2016; Sandi Zobrest to Dierenfield, email, July 27, 2017.

31. Santeford, questionnaire, Oct. 31, 2015; Zobrest family interview, June 23, 2015; Tamar Lewin, "Deaf Student's Need Could Alter Church-State Relations," *New York Times*, Feb. 22, 1993; Ernie Heltsley, "Catalina School District Is Sued by Deaf Teen on Interpreter Fees," *Arizona Daily Star*, Aug. 2, 1988; Foley, "Learning through Hands," 4.

32. Zobrest family interview, June 23, 2015; Santeford, questionnaire, Oct. 31, Nov. 23, 2015.

33. Santeford, questionnaire, Oct. 31, Nov. 23, 2015; Erickson, interview, March 14, 2016; Richard McBride, interview, April 4, 2016.

34. Santeford, questionnaire, Oct. 31, 2015.

35. Erickson, interview, March 14, 2016; Brubaker to Bruce Dierenfield, email, May 3, 2018.

36. Santeford, questionnaire, Oct. 31, 2015; Zobrest family interview, June 23, 2015.

37. Santeford, questionnaire, Oct. 31, 2015.

38. Terek Amin, interview, March 18, 2017; "Robert 'Lute' Olson," Hall of Famers, Naismith Basketball Hall of Fame, http://www.hoophall.com/hall-of-famers/lute-olson/; Hersha, interview, March 21, 2017.

39. Dan Steinberg, "The Nation's Only Deaf Men's College Basketball Team, on the Verge of Its First March Madness," *Washington Post*, Feb. 25, 2017, https://www.washingtonpost.com/news/dc-sports-bog/wp/2017/02/24/the-nations-only-deaf-mens-college-basketball-team-is-on-the-verge-of-its-first-march-madness; Hersha, interview, March 21, 2017; Hunter Clark, "Basketball and the Deaf," n.d., http://www.lifeprint.com/asl101/topics/basketball-and-the-deaf-2.htm; Koester, interview, Dec. 2, 2016.

40. Kristen Brackett, "This Is How Deaf Basketball Players Communicate on the Court," Hearing Like Me, March 28, 2017, https://www.hearinglikeme.com/deaf-basketball-players-communicate-court; Paul Corliss and Tresa Galvez, "The First Deaf NBA Player: Insights from Lance Allred," May 6, 2015, https://www.legendsofbasketball.com/the-first-deaf-nba-player-insights-from-lance-allred; Aaron Epstein, "The Interpreter and the Establishment Clause," in *A Year in the Life of the Supreme Court*, ed. Rodney A. Smolla (Durham, N.C.: Duke University Press, 1995), 133.

41. Hersha, interview, March 21, 2017; Koester, interview, Dec. 2, 2016. The assertions made regarding the game of basketball are based on Bruce Dierenfield's playing and coaching career.

42. Hersha, interview, March 21, 2017; Flannery, interview, June 25, 2015.

43. Santeford, questionnaire, Oct. 31, 2015.

44. Sandi Zobrest to Dierenfield, email, July 27, 2017; Hersha, interview, March 21, 2017; Richard McBride, interview, April 4, 2016.

45. "Jim Flannery," Pima County Sports Hall of Fame, http://pcshf.org/jim-flannery; Sam Zobrest, interview, Jan. 30, 2017; Brunenkant, interview, Nov. 7, 2016; Hersha, interview, March 21, 2017; Koester, interview, Dec. 2, 2016.

46. Sandi Zobrest to Dierenfield, email, July 27, 2017; Zobrest family interview, June 23, 2015; Hersha, interview, March 21, 2017; Sandi Zobrest to Dierenfield, email, July 27, 2017; Jim Zobrest to Dierenfield, email, July 25, 2017; Zobrest family interview,

June 23, 2015; Jack Rickard, "Lancer Great Now Stellar in San Diego," *Tucson Citizen*, Dec. 24, 1996.

47. Zobrest family interview, June 23, 2015; Flannery, interview, June 25, 2015; Jim Zobrest to Dierenfield, email, July 25, 2017; Santeford, questionnaire, Oct. 31, 2015; Hersha, interview, March 21, 2017; Sandi Zobrest to Dierenfield, email, July 27, 2017.

48. Oliva, *Alone in the Mainstream*, 77–81, 92–97.

49. Jim Zobrest to Dierenfield, email, July 25, 2017.

50. Josh Noel, "Ryan Tries Harder Playing as No. 2," *Tucson Citizen*, 4D; Greg Hansen, "6. Sean Flannery, Salpointe," *Arizona Daily Star*, July 20, 2017, https://tucson.com/sean-flannery-salpointe/article_678b133e-6d92-11e7-916d-0ba82fe933a2.html; Rob Walpole, "Shooting for the Title," Salpointe Catholic High School *Horizons* yearbook, 1992, 196–97.

51. Rotstein, "Justices to Give Tucson Student a Court Interpreter"; Santeford, questionnaire, Oct. 31, 2015.

52. Santeford, questionnaire, Oct. 31, 2015.

53. Cerney, *Deaf Education in America*, 28; Jim Zobrest to Dierenfield, email, July 25, 2017; Brubaker to Dierenfield, email, May 3, 2018.

CHAPTER 4. IN SEARCH OF RELIGIOUS LIBERTY

1. Ernie Heltsley, "Catalina School District Is Sued by Deaf Teen on Interpreter Fees," *Arizona Daily Star*, Aug. 2, 1988; Aaron Epstein, "Supreme Court Hears Case of Tucson Family Caught between . . . Church and State," *Phoenix Gazette*, Feb. 2, 1993; Zobrest family interview, June 23, 2015.

2. Zobrest family interview, June 23, 2015; Terry Downey, interview, June 23, 2015. The Zobrest suit was not moot with Jim Zobrest's graduation because his parents sought reimbursement for interpreter fees, a matter that remained outstanding.

3. Downey, interview, June 23, 2015; Robert Hetzel, interview, Feb. 8, 2016; John C. Richardson, interview, June 24, 2015.

4. Terry Downey, letter to JoAnn Sheperd, Jan. 8, 1988, James Zobrest file, Catalina Foothills School District (CFSD); Downey, interview, June 23, 2015; Richardson, interview, June 24, 2015; JoAnn Sheperd, interview, Nov. 30, 2015; JoAnn Sheperd, letter to Terry Downey, March 8, 1988, James Zobrest file, CFSD.

5. Virginia Ball Duncan, interview, May 22, 2015; Zobrest family interview, June 23, 2015. By the time of Sandi Zobrest's telephone call to Sandy Ball Duncan, William Bentley Ball had won more major First Amendment cases in the field of religious liberty than any other attorney in the history of American jurisprudence. He was, or had been, chairman of the Committee on Federal Court Relations, national chairman of the Committee on Constitutional Law of the Federal Bar Association, director of the Human Life and Natural Family Planning Foundation, and a member of the Appellate Court Rules Committee of the Pennsylvania Supreme Court and the National Advisory Board of the Center for Law and Religious Freedom. He was commonly regarded by his peers as "the experts' expert." See Kent Kelly, ed., *The Separation of Church and Freedom: A War Manual for Christian Soldiers* (Southern Pines, NC: Calvary Press, 1980), xii.

6. William B. Ball, letter to Sandi Zobrest, Aug. 18, 1988, Zobrest family papers; Zobrest family interview, June 23, 2015; William Bentley Ball, "Secularism: Tidal Wave of Repression," in *Caesar's Coin Revisited: Christians and the Limits of Government*, ed. Michael Cromartie (Washington, D.C.: Eerdmans, 1996), 49; Richard Connell, interview, May 22, 2015; Tamar Lewin, "Deaf Student's Need Could Alter Church-State Relations," *New York Times*, Feb. 22, 1993; Thomas Berning, interview, June 24, 2015. Ball would later refer to "secularists," meaning those who believe in the strict separation of church and state, as "barbarians in Brooks Brothers suits." For a fuller discussion of the Christian case against secularism, see William B. Ball, ed., *In Search of a National Morality: A Manifesto for Evangelicals and Catholics* (San Francisco: Ignatius Press, 1992; William B. Ball's generic letter to church-state accommodationists, Oct. 13, 1988, Zobrest family papers.

7. Berning, interview, June 24, 2015; Virginia Ball Duncan to authors, email, April 6, 2018; Ball Duncan, interview, May 22, 2015.

8. Michael W. McConnell, "Ball, William Bentley (1916–99)," in *The Yale Biographical Dictionary of American Law*, ed. Roger K. Newman (New Haven: Yale University Press, 2009), 26; Richard Vigilante, "Beyond the Burger Court: Four Supreme Court Candidates Who Could Lead a Judicial Counterrevolution," *Policy Review* 28 (Spring 1984): 25; Ball Duncan, interview, May 22, 2015; Caroline Ball, telephone interview, May 29, 2015; Philip Murren, interview, May 22, 2015, Aug. 16, 2016; William Bentley Ball, "Accountability: A View from the Trial Courtroom," *George Washington Law Review* 60/3 (March 1992): 809; Shawn Frances Peters, *The Yoder Case: Religious Freedom, Education, and Parental Rights* (Lawrence: University Press of Kansas, 2003).

9. William Bentley Ball, *Mere Creatures of the State? Education, Religion, and the Courts: A View from the Courtroom* (Notre Dame, Ind.: Crisis Books, 1994), 129–30; "William Bentley Ball," *Thomas Aquinas College Newsletter*, Thomas Aquinas College, Winter 1999–2000, https://thomasaquinas.edu/about/william-bentley-ball; William B. Ball, *Litigation in Education: In Defense of Freedom* (Wichita, Kans.: Center for Independent Education, 1977), 12–13; Wolfgang Saxon, "William Ball Is Dead at 82; Defended Religious Rights," *New York Times*, Jan. 18, 1999; Murren, interview, May 22, 2015; Richard Connell, interview, May 22, 2015; William Bentley Ball, ed. *In Search of a National Morality: A Manifesto for Evangelicals and Catholics* (Grand Rapids, Mich.: Baker Book House, 1992). The law partners William Ball and Joseph Skelly did not regard themselves as "lobbyists" for particular legislation, but rather as "counsel" for the Pennsylvania Catholic Conference, meaning they would analyze issues and legislation for interested organizations and state legislators. Ball discussed his new book, *Mere Creatures of the State?* in an interview entitled "No Mere Creatures," which aired on Eternal Word Television Network (EWTN) in 1995, https://www.ewtn.com/library/ISSUES/MERECREA.TXT (accessed Oct. 14, 2018).

10. Douglas W. Kmiec, "'God's Litigator': A Review Essay of *Mere Creatures of the State? Education, Religion, and the Courts: A View from the Courtroom*," *Notre Dame Law Review* 70/5 (1995): 1247–75; Elder Witt, *A Different Justice: Reagan and the Supreme Court* (Washington, D.C.: Congressional Quarterly, 1986, 155–56; Vigilante, "Beyond the Burger Court," 25–26; Joseph R. McKinney, "Special Education and the

Establishment Clause," *West's Education Law Reporter* 65 (March 14, 1991): 19; William Bentley Ball, *Mere Creatures of the State?*, x; William A. Donohue, "William Bentley Ball, R.I.P.," *Catholic League*, March 27, 1999, https://www.catholicleague.org/william-bentley-ball-r-i-p; William B. Ball, "Signum Fidei Medal Address," LaSalle College, Oct., 2, 1965, William Bentley Ball Papers, American Catholic History Research Center and University Archives, Catholic University of America, Washington, D.C.; Joseph Esposito, "Constitutional Scholar William Bentley Ball, 82, Dies," *National Catholic Register*, Jan. 17, 1999, http://www.ncregister.com/site/article/constitutional_scholar_william_bentley_ball_82_dies.

11. Ralph Albert Parlette, "Over the Lyceum and Chautauqua Field," *Lyceum Magazine* (Dec. 1928), 36; Michael W. McConnell, "Ball, William Bentley (1916–99)," in *The Yale Biographical Dictionary of American Law*, 26; Jim Lanese, "Cathedral Latin School," *Cleveland Historical*, May 11, 2012, https://clevelandhistorical.org/items/show/456; Western Reserve University commencement convocation, 1940, Case Western Reserve University Archives; Clarence H. Cramer, *Case Western Reserve: A History of the University, 1826–1976* (Boston: Little, Brown, 1976); Virginia Ball Duncan to Bruce Dierenfield, email, Oct. 20, 2017; Donald I. Warren, *Radio Priest: Charles Coughlin, the Father of Hate Radio* (New York: Free Press, 1996), 57–70; Albin Krebs, "Charles Coughlin, 30's 'Radio Priest' Dies," *New York Times*, Oct. 28, 1979.

12. William B. Ball diary, June 5–6, 1944; McConnell, "Ball, William Bentley (1916–99)," 26; Caroline Ball, interview, May 29, 2015; Vigilante, "Beyond the Burger Court," 25; Peters, *Yoder Case*, 60; Gray Thoron and A. E. Papale, memorandum to the Association of American Law Schools, Villanova Law School archives, Nov. 30, 1957; Harold Gill Reuschlein, "Villanova—Newest of the Catholic Law Schools," *Catholic Lawyer* 3 (Jan. 1957): 16–21; *Villanova University Law School Bulletin* (1956–1957): 26–37; "The Study of Law," *Villanova University Law School Bulletin* (1956–1957): 8; William B. Ball to John Cardinal Krol, March 25, 1964, Cardinal John Krol Papers, Catholic Historical Research Center of the Archdiocese of Philadelphia, Pennsylvania.

13. McConnell, "Ball, William Bentley (1916–99)," 26; William B. Ball to James A. McNulty, Oct. 20, 1966, Cardinal John Krol Papers; "Paying for Private Schools," *Washington Post*, Dec. 1, 1970; William B. Ball, "The Need of the Church for Legal Services," Nov. 1966, Catholic Historical Research Center, Philadelphia; Caroline Ball, interview, May 29, 2015; William Bentley Ball, "The American Horizon: What Fears? What Hopes!" *The Bridge* 76/7 (June 1985): 3–6; "Requiescat in Pace," *Permanent Things* (Russell Kirk Center for Cultural Renewal newsletter) 2, undated, n.p. The original name of the Pennsylvania Catholic Conference was the Pennsylvania Catholic Welfare Committee, a name that lasted until 1965.

14. James Youniss and John J. Convey, eds., *Catholic Schools at the Crossroads: Survival and Transformation* (New York: Teachers College Press, 2000), 55–71; Ball, *Litigation in Education*, 16; Ball, *Mere Creatures of the State?* 26, 52; William B. Ball, "Law and Religion in America: The New Picture," *Catholic Lawyer* 16/1 (Winter 1970): 3–5; John T. McGreevy, "Anti-Catholicism in the United States: The View from History," in *American Catholics, American Culture: Tradition & Resistance*, vol. 2, *American Catholics in the Public Square*, ed. Margaret O'Brien Steinfels (Lanham,

Md.: Rowman & Littlefield, 2004), 155–61; Philip Jenkins, *The New Anti-Catholicism: The Last Acceptable Prejudice* (New York: Oxford University Press, 2003), 23. See also John T. McGreevy, *Catholicism and American Freedom: A History* (New York: W. W. Norton, 2003). William Ball once wrote that the charters of religious schools are "really from God" and such schools should not be bound "in any way to the State." See Kelly, *The Separation of Church and Freedom*, 14.

15. William Bentley Ball, "What's a Constitution without Natural Law?," *The Laws of Nature and of Nature's God: The Ultimate Law* (Marlborough, N.H.: Plymouth Rock Foundation, 1992), 5–11; Mike Mallowe, "Cardinal Krol: The Kingdom and the Power," *Philadelphia* 66 (Dec. 1975): 131, 133–34, 190, 192; E. Michael Jones, *John Cardinal Krol and the Cultural Revolution* (South Bend, Ind.: Fidelity Press, 1995), 228–300; Richard Connell, interview, May 22, 2015; William B. Ball, "Memorandum of Law: Authorization, under Economic Opportunity Act, for Expenditure of Public Funds to Support Birth Control Programs, Jan. 29, 1966, William Bentley Ball Papers, American Catholic History Research Center and University Archives, Catholic University of America, Washington, D.C.; Philip Murren, interview, Aug. 16, 2016. The concept of natural law referred to the belief that the source of people's rights lay in a higher law—God's law—which preceded and superseded human law as found, for example, in the U.S. Constitution. Supporters of natural law, including William Ball, maintained the Declaration of Independence acknowledged America's dependence on "Nature's God," and that revolutionary and foundational document should be regarded as the "preamble to the Preamble of the Constitution.

16. Frank J. Sorauf, *The Wall of Separation: The Constitutional Politics of Church and State* (Princeton: Princeton University Press, 1976), 186; Ball to Krol, March 25, 1964, Nov. 21, 1966, William B. Ball to James A. McNulty, Nov. 6, 1966, Dec. 15, 1966, Jan. 9, 1967, Cardinal John Krol Papers; William B. Ball, "Legal Needs at the Church's National Office: Survey & Recommendations," Nov., 1966, Cardinal John Krol Papers; McConnell, "Ball, William Bentley (1916–1999)," 26; "Joseph G. Skelly," Skelly Dispute Resolution Center, http://www.skellydrc.com/joseph_g_skelly.html; Connell, interview, May 22, 2015; Murren, interviews, May 22, 2015, Aug. 16, 2016.

17. William B. Ball to John Cardinal Krol, Jan. 12, 1971, Nov. 29, 1972, Cardinal John Krol Papers; George Weigel, "The Neoconservative Difference: A Proposal for the Revival of Church and Society," in *Being Right: Conservative Catholics in America*, ed. Mary Jo Weaver and R. Scott Appleby (Bloomington: Indiana University Press, 1995), 138–40, 143, 150–51, 154–56; Damon Linker, *The Theocons: Secular America under Siege* (New York: Doubleday, 2006); William M. Shea, *The Lion and the Lamb: Evangelicals and Catholics in America* (New York: Oxford University Press, 2004), 3–5, 268; Charles C. Haynes and Oliver Thomas, *Finding Common Ground: A First Amendment Guide to Religion and Public Schools* (Nashville, Tenn.: First Amendment Center, 2007), 285–308, http://www.religiousfreedomcenter.org/wp-content/uploads/2015/01/Finding-Common-Ground-Williamsburg-Charter.pdf; "Evangelicals & Catholics Together: The Christian Mission in the Third Millennium," *First Things* (May 1994) https://www.firstthings.com/article/1994/05/evangelicals-catholics-together-the-christian-mission-in-the-third-millennium.

18. "History of the Center," Arizona Center for Disability Law, https://www.azdisabilitylaw.org/about-us/acdl-history; Rose Daly-Rooney, interview, June 26, 2015; Zobrest family interview, June 23, 2015.

19. Berning, interview, June 24, 2015; Nancy Guthrie, "Court Denies Interpreter to Deaf Catholic Student," *Tucson Territorial*, July 21, 1989.

20. Berning, interview, June 24, 2015; William B. Ball letter to Thomas J. Berning, September 12, 1988, Zobrest family papers.

21. JoAnn Sheperd, Opinion No. 88–04, April 26, 1988, James Zobrest file, CFSD; Bob Corbin letter to Stephen D. Neely, June 27, 1988, James Zobrest file, CFSD; Robert Hetzel, interview, Feb. 8, 2016.

22. John C. Richardson, interview, June 24, 2015; Hetzel, interview, Feb. 8, 2016.

23. Hetzel, interview, Feb. 8, 2016; Terek Amin, interview, March 18, 2017; Zobrest family interview, June 23, 2015.

24. Ernie Heltsley, "Catalina School District Is Sued by Deaf Teen on Interpreter Fees"; McKinney, "Special Education and the Establishment Clause," 1, 5, 18.

25. "John C. Richardson," DeConcini MacDonald Yetwin & Lacy, P.C., Attorneys, http://www.deconcinimcdonald.com/attorney/richardson-john-c; Dennis DeConcini and Jack L. August Jr., *Senator Dennis DeConcini: From the Center of the Aisle* (Tucson: University of Arizona Press, 2006), 59; Richardson, interview, June 24, 2015.

26. For a careful explication of the origins and meaning of the Establishment Clause, see Leonard W. Levy, *The Establishment Clause: Religion and the First Amendment*, 2nd. ed. (Chapel Hill: University of North Carolina Press, 1994); Daniel Dreisbach, *Thomas Jefferson and the Wall of Separation between Church and State* (New York: New York University Press, 2002), 34.

27. *Pierce v. Society of Sisters of the Holy Names of Jesus and Mary*, 268 U.S. 510 (1925); William Bentley Ball, "Address of William Bentley Ball," *The Red Mass*, Oct. 30, 1977, no publisher, date, or page given; *Cochran v. Louisiana State Board of Education*, 281 US 370 (1930); Joseph M. McMillan, "*Zobrest v. Catalina Foothills School District*: Lowering the Establishment Clause Barrier in School-Aid Controversies," *St. Louis University Law Journal* 39 (1994–1995): 342–44, 346–47, 351–52; *Everson v. Board of Education*, 330 U.S. 1 (1947). The U.S. Supreme Court had first referred to Jefferson's "wall" metaphor in a Mormon bigamy case called *Reynolds v. United States* (1869). See Donald L. Drakeman, "Reynolds v. U.S.: The Historical Construction of Constitutional Reality," *Constitutional Commentary* 21 (2004): 697–726; *Everson v. Board of Education*, 330 U.S. 1, 18 (1947); Ronald B. Flowers, *That Godless Court? Supreme Court Decisions on Church-State Relationships* (Louisville, Ky.: Westminster John Knox Press, 2005), 73; Barbara A. Perry, "Justice Hugo A. Black and the 'Wall of Separation between Church and State,'" *Journal of Church and State* 31 (Winter 1989): 55.

28. William Bentley Ball, "The Byzantine World of Religious Jurisprudence," *First Things* (April 1996), https://www.firstthings.com/article/1996/04/002-the-byzantine-world-of-religious-jurisprudence.

29. *McCollum v. Board of Education*, 333 U.S. 203 (1948); Philip B. Kurland, *Religion and the Law: Of Church and State and the Supreme Court* (Chicago: Aldine, 1962),

86–90; *Abington School District v. Schempp*, 374 U.S. 203 (1963); William B. Ball, "Keynote Address: 1981 Seminar on Church, Family, State, and Education," *Journal of Christian Jurisprudence* 3 (1982): 17.

30. William B. Ball, "Sense and Nonsense on Education Aid," *NCEA Bulletin* 65/4 (May 1969): 3, 7; Douglas Laycock, *Religious Liberty*, vol. 1: *Overviews and History* (Grand Rapids, Mich.: William B. Eerdmans, 2010), 315–19; *Board of Education v. Allen*, 292 U.S. 236 (1968); Joseph M. McMillan, "*Zobrest v. Catalina Foothills School District*: Lowering the Establishment Clause Barrier in School-Aid Controversies," 342–48, 349; James Hitchcock, *The Supreme Court and Religion in American Life*, vol. 1 (Princeton: Princeton University Press, 2004), 122–23; Dennis J. Hutchinson, *The Man Who Once Was Whizzer White: A Portrait of Justice Byron R. White* (New York: Free Press, 1998), 348; Jones, *John Cardinal Krol and the Cultural Revolution*, 470. The Rhode Island companion cases to *Lemon* were *Early v. DiCenso* and *Robinson v. DiCenso*. William Bentley Ball unequivocally affirmed E. Michael Jones's "accuracy" of events, particularly with regard to "freedom of parental choice in education." Ball noted Jones received "full access to the Krol files." See William B. Ball, "More than a Rant," *First Things* 59 (Jan. 1996): 5.

31. Sorauf, *Wall of Separation*, 59–85; William B. Ball to John Cardinal Krol, Dec. 17, 1963, Cardinal John Krol Papers.

32. Jones, *John Cardinal Krol and the Cultural Revolution*, 469–70, 474, 492–94; William B. Ball, "A Roman Catholic Viewpoint," *Public Controls for Nonpublic Schools*, ed. Donald A. Erickson (Chicago: University of Chicago Press, 1969), 187–97; William Bentley Ball, "Freedom of Religion, the American Constitution and the Catholic Church," in *Church and State in America: Catholic Questions*, ed. George A. Kelly (New York: St. John's University, 1992), 152; *Lemon v. Kurtzman*, 403 U.S. 602 (1971); Murren, interview, May 22, 2015; *Yoder Case*, 60–61; David H. Kurtzman, "The Pennsylvania Nonpublic Elementary and Secondary Education Act—Pioneer and Precedent," paper presented to the annual meeting of the Education Commission of the States, Denver, July 7, 1969, 1–2, https://files.eric.ed.gov/fulltext/ED033473.pdf; *Lemon v. Kurtzman* 403 U.S. 602 (1971)," Justia US Supreme Court, https://supreme.justia.com/cases/federal/us/403/602; Adam Liptak, "Alton T. Lemon, Who Challenged State Aid to Religious Schools, Dies at 84," *New York Times*, May 25, 2013; Donald R. Barbera, *Black and Not Baptist: Nonbelief and Freethought in the Black Community* (Lincoln, Neb.: iUniverse, 2003), 219; David L. Hudson Jr., "Lemon Plaintiff, Out of Limelight, Still Tracks Church-State Issues," Freedom Forum Institute, May 19, 2004, http://www.freedomforuminstitute.org/2004/05/19/lemon-plaintiff-out-of-limelight-still-tracks-church-state-issues; Christopher Thomas Anglim, *Religion and the Law: A Dictionary* (Santa Barbara: ABC-CLIO, 1999), 212.

33. Sorauf, *Wall of Separation*, 190; Gregg Ivers, *To Build a Wall: American Jews and the Separation of Church and State* (Charlottesville: University Press of Virginia, 1995), 74; Ball to Krol, Dec. 17, 1963, Cardinal John Krol Papers; Leo Pfeffer, *God, Caesar, and the Constitution: The Court as Referee of Church-State Confrontation* (Boston: Beacon Press, 1974), 20.

34. "Church and State Conference Held at Law School," (University of Pennsylvania) *Law Alumni Journal* 1/1 (Fall 1965): 4, http://scholarship.law.upenn.edu/cgi/viewcontent.cgi?article=1100&context=plj; William B. Ball, "Legal Needs at the Church's National Office: Survey & Recommendations," Nov. 1966, Cardinal John Krol Papers, Catholic Historical Research Center of the Archdiocese of Philadelphia; William B. Ball to James A. McNulty, Dec. 15, 1966, Cardinal John Krol Papers; Jones, *John Cardinal Krol and the Cultural Revolution*, 471, 482.

35. William B. Ball to John Cardinal Krol, Feb. 12, 1971, Cardinal John Krol Papers; *Lemon v. Kurtzman*, 403 U.S. 602, 612–13, 619, 667; James Hitchcock, *The Supreme Court and Religion in American Life*, vol. 1 (Princeton: Princeton University Press, 2004), 124–25. There was one dissenter in the Rhode Island case—Byron White.

36. Jones, *John Cardinal Krol and the Cultural Revolution*, 494–500; William B. Ball to John Cardinal Krol, July 17, 1971, Cardinal John Krol Papers, Catholic Historical Research Center of the Archdiocese of Philadelphia; C. Matthew McMahon, "The Reformed Theologian, Loraine Boettner," A Puritan's Mind, https://web.archive.org/web/20070202111009/http://www.apuritansmind.com/ChristianWalk/LoraineBoettnerBio.htm; Loraine Boettner, *Roman Catholicism* (Philadelphia: Presbyterian & Reformed Publishing, 2000), 359; Paul Freund, "Public Aid to Parochial Schools," *Harvard Law Review* 82 (1969): 1680; Ball, *Mere Creatures of the State?*, 27, 34, 37; William Bentley Ball, "The Effect of Current Judicial Decisions on the Place of Catholics in the Life of the Country," in *When Conscience and Politics Meet: A Catholic View* (San Francisco: Ignatius Press, 1993), 71; Ball, *In Search of a National Morality*, 212; McKinney, "Special Education and the Establishment Clause," 9.

37. *Meek v. Pittenger*, 421 U.S. 349 (1975); Joseph G. Skelly, "*Meek v. Pittenger*: Will It Precipitate a Solution?" *Catholic Lawyer* 20 (Autumn 1974): 335–46.

38. Ball, *Mere Creatures of the State?*, 43; oral argument, *Meek v. Pittenger*, 421 U.S. 349 (1975), https://www.oyez.org/cases/1974/73-1765; Elizabeth Lugg, "Providing Title I Services on Parochial School Grounds: *Aguilar v. Felton* Is No Longer the Law," *Urban Lawyer* 31 (1999): 151; McMillan, "*Zobrest v. Catalina Foothills School District*," 355–57.

39. McMillan, "*Zobrest v. Catalina Foothills School District*," 361, 363; *Wolman v. Walter*, 433 U.S. 229, 244 (1977); Joseph E. Bryson and Samuel H. Houston Jr., *The Supreme Court and Public Funds for Religious Schools: The Burger Years, 1969–1986* (Jefferson: McFarland, 1990), 93–99; Levy, *Establishment Clause*, 154–55, 171, 174–79; Flowers, *That Godless Court?*, 79–80, 82–83, 86–87; James John Jurinski, *Religion on Trial: A Handbook with Cases, Laws, and Documents* (Santa Barbara, Calif.: ABC CLIO, 2004), 125–26; Stephen V. Monsma, *Positive Neutrality: Letting Religious Freedom Ring* (Westport, Conn.: Greenwood Press, 1993), 27, 236; *Aguilar v. Felton*, 473 U.S. 402 (1985); *School District of Grand Rapids v. Ball*, 473 U.S. 373, 385, 394, 397 (1985); Charles J. Russo et al., "The Delivery of Special Education Services in Catholic Schools: One Hand Gives, the Other Hand Takes Away," *Catholic Education: A Journal of Inquiry & Practice* 3/3 (Oct. 2013): 376; Stephen V. Monsma, *When Sacred and Secular Mix: Religious Nonprofit Organizations and Public Money* (Lanham, Md.:

Rowman & Littlefield, 1996), 33, 37–39; Leslie C. Griffin, ed., *Law & Religion: Cases in Context* (New York: Aspen, 2010), 207; Laycock, *Religious Liberty*, vol. 1, 19–20, 140, 317, 322–23; Bryson and Houston, *Supreme Court and Public Funds for Religious Schools*, 115–24; Joyce Martin, "Special Education and the Non-Public School Child: A Handicap Is a Non-Sectarian Condition," *Law & Inequality: A Journal of Theory and Practice* 5/3 (1987): 571–72; *Witters v. Washington Department of Services for the Blind*, 474 U.S. 481 (1986); "Blind Student Tries Case for Return of Aid," *Daily Guardian* (Wright State University), May 14, 1985, 1–2; Laurie Goodstein, "The Nation: In States, Hurdles Loom," *New York Times*, June 30, 2002, https://www.nytimes.com/2002/06/30/weekinreview/the-nation-in-states-hurdles-loom.html; John Witte Jr., *Religion and the American Constitutional Experiment: Essential Rights and Liberties* (Boulder: Westview Press, 2000), 176–77; Henry J. Reske, "The Supreme Court, in Its First Decision in a . . . ," UPI archives, Jan. 27, 1986; Leslie C. Griffin, ed. *Law & Religion: Cases in Context* (New York: Aspen, 2010), 264; Michael McConnell, "Equal Treatment and Religious Discrimination," in *Equal Treatment of Religion in a Pluralistic Society*, ed. Stephen V. Monsma and J. Christopher Soper (Grand Rapids, Mich.: William B. Eerdsmans, 1998), 45–46. The U.S. Supreme Court remanded the *Witters* case to the Washington Supreme Court, which used the state constitution to block the scholarship for anyone attending religious schools.

40. *Wallace v. Jaffree*, 472 U.S. 38, 111–112 (1985). For a discussion of the Rehnquist court's jurisprudence regarding church and state questions, see Tinsley E. Yarbrough, *The Rehnquist Court and the Constitution* (New York: Oxford University Press, 2000), 155–77.

41. Derek Davis, *Original Intent: Chief Justice Rehnquist and the Course of American Church/State Relations* (Buffalo: Prometheus Books, 1991), 114–17; McMillan, "*Zobrest v. Catalina Foothills School District*," 359–61.

CHAPTER 5. SIGNING, SECTARIAN SCHOOLS, AND THE LAW

1. Arthur H. Rotstein, "Justices to Give Deaf Tucson Student a Court Interpreter," *Arizona Daily Star*, Feb. 22, 1993; Joan Biskupic, "Deaf Student's Case Sets Up Church-State Test," *Washington Post*, Feb. 21, 1993; Ellen Gamerman, "Zobrest Case May Set New Standards," *Arizona Daily Star*, Feb. 28, 1993.

2. Margret A. Winzer, *From Integration to Inclusion: A History of Special Education in the 20th Century* (Washington, D.C.: Gallaudet University Press, 2009), 121; Rotstein, "Justices to Give Deaf Tucson Student."

3. "Richard M. Bilby: U.S. District Court Judge of District of Arizona," *University of Arizona Law Record* 20/1 (Fall 1998): 10; Dennis DeConcini and Jack L. August Jr., *Senator Dennis DeConcini: From the Center of the Aisle* (Tucson: University of Arizona Press, 2006), 62, 120–121, 245–246; Robert McCormick, "Injunction to Pay Deaf Student's Interpreter Denied," *Tucson Citizen*, Aug. 13, 1988; *Wolman v. Walter* 433 U.S. 229 (1977).

4. McCormick, "Injunction to Pay Deaf Student's Interpreter"; Ernie Heltsley, "U.S. Judge Denies State-Paid Interpreter for Deaf Teen," *Arizona Daily Star*, Aug.

13, 1988; John C. Richardson, letter to Thomas Berning, Sept. 23, 1988, James Zobrest file, Catalina Foothills School District (CFSD).

5. Zobrest family interview, June 23, 2015; Larry Copenhaver, "Public School Asked to Pay for Interpreter," *Tucson Citizen*, July 19, 1989.

6. Kirk A. Kennedy, "Opportunity Declined: The Supreme Court Refuses to Jettison the Lemon Test in *Zobrest v. Catalina Foothills School District*, 113 S. Ct. 2462 (1993)," *Nebraska Law Review* 73 (1994): 410; McCormick, "Injunction to Pay Deaf Student's Interpreter"; Nancy Guthrie, "Court Denies Interpreter to Deaf Catholic Student," *Tucson Territorial*, July 21, 1989, 12.

7. Zobrest family interview, June 23, 2015; Sandi Zobrest to Bruce Dierenfield, email, Jan. 31, 2018; Joe Burchell and John F. Rawlinson, "Fire Ruins Main Plant of Oliver's, *Arizona Daily Star*, Aug. 13; Stella Pena and David L. Teibel, "Arsonists Cause $3 Million Damage," *Tucson Citizen*, Aug. 18, 1989; Ernie Heltsley, "Glover Files Chapter 11 after Competitor's Fire," *Arizona Daily Star*, undated; Tamar Lewin, "Deaf Student's Need Could Alter Church-State Relations," *New York Times*, Feb. 22, 1993.

8. Zobrest family interview, June 23, 2015; Aaron Epstein, "Supreme Court Hears Case of Tucson Family Caught between . . . Church and State," *Phoenix Gazette*, Feb. 2, 1993; Lewin, "Deaf Student's Need."

9. Rev. Leo McCarthy letter to Rev. Jack Lord, March 28, 1990, Zobrest family papers; Zobrest family interview, June 23, 2015; Rev. Leo McCarthy to James Zobrest, May 30, 1990, Zobrest family papers; Stanley D. Hayden, letter to Rev. Leo McCarthy, Nov. 6, 1990, Zobrest family papers; Jim Click Jr., letter to James Zobrest, July 23, 1990, Zobrest family papers; Glenn Luglan letter to Jim Zobrest, Sept. 12, 1990, Zobrest family papers.

10. Matt Rees, "The Judge the Supreme Court Loves to Overturn," *Weekly Standard* (May 5, 1997); *Vander Malle v. Ambach*, 673 F.2d 49 (2d Cir 1982); *Tilton v. Jefferson City Board of Education*, 705 F.2d 800, 804 (6th Cir., 1983); Michael Kirkland, "Court Rejects Va. Christian School Case," UPI archives, Jan. 8, 1996, https://www.upi.com/Archives/1996/01/08/Court-rejects-Va-Christian-school-case/9131821077200/; Charles J. Russo et al., "The Delivery of Special Education Services in Catholic Schools: One Hand Gives, the Other Hand Takes Away," *Catholic Education: A Journal of Inquiry & Practice* 3/3 (Oct. 2013): 380; *Goodall v. Stafford County School Board*, 930 F.2d 363 (4th Cir.) (Goodall I), cert. denied, 502 U.S. 864, 116 L. Ed. 2d 149, 112 S. Ct. 188 (1991).

11. *Goodall v. Stafford County School Board*, 60 F.3d 168 (4th Cir. 1995) cert. denied, 516 U.S. 1046 (1996).

12. News staff of the *San Francisco Chronicle*, *The Quake of '89* (San Francisco: Chronicle Books, 1989); Randy Shilts and Susan Sward, "Oakland Freeway Collapses—Bay Bridge Fails," *San Francisco Chronicle*, Oct. 18, 1989; John C. Richardson, interview, June 24, 2015; *Zobrest v. Catalina Foothills School District*, 963 F.2d 1190 (9th Cir), cert. granted, 113 S. Ct. 52 (1992). John Paul Stevens argues that had Thurgood Marshall remained on the court, he would have made the difference in "most, if not all," of the decisions in which there were four dissenters; see John Paul Stevens, *Five Chiefs: A Supreme Court Memoir* (New York: Little, Brown, 2011), 187.

13. Mr. and Mrs. Larry Zobrest, letter to Thomas Tang, November 11, 1991, James Zobrest file, CFSD.

14. William B. Ball, letter to Betty B. Fletcher, March 27, 1992, James Zobrest file, CFSD. Three days after excoriating the Ninth Circuit Court judges for their prolonged delay in deciding the *Zobrest* case, attorney Ball thought better of his blistering personal attack and apologized to each of them in turn for "implying a betrayal of public trust upon your part and 'neglect.'" Still, Ball felt constrained to add that the judges could "little imagine the distress which your delay has caused my clients."

15. Richardson, interview, June 24, 2015; "Court Rejects State-Paid Interpreter, *Arizona Daily Star*, May 3, 1992; Rees, "Judge the Supreme Court Loves"; Kennedy, "Opportunity Declined," 410–11; "Court Rejects State-Paid Interpreter," *Arizona Daily Star*, May 3, 1992; Judith Sharon Rosen, "Constitutional Law—*Zobrest v. Catalina Foothills School District*: Should the Wall between Church and State Come Crumbling Down? Funding Sign Language Interpreters and the First Amendment," *Golden Gate University Law Review* 23 (1993): 90–91; Mark Walsh, "Court Rejects Interpreter for Deaf Church-School Student," *Education Week* 11/34 (May 13, 1992): 11.

16. Wolfgang Saxon, "Thomas Tang, 73, Senior Judge for a Federal Court of Appeals," *New York Times*, July 21, 1995; Judith Sharon Rosen, "Constitutional Law," 91–95; *Zobrest v. Catalina Foothills School District*, 963 F.2d (9th Cir.) at 1202.

17. Judith Sharon Rosen, "Constitutional Law," 95–97; Allan G. Osborne Jr., "Providing Special Education and Related Services to Parochial School Students in the Wake of Zobrest," *West's Education Law Reporter* 87 (Feb. 1994): 334; *Zobrest v. Catalina Foothills School District*, 963 F.2d at 1203–04.

18. Richardson, interview, June 24, 2015; William Ball, "God Save This Honorable Court," *Crisis* (October 1992): 26; William Bentley Ball diary, May 28, 1992.

19. Rob Boston, "Hearing Problem: Why a Deaf Student's Supreme Court Case Has Church-State Separationists Worried," *Church & State* 6/2 (February 1993): 4; William Bentley Ball diary, October 5–6, 8, 1992; "Michael W. McConnell," Stanford Law School directory, https://law.stanford.edu/directory/michael-w-mcconnell/#slsnav-key-works; *School District of Grand Rapids v. Ball* 473 U.S. 373 (1985). The case of *School District of Grand Rapids v. Ball* involved Phyllis Ball and other parents who objected to government aid to students in religious schools, not William Bentley Ball, the Zobrests' attorney.

20. Boston, "Hearing Problem," 6; Lewin, "Deaf Student's Need"; *Witters v. Washington Department of Services for the Blind*, 474 U.S. 481 (1986); Al Kamen, "Court Accepts Church-State Case," *Washington Post*, April 2, 1985, https://www.washingtonpost.com/archive/politics/1985/04/02/court-accepts-church-state-case/04ebeb54-b7e9-4e3d-8b5e-444a90432fc7; William Bentley Ball, "First Amendment Watch," *Crisis* (Sept. 1993): 44.

21. Brief filed by the U.S. Department of Justice, 4–7, 12–15, *Zobrest v. Catalina Foothills School District*, 509 U.S. 1 (1993).

22. All briefs mentioned in this paragraph were filed as part of *Zobrest v. Catalina Foothills School District*, 509 U.S. 1 (1993): brief filed by the Christian Legal Society, the National Association of Evangelicals, the National Council of Churches of Christ in

the USA, the Catholic League for Religious and Civil Rights, the Christian Life Commission of the Southern Baptist Convention, the Association of Christian Schools International, the Family Research Council, the Church of Jesus Christ of Latter-Day Saints, Joni and Friends, and the Lutheran Church—Missouri Synod, 1–6; Boston, "Hearing Problem," 6, 8; brief filed by the United States Catholic Conference, 2; brief filed by Arizona School Boards Association, 2, 5, 10; brief filed by the National School Boards Association, 2–3, 10–12; brief filed by Arizona School Boards Association, 5; brief filed by the National School Boards Association, 20–22.

23. Epstein, "Supreme Court Hears Case of Tucson Family"; Boston, "Hearing Problem," 8. All briefs mentioned were filed as part of *Zobrest v. Catalina Foothills School District*, 509 U.S. 1 (1993): brief filed by the American Civil Liberties Union, Americans United for Separation of Church and State, the American Jewish Committee, and the Anti-Defamation League, 5–6, 8–9, 12–17; brief filed by the American Jewish Congress, the Union of American Hebrew Congregations, and the Baptist Joint Committee on Public Affairs, 44.

24. Brief filed by the Alexander Graham Bell Association for the Deaf, 1-7, *Zobrest v. Catalina Foothills School District*, 509 U.S. 1 (1993).

25. Philip Murren to Bruce Dierenfield, email, Jan. 2, 2018; William Bentley Ball's notes for *Zobrest v. Catalina Foothills School District* (1993), 8, 12; Richard Connell, interview, May 22, 2015; Philip Murren, interviews, May 22, 2015, Aug. 16, 2016; Thomas Berning, interview, June 24, 2015; Virginia Ball Duncan to Bruce Dierenfield, email, Jan. 17, 2018. As William Ball prepared for oral argument, he may have recalled a pessimistic passage he had once written: "We must not pin any ultimate hopes on our courts (including the Supreme Court)" because American judges come from a "mancentered" society steeped in "materialism, hedonism, dishonesty and violence." See Kelly, *The Separation of Church and Freedom*, 20.

26. Richardson, interview, June 24, 2015; Brett Dunkelman, interview, Sept. 25, 2015; Thomas M. Keck, *The Most Activist Supreme Court in History: The Road to Modern Judicial Conservatism* (Chicago: University of Chicago Press, 2004), 228–29; Aaron Epstein, "The Interpreter and the Establishment Clause," in *A Year in the Life of the Supreme Court*, ed. Rodney A. Smolla (Durham, N.C.: Duke University Press, 1995), 135; John C. Richardson to David Gerber, email, June 29, 2015.

27. David G. Savage, *Turning Right: The Making of the Rehnquist Court* (New York: John Wiley & Sons, 1992), 110–11, 250; Nancy Maveety, *Justice Sandra Day O'Connor: Strategist on the Supreme Court* (Lanham, Md.: Rowman & Littlefield, 1996), 36, 63, 130; Robert W. Van Sickel, *Not a Particularly Different Voice: The Jurisprudence of Sandra Day O'Connor* (New York: Peter Lang, 1998), 133; Joan Biskupic, *Sandra Day O'Connor: How the First Woman on the Supreme Court Became Its Most Influential Justice* (New York: Harper Perennial, 2005), 282–86, 288; Derek Davis, *Original Intent: Chief Justice Rehnquist and the Course of American Church/State Relations* (Buffalo: Prometheus Books, 1991), 160–61.

28. Linda Greenhouse, "Reagan Nominates Anthony Kennedy to Supreme Court," *New York Times*, Nov. 12, 1987; Edward Lazarus, *Closed Chambers: The First Eyewitness Account of the Epic Struggles inside the Supreme Court* (New York: Times Books, 1998),

251, 471; Helen J. Knowles, *The Tie Goes to Freedom: Justice Anthony M. Kennedy on Liberty* (Lanham, Md.: Rowman & Littlefield, 2009), 92; *Lee v. Weisman*, 505 U.S. 577 (1992); James F. Simon, *The Center Holds: The Power Struggle inside the Rehnquist Court* (New York: Simon & Schuster, 1995), 254, 257–89; Epstein, "Interpreter and the Establishment Clause," 135; David M. Ackerman and Kimberly D. Jones, *The Law of Church and State in the Supreme Court Revisited* (New York: Nova Science, 2006), 27; Boston, "Hearing Problem," 5; Maveety, *Justice Sandra Day O'Connor*, 63–64, 81; Patrick M. Garry, *Wrestling with God: The Courts' Tortuous Treatment of Religion* (Washington, D.C.: Catholic University Press of America, 2006), 59; David L. Hudson Jr., *The Rehnquist Court: Understanding Its Impact and Legacy* (Westport, Conn.: Praeger, 2006), 73.

29. Richardson, interview, June 24, 2015; Hudson, *Rehnquist Court*, 74; Dunkelman, interview, September 25, 2015.

30. William Bentley Ball diary, February 25, 1993; Deborah McQuaid, "Former Erie Family Argues Case before U.S. Supreme Court," *Erie (Pa.) Morning News*, Feb. 25, 1993; Linda P. Campbell, "Use of Sign-Language Interpreter Keys Church-State Court Case," *Chicago Tribune*, Feb. 24, 1993; Deborah McQuaid, "A Family's Fight Takes on National Significance," *Erie (Pa.) Morning News*, Feb. 18, 1993; Rotstein, "Justices to Give Deaf Tucson Student."

31. William Bentley Ball diary, Feb. 25, 1993; Kennedy, "Opportunity Declined," 427–31; Virginia Ball Duncan, interview, May 22, 2015.

32. William Bentley Ball diary, May 25, 1992, Feb. 24, 1993; Ball Duncan, interview, May 22, 2015.

33. Ball Duncan, interview, May 22, 2015; Zobrest family interview, June 23, 2015; Richardson, interview, June 23, 2015; William Bentley Ball diary, Feb. 25, 1993; Virginia Ball Duncan to Bruce Dierenfield, email, Oct. 31, 2017; Leigh Jackson, "For the Deaf, a Sign of Improvement," *Washington Post*, Feb. 15, 1990, https://www.washingtonpost.com/archive/local/1990/02/15/for-the-deaf-a-sign-of-improvement/34ea7d7d-2739-4d32-b7fc-31a2ce5efbcd.

34. Ball Duncan, interview, May 22, 2015; Ellen Gamerman, "Justices Weigh Church-State Issue, Handicap Rights in Tucsonan's Case," *Arizona Daily Star*, Feb. 25, 1993; Zobrest family interview, June 23, 2015.

35. Epstein, "Supreme Court Hears Case of Tucson Family"; Joseph R. McKinney, "Special Education and the Establishment Clause," *West's Education Law Reporter* 65 (March 14, 1991): 20–22; Richardson, interview, June 24, 2015; Peter Irons, ed., *May It Please the Court: Courts, Kids, and the Constitution* (New York: New Press, 2000), 315–17; Ken Foskett, *Judging Thomas: The Life and Times of Clarence Thomas* (New York: HarperCollins, 2004), 3, 54–66, 73–88, 96–97; Joan Biskupic, *American Original: The Life and Constitution of Supreme Court Justice Antonin Scalia* (New York: Sarah Crichton Books, 2009), 20–26; Lazarus, *Closed Chambers*, 192; Mark Tushnet, *A Court Divided: The Rehnquist Court and the Future of Constitutional Law* (New York: W. W. Norton, 2006), 73–75; William M. Wiecek, *The History of the Supreme Court of the United States*, vol. 12: *The Birth of the Modern Constitution: The United States Supreme Court, 1941–1953* (New York: Cambridge University Press, 2006), 273; Davis, *Original Intent*, 83, 85–88, 118; Boston, "Hearing Problem," 5.

36. Irons, *May It Please the Court*, 315; Richardson, interview, June 23, 2015.

37. William Bentley Ball diary, February 25, 1993; Oral argument, *Zobrest v. Catalina Foothills School District*, 1993, Westlaw 754944, 4.

38. Oral argument, *Zobrest v. Catalina Foothills School District*, 1993, Westlaw 754944, 6–7.

39. Oral argument, *Zobrest v. Catalina Foothills School District*, 1993, Westlaw 754944, 7, 10.

40. Tinsley Yarbrough, *David Hackett Souter: Traditional Republican on the Rehnquist Court* (New York: Oxford University Press, 2005), 7, 113, 255; Lazarus, *Closed Chambers*, 515; Melissa Rogers, "Justice Souter and the Supreme Court's Church-State Balance," Brookings Institution, May 19, 2009, https://www.brookings.edu/opinions/justice-souter-and-the-supreme-courts-church-state-balance/; *Zobrest v. Catalina Foothills School District* (1993); Oral argument, *Zobrest v. Catalina Foothills School District*, 1993, Westlaw 754944, 13–14; William Bentley Ball, *Mere Creatures of the State? Education, Religion, and the Courts* (Notre Dame, Ind.: Crisis Books, 1994), 53; William Bentley Ball diary, Feb. 25, 1993.

41. Oral argument, *Zobrest v. Catalina Foothills School District*, 1993, Westlaw 754944, 16; William Bentley Ball diary, Feb. 25, 1993.

42. "William C. Bryson, Circuit Judge," United States Court of Appeals for the Federal Circuit, http://www.cafc.uscourts.gov/judges/william-c-bryson-circuit-judge; Richardson, interview, June 24, 2015; Oral argument, *Zobrest v. Catalina Foothills School District*, 1993, Westlaw 754944, 20, 24.

43. Oral argument, *Zobrest v. Catalina Foothills School District*, 1993, Westlaw 754944, 25, 48; William Bentley Ball diary, Feb. 25, 1993; Richardson, interview, June 24, 2015; Brett Dunkelman, interview, Sept. 25, 2015; Davis, *Original Intent*, 115; Bill Barnhart and Gene Schlickman, *John Paul Stevens: An Independent Life* (DeKalb: Northern Illinois University Press, 2010), 246–48; Eduardo Moisés Peñalver, "Treating Religion as Speech: Justice Stevens's Religion Clause Jurisprudence," *Fordham Law Review* 74 (2006): 2243; Erwin Chemerinsky, "A Fixture on a Changing Court: Justice Stevens and the Establishment Clause," *Northwestern University School of Law* 106/2 (2012): 587, 589–93.

44. Oral argument, *Zobrest v. Catalina Foothills School District*, 1993, Westlaw 754944, 25, 34, 40, 42, 48; Dunkelman, interview, Sept. 25, 2015; Davis, *Original Intent*, 115; Barnhart and Schlickman, *John Paul Stevens*, 246–48; Peñalver, "Treating Religion as Speech," 2243; Chemerinsky, "Fixture on a Changing Court," 587, 589–93; Marjorie Williams, "How Sandra Day O'Connor Became the Most Powerful Woman in 1980s America," *Washington Post*, March 29, 2016, https://www.washingtonpost.com/news/arts-and-entertainment/wp/2016/03/29/how-sandra-day-oconnor-became-the-most-powerful-woman-in-1980s-america; Richardson, interview, June 24, 2015.

45. Richard L. Hasen, *The Justice of Contradictions: Antonin Scalia and the Politics of Disruption* (New Haven, CT: Yale University Press, 2018), ix–x, 2, 5–6, 40–63, 172–73; Elizabeth Dias, "How Scalia's Faith Reshaped the Supreme Court," *Time*, Feb. 13, 2016, http://time.com/4220768/antonin-scalia-dead-catholic-legacy/; Biskupic, *American*

Original, 40–41, 87–88, 117–18, 139, 185–88, 190–92, 206, 208–10, 284, 351–52; William B. Ball, "Signum Fidei Medal Address," LaSalle College, Oct. 2, 1965, William Bentley Ball Papers, American Catholic History Research Center and University Archives, Catholic University of America, Washington, D.C.; Erwin Chemerinsky, "The Jurisprudence of Justice Scalia: A Critical Appraisal," *University of Hawaii Law Review* 22 (2000): 385, 388–89, 392; Jay Schlosser, "Establishment Clause and Justice Scalia: What the Future Holds for Church and State," *Notre Dame Law Review* 63/3 (1988): 387. Scalia did disagree with the Catholic Church when it came to the death penalty. See Richard A. Brisbin Jr., *Justice Antonin Scalia and the Conservative Revival* (Baltimore: Johns Hopkins University Press, 1997), 217, 220, 301.

46. Oral argument, *Zobrest v. Catalina Foothills School District*, 1993, Westlaw 754944, 42–44, 48; *Everson v. Board of Education*, 330 U.S. 1 (1947).

47. Oral argument, *Zobrest v. Catalina Foothills School District*, 1993, Westlaw 754944, 34–35; Rex E. Lee and Richard G. Wilkins, "On Greatness and Constitutional Vision: Justice Byron R. White," *Brigham Young University Law Review* 1994/2 (1994): 297, 305, 312; Epstein, "Interpreter and the Establishment Clause," 134.

48. Lazarus, *Closed Chambers*, 253; Gregory C. Sisk, "The Willful Judging of Harry Blackmun," *Missouri Law Review* 70/4 (Fall 2005): 1061, 1063; Simon, *Center Holds*, 213–15, 284.

49. Jane Mayer and Jill Abramson, *Strange Justice: The Selling of Clarence Thomas* (New York: Plume, 1994), 17; Laura Blumenfeld, "The Nominee's Soul Mate," *Washington Post*, Sept. 10, 1991; Scott Douglas Gerber, *First Principles: The Jurisprudence of Clarence Thomas* (New York: New York University Press, 1999), 59–60; Lazarus, *Closed Chambers*, 449–51.

50. William Bentley Ball diary, Feb. 25, 1993.

51. William Bentley Ball diary, Feb. 25, 1993; Ball Duncan, interview, May 22, 2015; Zobrest family interview, June 23, 2015.

52. Radhika Rao, letter to Harry Blackmun, Feb. 25, 1993 case file: *Zobrest v. Catalina Foothills School District*, Harry A. Blackmun papers, Library of Congress, Washington, D.C.

53. Davis, *Original Intent*, 83; *Meek v. Pittenger*, 421 U.S. 349 (1975), 396; David L. Hudson Jr., *The Rehnquist Court: Understanding Its Impact and Legacy* (Westport, Conn.: Praeger, 2006), 71–72, 77; Gerber, *First Principles*, 142; Jeffrey Rosen, "Rehnquist the Great?," *Atlantic*, April 2005, https://www.theatlantic.com/magazine/archive/2005/04/rehnquist-the-great/303820/; Herman J. Obermayer, *Rehnquist: A Personal Portrait of the Distinguished Chief Justice of the U.S.* (New York: Threshold Editions, 2009), 109; *Wallace v. Jaffree*, 472 U.S. 38 (1985); Simon, *Center Holds*, 11, 303–04; Mark Tushnet, *A Court Divided: The Rehnquist Court and the Future of Constitutional Law* (New York: W. W. Norton, 2006), 11.

54. William Bentley Ball diary, June 11, 18, 1993.

55. Jeffrey Rosen, "Rehnquist the Great?"; Kennedy, "Opportunity Declined," 411; Linda Greenhouse, "Court Says Government May Pay for Interpreter in Religious School," *New York Times*, June 19, 1993; Joseph M. McMillan, "Zobrest v. Catalina Foothills School District: Lowering the Establishment Clause Barrier in School-

Aid Controversies," *St. Louis University Law Journal* 39 (1994–1995): 338; Michaelle Greco Cacchillo, "*Zobrest v. Catalina Foothills School District*: A Victory for Disabled Children, A Snub for the Lemon Test," *Loyola University Chicago Law Journal* 25/3 (Spring 1994): 445.

56. *Zobrest v. Catalina Foothills School District*, 509 U.S. 1–3, 8, 10, 14, 20 (1993); Cacchillo, "*Zobrest v. Catalina Foothills School District*," 445; Flowers, *That Godless Court?*, 87; Greenhouse, "Court Says Government May Pay for Interpreter."

57. *Zobrest v. Catalina Foothills School District*, 509 U.S. 1, 13 (1993).

58. *Zobrest v. Catalina Foothills School District*, 509 U.S. 1, 7–8, 16 (1993); Kennedy, "Opportunity Declined," 412, 419; Epstein, "Interpreter and the Establishment Clause," 139.

59. *Zobrest v. Catalina Foothills School District*, 509 U.S. 1, 2, 10 (1993).

60. *Zobrest v. Catalina Foothills School District*, 509 U.S. 1, 13 (1993); James Santeford, questionnaire, October 31, 2015.

61. *Zobrest v. Catalina Foothills School District*, 509 U.S. 1, 14, 17, 24 (1993); Kaarin Long, "Zobrest v. Catalina Foothills School District: A Misapplication of Establishment Clause Precedent," *South Dakota Law Review* 39 (1994): 409–10; Kennedy, "Opportunity Declined," 411–12. Justice Sandra Day O'Connor filed a separate dissent making essentially the same point Blackmun did.

62. *Zobrest v. Catalina Foothills School District*, 509 U.S. 18–19, 22 (1993).

63. Zobrest family interview, June 23, 2015; Heather Newman, "Case Will Help Others, Deaf Student Says," *Tucson Citizen*, June 19, 1993; Maureen O'Connell, "Deaf Salpointe Graduate Wins Case," *Arizona Daily Star*, June 19, 1993.

64. "Tucsonan Wins High Court Case," *Tucson Citizen*, June 18, 1993; James J. Kilpatrick, "One More Look at a Famous Wall," *Indianapolis Star*, July 17, 1993; William Bentley Ball, *Mere Creatures of the State?*, 51.

CHAPTER 6. THE AFTERMATH

1. Thomas Berning, interview, June 24, 2015.

2. Rob Boston, "Hearing Problems: Why a Deaf Student's Supreme Court Case Has Church-State Separationists Worried," *Church & State* 6/2 (Feb. 1993): 5.

3. Quoted in "Deaf Ex-Salpointe Student Wins Supreme Court Decision," *Tucson Citizen*, June 18, 1993.

4. As evidenced in these writings by William Bentley Ball: "Like in an Occupied Country," in *In Search of a National Morality: A Manifesto for Evangelicals and Catholics*, ed. William Bentley Ball (San Francisco: Ignatius Press, 1992), 9–13; *Mere Creatures of the State? Education: Education, Religion, and the Courts—A View from the Courtroom* (Notre Dame, Ind.: Crisis Books, 1994); "Testimonies," in *Why I Am Still a Catholic*, ed. Kevin and Marilyn Ryan (New York: Riverhead Books, 1998), 147–61; and with considerable vehemence in an interview, "No Mere Creatures: A Constitutional Lawyer Turns Author in an Effort to Raise Public Awareness of Growing Threats to Religious Freedom in the United States," *Catholic World Report*, Aug./Sept. 1995, 54–57. Ball's ideological position, at the juncture of modern American political conservatism and postconciliar American Catholicism, and his sense of

moral urgency connect closely with those of the late twentieth-century Catholic neoconservative public intellectuals; George Weigel, "The Neoconservative Difference: A Proposal for Renewal of Church and Society," in *Being Right: Conservative Catholics in America*, ed. R. Scott Appleby and Mary Jo Weaver (Bloomington: Indiana University Press, 1995), 138–58.

5. Michelle Greco Cocchillo, "A Victory for Disabled Children, a Snub for the Lemon Test," *Loyola University of Chicago Law Journal* 25 (Spring 1994): 445–79. Not invoking the Lemon Test could be easily confused with overruling it; Julie Marie Hood, "What's Past Is Prologue: Establishment Clause Jurisprudence after *Zobrest v. Catalina Foothills School District*," *Wisconsin Law Review* 6 (1994): 1327–44.

6. *Agostini v. Felton*, 521 U.S. 203 (1997); *Mitchell v. Helms*, 530 U.S. 793 (2000); *Zelman v. Simmons-Harris*, 536 U.S. 639 (2002).

7. William Bentley Ball, "Supreme Court Review: Church-State Jurisprudence," *Catholic Lawyer*, 36/3 (1999–2000): 249–50.

8. *Zelman v. Simmons-Harris*, 536 U.S. 639 (2002), https://caselaw.findlaw.com/us-supreme-court/536/639.html (accessed Sept. 15, 2017).

9. A point made repeatedly in Justice Blackman's dissent in the *Zobrest* decision, in which he emphasized the unprecedented approval by the majority of an ongoing role of an employee, paid for with public funds, interpreting Catholic doctrine routinely during the school day in a Catholic institution. Commentators concerned with the implications of the decision for the coherence of the Establishment Clause reiterated this point. See, for example, Jesse Choper, "The Unpredictability of the Supreme Court's Doctrine in Establishment Clause Cases," *Wayne Law Review* 43 (1996–97): 1443–46.

10. David G. Savage, *Turning Right: The Making of the Rehnquist Court* (New York: John Wiley and Sons, 1992), 248–93, 303–32, and summarized, 325–26.

11. *Agostini v. Felton*, 521 U.S. 203 (1997), https://caselaw.findlaw.com/us-supreme-court/521/203.html (accessed Sept. 15, 2017).

12. *Mitchell v. Helms*, 530 U.S. 793 (2000), https://caselaw.findlaw.com/us-supreme-court/530/793.html (accessed Sept. 15, 2017).

13. See Appendix 1.

14. Paul Siegal, "What They Didn't Know May Have Helped Us: How the Supreme Court Misinterpreted the Role of Sign Language Interpreters," *Annals of the Deaf* 140/5 (Dec. 1995): 386–95.

15. Robert F. Drinan, "A Glimmer of Hope for Aid to Catholic Schools," *America* 169 (Sept. 18, 1993): 4–5.

16. Aaron Epstein, "U.S. Supreme Court to Rule on Interpreters in Religious Schools," *Silent News* (March 1993), reprinted from the *Detroit Free Press*. Titles of articles in widely circulated newspapers suggest the order of importance—church-state doctrine and then disability as human interest—attached by the authors or publications to the two parts of the Zobrest lawsuit. (It should be noted that another—though exclusively—church-state case, *Lamb's Chapel v. Moriches Union*, was heard the same day and is referred to in some of these titles). See, for example, Joan Biskupic, "Deaf Student Sets Up Church-State Issues," *Washington Post*, Feb. 21, 1993, and "Quips, Hypotheses

Punctuate Court Arguments in Two Religion Cases," *Washington Post*, Feb. 25, 1993; Linda P. Campbell, "Use of Sign-Language Interpreter Keys Church-State Court Case," *Chicago Tribune*, Feb. 24, 1993; Dennis Cauchon, "Two Key Church-State Cases Argued Today: Deaf Catholic Student Seeks Government Paid Interpreter," *USA Today*, Feb. 24, 1993. Unnamed local reporters and news staffs in Tucson ran similarly weighted stories: "Tucsonan Wins High Court Case: Public Schools May Provide Interpreter for Deaf Students Who Choose Religious School," *Tucson Citizen*, June 18, 1993; "Deaf Ex-Salpointe Student Wins Supreme Court Decision—Public Funds to the Deaf OK at Private School, Says Court," *Tucson Citizen*, June 18, 1993.

The only reporter writing in some depth about the case from a disability point of view was Ellen Gamerman. Gamerman inquired into what sign interpreters actually do in the classroom, to the extent that she implicitly questioned Berning and Ball's argument: see Gamerman, "Justices Weigh Church-State Issues, Handicap Rights in Tucsonan's Case," *Arizona Daily Star*, Feb. 25, 1993. Several days later she published another article that was exclusively oriented to church-state jurisprudence: Ellen Gamerman, "Zobrest Case May Set New Standards," *Arizona Daily Star*, Feb. 28, 1993.

17. Mary Benson, "Mercyhurst Grad Takes Deaf Son's Case to U.S. Supreme Court," *Lake Shore Visitor* (Erie, Pa.), Feb. 26, 1993.

18. Keith Rosenblum, "Deaf Teen's Case Hits Top Court," *Arizona Republic*, Feb. 24, 1993.

19. Sandi Zobrest to William Bentley Ball, March 3, 1997, in the possession of Larry and Sandi Zobrest.

20. Mary Jo Green to Mr. and Mrs. Zobrest and James, June 20, 1993, in the possession of Larry and Sandi Zobrest.

21. Pub.L. No. 94-142, 89 Stat 777 (1975). The relevant federal regulation, as it then stood, is §34CFR300, 451.

22. The confusion, post-*Zobrest*, about what the EAHCA/IDEA said regarding assistance to disabled students in nonpublic schools mirrored the confusion to the *Zobrest* court itself. See Ralph D. Mawdsley and Cynthia Dietrich, "Limiting Services to Parochial School Students: What Does Zobrest Mean?," *West's Education Law Reporter* 112 (1996): 555–82; Ralph D. Mawdsley, "Providing Educational Services to Students in Parochial School," *West's Education Law Quarterly* 5/2 (April 1996): 254–69; and Larry Bartlett, "Post-'Zobrest': Where Are We on the Issue of Special Education Programs and Services to Students in Parochial Schools," *West's Education Law Quarterly* 5/3 (July 1996): 517–42.

Regarding changes in the law since 1993: Lauri M. Traub, "The Individuals with Disabilities Education Act: A Free Appropriate Public Education—At What Cost?," *Hamline Law Review* 3/22 (1999): 666, 670; Office of Innovation and Improvement, Office of Non-Public Education, *The Individuals with Disabilities Education Act: Provisions Related to Children with Disabilities Enrolled by Their Parents in Private Schools* (Washington, D.C.: U.S. Department of Education, 2011).

23. *Goodall v. Stafford County School Board*, 60 F. 3d 168 (4th Circuit 1995); Traub, "Individuals with Disabilities Education Act," 677–79.

24. *M.L. v. Bowers*, et al., U.S. Court of Appeals, 4th Circuit 15-2017.

25. Quoted in Jennifer Sterba, "Foothills School District Looks Back at '93 High Court Ruling," *Arizona Daily Star*, June 18, 2003.

26. "Federal Report Says Voucher Programs Can Leave Disabled Students Behind," *Church & State* 69 (Nov. 2016): 20–21.

27. Terry Downey, interview, June 23, 2015; Aaron Epstein, "High Court Case Pits Two Values on Religion," *Arizona Republic*, February 2, 1993.

28. Zobrest family interview, June 23, 2015.

29. "Zobrest Victory," editorial, *Arizona Daily Star*, June 19, 1993.

30. "Separation," *Tucson Citizen*, editorial, Feb. 27, 1993.

31. Jennifer Stephens, "Opinion Poll: Zobrest Is Entitled to Money, Students Say," *Crusader*, March 12, 1993.

32. Stephens, "Opinion Poll."

33. "State May Provide Services for Handicapped Parochial School Students," *Catholic League Newsletter*, July 20, 1993, http://www.catholicleague.org/tag/july-august-issue-1993 (accessed Jan. 11, 2013; Dec. 21, 2019).

34. John C. Richardson, interview, June 24, 2015; Berning, interview, June 24, 2015; Maureen O'Connell, "School District Seeks One-Time Tax to Help Pay for Court Case," *Arizona Daily Star*, July 3, 1993.

35. Richardson interview, June 24, 2015; Berning interview, June 24, 2015; Heather Newman, "Case Will Help Others, Deaf Student Says," *Tucson Citizen*, June 19, 1993. Thomas Berning to Larry and Sandi [Zobrest], June 29, 1993, John C. Richardson to William Bentley Ball, July 1, 1993, and *Settlement Agreement*, no date, signed by Sandi Zobrest, Larry Zobrest, Jim Zobrest, William Bentley Ball, Thomas Berning, John C. Richardson, and David W. Noel [Governing Board President, Catalina Foothills Schools District], all in the possession of Larry and Sandi Zobrest.

36. O'Connell, "School District Seeks One-Time Tax"; Governing Board, Catalina Foothills School District, *Minutes, 1988–1995*, July 13, 1993; Rhonda Bodfield, "Catalina to Face Tough Sell," *Tucson Citizen*, July 20, 1993.

37. "More Money than Brains Is an Apt Description," editorial, *Tucson Citizen*, July 22, 1993.

38. Quoted in Rhonda Bodfield, "Catalina to Face Tough Sell."

39. Charlotte Ackerman to Editor, *Tucson Citizen*, Aug. 14, 1993.

40. Rhonda Bodfield, "County Oks One-Time Levy," *Tucson Citizen*, July 21, 1993; Chris Limbris, "Board Delays Decision to Buy New Dump Site," *Arizona Daily Star*, July 21, 1993.

41. Sandi Zobrest to David Gerber, email, Aug. 21, 2017; Mary Prus, interview, Feb. 22, 2017.

42. Ball wrote the Zobrests at the time of the announcement of the decision in *Agostini v. Felton* (1997) and told them how heavily indebted the decision was to their own case; William Bentley Ball to Larry, Sandi, and Jim [Zobrest], June 23, 1997, in the possession of the Zobrests; Aaron Epstein, "The Interpreter and the Establishment Clause," in *A Year in the Life of the Supreme Court*, ed. Rodney A. Smolla (Durham,

N.C.: Duke University Press, 1995): 126–40; Peter Irons, ed., "Zobrest v. Catalina Foothills School District (1993)," in *Courts, Kids, and the Constitution* (New York: New Press, 2000), 307–25; Robert S. Alley, *The Constitution and Religion: Leading Supreme Court Cases on Church and State* (Amherst, N.Y.: Prometheus Press, 1999), 270–79.

43. Marco Enriquez to David Gerber, email, July 20, 2015.

44. Quoted in Kristen Cook, "Justices to Weigh Appeal by Deaf Tucson Student," *Arizona Daily Star*, October 6, 1992.

45. William Bentley Ball to "Dear____," Nov. 4, 1988 (template for fund-raising letter), in the possession of Sandi and Larry Zobrest.

46. Zobrest family interview, June 23, 2015; Jim Zobrest to Bruce Dierenfield, email, July 27, 2017; Sandi Zobrest to David Gerber, emails, Sept. 16–17, 2017.

47. Sandi Zobrest to Gerber, emails, Sept. 16–17, 2017; Zobrest family interview, June 23, 2015; Sam Zobrest, interview, Jan. 30, 2017.

48. Robert Putnam and David E. Campbell, *American Grace: How Religion Unites and Divides Us* (New York: Simon and Schuster, 2010), 96–97. Sandi Zobrest did not reference the sexual abuse scandals that have deeply hurt the reputation of institutional Catholicism as a source of her disaffection.

49. Sandi Zobrest to David Gerber, email, Aug. 21, 2017.

50. Zobrest family interview, June 23, 2015; Prus, interview, Feb. 22, 2017; Virginia Ball Duncan, interview, Aug. 16, 2016.

51. Carrie Lou Garberoglio, Stephanie Cawthon, and Mark Bond, *Deaf People and Employment in the United States, 2016* (Washington, D.C.: National Deaf Center on Post-Secondary Outcomes, 2016).

52. Zobrest family interview, June 23, 2015; Sam Zobrest, interview, Jan. 30, 2017, Prus, interview, Feb. 22, 2017; Virginia Ball Duncan, interviews, May 22, 2015, Aug. 16, 2016.

INDEX

BRUCE J. DIERENFIELD is a professor of history and director of the All-College Honors Program at Canisius College. His five previous books include the prizewinning *The Battle over School Prayer: How* Engel v. Vitale *Changed America*.

DAVID GERBER is a University at Buffalo Distinguished Professor of History Emeritus and director emeritus of the University at Buffalo Center for Disability Studies. He is the author of *Authors of Their Lives: The Personal Correspondence of British Immigrants to North America in the Nineteenth Century* and editor of *Disabled Veterans in History*.

DISABILITY HISTORIES

Disability Histories edited by Susan Burch and Michael Rembis
Between Fitness and Death: Disability and Slavery in the Caribbean Stefanie Hunt-Kennedy
Money, Marriage, and Madness: The Life of Anna Ott Kim E. Nielsen
Disability Rights and Religious Liberty in Education: The Story behind Zobrest v. Catalina Foothills School District Bruce J. Dierenfield and David A. Gerber

The University of Illinois Press
is a founding member of the
Association of University Presses.

Composed in 10.5/13 Minion Pro
with DIN Condensed and Avenir display
by Lisa Connery
at the University of Illinois Press
Cover designed by Jim Proefrock
Cover illustration: Jim, Larry, and Sandi Zobrest in front of a highway sign they had petitioned the Pennsylvania Department of Transportation to post. (Reprinted with permission from Times Publishing Company, Erie, PA. Copyright 2019)

University of Illinois Press
1325 South Oak Street
Champaign, IL 61820-6903
www.press.uillinois.edu